Buffet Catering

To Anne & John Gross,
my good friends:
Happy cooking

Charles Finance

Texas 1983

Buffet Catering

Charles Finance

Design and Layout: Edmund Annand

AHRENS PUBLISHING COMPANY, INC.
Rochelle Park, New Jersey

18 19 20 21 22 23 24 25 26   PRINTING

80 81 82 83 84 85 86 87 88   YEAR

Foreword

This is a book of which both the author, Charles Finance, and the publisher can be justly proud; the author because it represents his years of international experience and displays his artistic ability in catering as well as in photography; the publisher, because we have been so fortunate as to bring to our readers this very beautiful and practical book, sorely needed by the catering industry.

Mr. Finance has won a distinguished list of awards both in Europe and America. During the decade between 1939 and 1949, while Professor of Culinary Art at the Swiss Hotel School in Lucerne and editor of the magazine *Hotellerie*, Mr. Finance wrote and published a cook book of 550 pages for the restaurant business in Switzerland, Germany, and France. The French edition is also published in Belgium.

He has served as Chef in the largest Swedish restaurant in Stockholm. He has been a consultant in the hotel schools and the major restaurants in Copenhagen, Oslo, and Helsinki. In 1950 he served as Executive Chef at the Balmoral Club, Nassau in the Bahamas.

Coming to the States, he was Executive Chef for Western Hotels, working for their hotels in San Francisco, Palm Springs, and Los Angeles. Later, while Executive Chef at the Caribe Hilton he worked for the Insular Government of Education in training young Puerto Ricans for work in the culinary field. Subsequently he served as Executive Chef at the Greenbrier Hotel, White Sulphur Springs and the Ridglea Country Club, Fort Worth.

Mr. Finance was the first man to lead an American Culinary team to the Culinary Olympics in Switzerland where his team was among the top three to win honors. In addition to the long list of prizes he has won for his catering work both in Europe and in the States, he has also won, as an amateur, recognition for his photography at the International Photography Show in Luxembourg, also in Tulsa and in Denver.

This book offers ample proof of all the "know-how" evidenced by the foregoing. While some of the finished dishes appear difficult, his ability as a teacher shows up in his step-by-step pictures which lead so gradually to the grand finale that even the most difficult pieces may be attempted by the uninitiated with assurance of success.

We offer this book with confidence, knowing that it will prove a great boon to the catering industry which the author and we so proudly serve.

D. L. Nichols
Publisher

Preface

Years have passed since I first made the attempt to gather in one place my personal recipes resulting from a varied career in many countries. Perhaps this might not have been accomplished without the inspiration of many of my friends and colleagues who have persuaded me to write a book on culinary art, specializing in cold cuisine. To them I am deeply indebted.

I am grateful to the Western Hotels, the Hilton Hotels International, and the Ridglea Country Club, Texas, where I was able to display and photograph some of my material. I particularly thank Hank Green and Charles Hiltebrand of the Ridglea Country Club for the opportunity to assemble the material and photograph many of the illustrations in this book.

Photographs of many of the pieces from outstanding culinary shows have been added, emphasizing the fact that teamwork achieves culinary awards. This may prove helpful in the future, in presenting and judging pieces in culinary shows throughout the country.

I appreciated the opportunity of leading the first American Team ever to compete at the International Culinary Show (Hospes) in Switzerland in 1954. The American Team was sponsored by the American Culinary Federation and the Société Culinaire Philanthropique, whose president at that time was Hermann Rusch. I express thanks to Louis Bartenbach, Clement Maggia, Ernest Meyer, Hippolyte Haultcoeur, Robert Angelvin, members of the Team, and to Charles Daniel for their great assistance in the preparation of several of my buffet pieces during the Show; also to Wesley Penn, James Kelley, Hans Roth, Emil Maag, Armin Jung, and Henry Goldstein for their assistance on other pieces.

I also appreciate the cooperation of Otto Spitzer, Editor and Publisher of the *Chefs' and Stewards' Food and Equipment Manual*, in releasing all articles and pictures I have contributed to his magazine for use in this book.

With few exceptions, all photographs and sketches were made by me with three different cameras: a Nettel 6-9 cm.; a Nettel 35 mm., and an Exacta 66. The mirror reflex camera, Exacta 66, gave me the best results on food. The image and light on the picture is readily seen in the larger mirror view finder; also close-up shots with a telephoto lens were not distorted.

I have been greatly assisted by Grace H. Woolley for her editing and layout of this book.

The illustrations and recipes in the book are compiled from daily practical experience. Emphasis is placed on the natural and appetizing appearance of cold food. From the simple to the most complicated forms of culinary art, let me emphasize that nothing should be used that is inedible and that no colors be used that are not true to food. There should be no over-loading or over-decorating of platters and no combinations of foods that are not related.

It is my hope that this book may serve as an aid in setting a standard reference book—something that is greatly needed.

CHARLES P. FINANCE
San Francisco

August, 1958

Contents

Foreword by Publisher   **5**

Preface   **7**

List of Illustrations   **13**

   I   *The Set-Up of a Cold Buffet*   **15**
       Cold Hors d'Oeuvre—Soups—Fish—Entrées—Grosse Pieces—Roasts—
       Vegetables and Salads—Desserts—Napkin Folding—Center Pieces—
       Layout and Carpenter's Work—Buffet Selections.

  II   *Organization of the Cold Section in the Kitchen*   **28**
       Refrigeration Section—Pantry Section—Cold Meat Section.

 III   *Decorating Material*   **30**
       Recommended Materials—Truffles for Large Scale Decoration—Butter
       Modeling.

  IV   *Selection and Preparation of Raw Material*   **43**
       Caviar—Herring—Sardines and Anchovies—Smoked Salmon—Fresh
       Fish—Meat—Poultry—Game—Vegetables.

   V   *Hot Hors d'Oeuvre Selections for Cocktail Buffets*   **48**
       Bacon-Wrapped Hors d'Oeuvre—Barquettes—Batons—Bouchées—Beur-
       recks—Blinis—Canapé Lorenzo—Cheese Balls—Clam Fritters—Croissants—
       Croutes—Croquettes and Cromesquis—Dartoise—Eggs Benedict—Eggs
       Foo Yong—Fish and Meat Balls—Kidney Stew—Orlys—Oysters—Pizza alla
       Napoletana—Quiche Lorraine—Rissoles—Scotch Woodcock—Tartlets.

VI *Cold Hors d'Oeuvre for the Buffet*   **56**
Fruit Cocktails—Melon Cocktails—Fish Cocktails—Meat Hors d'Oeuvre—
Canapés—Antipasto.

VII *Cold Sauces and Dressings*   **75**
Salad Dressings—Sauces—Chaudfroid Sauces.

VIII *Preparation of Fish, Crustaceans, and Mollusks*   **84**
Methods of Cooking—Court Bouillon—Preparation and Service of Sal-
mon—Salmon Filets—Salmon Mousse—Halibut, Sole, and Trout—Lobster—
Langouste—Crab—Ecrevisse—Shrimp—Oysters—Clams.

IX *Eggs*   **119**
Eggs Cardinal—with Caviar—with Shrimp—Russian Style—Jardiniere—
Gourmet—Italian Style—Danish Style—Soft Boiled Eggs Bristol—Soft
Boiled Eggs San Francisco.

X *Aspic*   **124**
Preparation—Recipes—Use.

XI *The Galantine—Pâté—Terrine—Mousse*   **132**
Preparation of a Capon Galantine—of a Suckling Pig—of Pheasant—
of Veal—Preparation of the Pâté—Baking the Pâté—Preparation of
Aspic for the Pâté—Pâté de Foie Gras—Pâté Family Style—Pheasant
Pâté—Ham and Veal Pâté—Rabbit or Hare Pâté—Liver Pâté—Salmon
Pâté—Preparation of a Terrine—Pain de Foie—Preparation and Service
of Mousse.

XII *Cold Ham*   **153**
Preparation and Service.

XIII *Poultry on the Cold Buffet*   **159**
Chaudfroid of Capon—Turkey—Pheasant.

XIV *Roasts on the Cold Buffet*   **171**
Preparation of Roasts for Display—Cold Beef Tenderloin, Belle Jardi-
niere—Tenderloin of Beef Wellington—Cold Prime Ribs of Beef—Filet
Mignon Rossini—Tournados Richelieu—Corned Beef—Beef à la Mode—
Cured Ox Tongue.

XV *Game*   **178**
Saddle of Deer—Pâté of Hare or Venison—Stuffed Boar's Head—
Marinades.

XVI   *Various Buffet Styles*   **182**
The Smorgasbord—Buffet on the Terrace—Beach Buffet—Breakfast Buffet—Hunt Breakfast.

XVII   *Salads*   **195**
General Information on Salads—Simple Green Salad Combinations—Vegetable Salads—Fruit Salads—Combined Salads—Molded and Frozen Salads—Salad Specialties of Other Countries—Fish Salads.

XVIII   *Suggestions for Hot Buffet Dishes*   **220**
Roasts—Seafood.

XIX   *Ice Carving for the Buffet*   **224**
Tools Used—Techniques.

Index   **250**

List of Illustrations

Many of the illustrations are listed individually as an aid in locating them easily. Others, such as the 50 illustrations of canapés, are grouped. For more definite information, reference should be made to the Index, pages 250 through 256.

Buffet Arrangement with Ice Carving	16	Aspic of Shrimp and Maine Lobster	102-103
Arrangement for Wedding Reception	17	Aspic of Lobster with Truffles	104
Low-Price Buffet	19	Maine Lobster en Bellevue	107
Large Functional Buffet	20	Langouste à la Parisienne	108
Napkin Folding	23	Preparation of Bread for Socles	109
Various Table Arrangements for Buffets	25	Langouste à la Parisienne with Assorted Hors d'Oeuvre	110
Tools for Decorative Work	31	Cracked Crab	112-113
Decoration Materials	32-40	Monterey Crab Delight	114
Materials and Methods for Making Truffles	41	Dressed Crab Irlandaise	115
Butter and Margarine Modeling	42	Egg Hors d'Oeuvre	120-122
Hot Hors d'Oeuvre for Cocktail Parties	48-55	Preparation of Aspics	126
Styles of Cocktail Glasses	57	Aspic of Filet of Dover Sole	128
Fruit Cocktails	58	Shrimp Aspic	130
Fruit Cocktails Supréme in Melon Basket	59	Galantine of Capon	133-134
Pineapple Tropical Cocktail	60	Galantine of Capon and Foie Gras	135
A Meal from Fruit	61	Galantine of Capon Argenteuil	135
Fruit Platter	61	Preparation of Suckling Pig	137-139
Papaya Cocktail	61	Preparation of Pâté	142-143
Arrangement of Cocktail Items for Speedy Service	63	Pâté of Deer and Other Game	143
Mixed Hors d'Oeuvre	64	Terrine from Duck	147
Hors d'Oeuvre Riche	64	Decorated Ham with Mousse Cubes	150
Canapés	66-70	Virginia Ham Cornets	150
Canapés in Preparation for Service	71-73	Preparation of Cold Ham for Buffet	154-158
Italian Antipasto	74	Chaudfroid of Capon	160-162
Preparation of Cold Whole Salmon	86-87	Capon Neva	163
Salmon Masterpiece	91	Chaudfroid of Turkey	164-166
Salmon Medallions	93	Cold Cornish Game Hen with Mandarins	167
Salmon Filets	93-94	Chaudfroid of Duckling	167
Salmon Mousse	96	Cold Roast Duckling	167
Cold Maine Lobster Parisienne	98	Pheasant	169
Maine Lobster Victoria	99	Faisan en Voliere	169
Seafood Buffet	100		

Tenderloin of Beef Wellington 173
Preparation of a Cold Prime Rib of
  Beef 174
Preparation of Pork Loin for Buffet 175
Ox Tongue with Tongue Aspic 176
Saddle of Venison Orientale 179
Stuffed Boar's Head 181
Cheese Platter 184
Crayfish and Dill Platter 184
Fruit Platter 184
Fish Platter 185
Platter with Wild Fowl 185
Arrangement of Smorgasbord 186-187
Large Buffet Breakfast 190
Easy-to-Serve Buffet Breakfast 191
Canadian Bacon and Sausage Links 193
Sweet Roll Display for Buffet 194
Preparation of Salad Bowl 198
Argenteuil Salad ⎫
Beatrice Salad ⎬ 199
Bon Ton Salad ⎭
Preparation of Caesar Salad 200
Cendrillon Salad ⎫
Carmelite Salad ⎬ 201
Chatelaine Salad ⎭
Cubane Salad ⎫
Dolly Salad ⎪
Geneva Salad ⎬ 202
George Salad ⎭
Grand Union Salad ⎫
Jockey Club Salad ⎬ 203
Jordan Salad ⎭
Monte Carlo Salad ⎫
Princess Salad ⎬ 204
Printemps Salad ⎭
Tosca Salad ⎫
Alma Salad ⎬ 205
Antoinette Salad ⎭
Group of Fruit Salads 206
Banana Salad ⎫
Bombay or Caribi Salad ⎬ 207

Diana Salad ⎫
Diplomat Salad ⎬ 207
Excelsior Salad ⎫
Floridienne Salad ⎬ 208
Frontenac Salad ⎭
Hawaiian Salad ⎫
Japonaise Salad ⎪
Ladies' Delight Salad ⎬ 209
Saratoga Salad ⎪
Sunburst Salad ⎭
Veronique Salad ⎫
Waldorf Salad ⎪
American Beauty Salad ⎬ 210
Anna Salad ⎪
Belge Salad ⎪
Caprice Salad ⎭
Chicken Salad Bowl 211
Doctor's Salad ⎫
Dumas Salad ⎪
Hawley Salad ⎪
Hortense Salad ⎬ 213
Iron Salad ⎪
Louise Salad ⎪
Palm Beach Salad ⎪
Poinsettia Salad ⎭
Shrimp Salad Bowl 216
Crab or Seafood Salad 216
Avocado Salad Stuffed with Shrimp 217
Salad for a New Year Buffet 218
Crab Louis Salad 219
Ice Carving for a Wedding 225
Ice Carving Tools 226
Steam Hose for Ice Carving 227
Small Ice Socles 228
Ice Carving: Bird on Branch 229
Ice Carving: Donkey 230
Ice Carving: Ship 230
Ice Carving: Fish 231
Ice Carving: Valentine Heart 232
Ice Carving: Flower with Leaves 232
Ice Carving: Boot and Spurs 233

Several pages have been reserved in the back of the book for the use of the reader in filling in special menus, plans for table arrangements, and different buffet set-ups which may have proved successful for him or for others.

CHAPTER I

The Set-Up of a Cold Buffet

Setting up a buffet calls for the creative touch. The one in charge of this operation will do well to keep in mind the old saying: "The eye is the first to feast." In no other phase of the art of cuisine is such a demand placed upon tasteful arrangement, display, and decoration. The choice of the person in charge of the display should be based upon someone with creative ability and experience in food presentation, whether the chef, maitre d', manager, or hostess.

A few primary points should be observed:

1. The relationship of food among the various dishes;
2. Selection and placement;
3. Presentation which gives the food item the best advantage in relation to the overall display;
4. Inedible items and additional decorations;
5. Center piece;
6. Layout and carpenter's work.

In arranging cold food on a buffet the same rules must be followed as for food service in the hot cuisine. If the guest is urged to step up on the right side of the buffet to follow the line to the left, the food items should be placed from left to right in the order of a regular menu: small hors d'oeuvre items, soup, fish, entrees, grosse pieces, roasts, vegetables, salads, sweets and desserts such as pastries, fruits, and cheeses.

The rare exceptions when this system is not followed are in the arrangement of smorgasbord, buffet de luxe, or when guests make their selections at the buffet but order and are served by a waiter at the table. Occasionally also, a few guests are enjoying a buffet supper and the food is placed irregularly and to the best advantage of eye appeal.

Buffet Arrangement with Ice Carving

In this set-up the guest is moving from right to left. Therefore, the fish items come first—shrimps with cocktail and remoulade sauce; antipasto with tuna and sardines; cold salmon with vegetables, mayonnaise, and deviled eggs; sour cream cucumber salad; olives, potato salad, and beets.

Next come the poultry items, the roasts, and ham with adequate sauces in front and garnishes beside the carved meat.

A large iced bowl with stewed fruits and cottage cheese is next. At the left end are stacks of dessert plates where all the cakes and pastries are in reach.

Also, one must be careful with sauces, dressings, and garnitures. They must be placed near the food with which they are served—the mayonnaise with the salmon, the mustard with the roasts, the cranberry sauce beside the turkey platter, etc.

Vegetable salads should be placed near those platters containing the food with which they are served. This prevents the guests making irregular choices. Cucumber salad should be near the fish, potato salad near the meats, and spiced fruits beside poultry or game. It is better to have the main dishes placed on a higher level with the garnishes, salads and dressings in front and on a lower level.

Selection and Placement

A good selection of food items for a regular buffet should include those listed on a complete menu. The classical buffet menu is divided into several groups and the guest makes selections with or without regard to the groupings. One should keep in mind, however, that good eating, for pleasure as well as nutrition, calls for careful selection in combining foods for a complete meal.

Cold Hors d'Oeuvre

Among these are many delicacies such as caviar on ice, foie gras, oysters on ice, sardines, smoked salmon, smoked oysters and eel, special antipasto, all canapés, puff paste with fillings, miniature éclairs and turnovers with fillings, patty shells filled with delicacies, and many more.

Soups

It is not usual to serve soup on a cold buffet but occasionally a jellied consommé, bouillon or a cold, thick soup such as Vichyssoise may be served. Even a hot consommé can be served, presented in a silver tureen in all its splendor surrounded by the cups, saucers, and bouillon spoons.

Fish

Fish and seafood are placed next with their correct sauces nearby.

Entrées

The entrées are precut from meat, poultry, or game, prepared and displayed as appetizingly as possible. Small chops or escallops of any meat, medallions of foie gras in aspic, ham rolls, etc., are entrées and may be garnished with appropriate vegetables, fruits, or salads designated for cold service. Egg dishes belong in this category also.

Grosse Pieces

A grosse piece is a large piece of meat which is partially carved. Often it is carved in front of the guest with the garnish to one side instead of on the same platter in the manner of classical presentation. A whole decorated ham garnished with asparagus tips and perhaps stuffed apple slices is a typical grosse piece. A prime rib of beef garnished with vegetables à la jardinière is another. With such large pieces a center piece may be achieved if there is no ice carving or flower arrangement available.

Arrangement for a Wedding Reception

Hot and cold hors d'oeuvre for a party up to 150 persons may be handled in this manner. From left to right, chafing dishes contain hot hors d'oeuvre—chicken livers wrapped in bacon, oysters in the shell, cheese tartlets, meat balls, etc. Cold assorted canapés are on the large trays with napkins. Small plates are at each end of the large table with cocktail napkins and cocktail forks in front. A suitable ice carving and candelabra give the table a more festive appearance.

Roasts

Cold roasts should be presented with their jellied natural gravy. But no gravy will be poured over a cold roast. Instead, an adequate quantity of aspic in cubes or other presentable form will be placed with the roast on the platter—for a beef roast, beef aspic—for a chicken roast, chicken aspic. With roast game, serve a Cumberland sauce, cold bread sauce, cranberry sauce, crabapple jelly, etc. A green salad is most likely to be chosen with a roast. Therefore, the green salad bowl should be placed nearby.

Vegetables and Salads

In addition to the adequate choices of vegetables and salads for the above items, vegetable specialties alone may be placed on the buffet such as artichokes, asparagus, salsify, hearts of palm, etc.

Desserts

These sweet dishes are very important on the buffet and a pastry chef is capable of glorifying the board to the delight of the gourmet with his fine works of artistry from sugar, pastillage, etc. Often the pastry chef might contribute the center piece.

French, Swiss, and Italian pastry furnish many tasty creations that are easy to serve. There are the petit fours with their minute and dainty decorations that attract the eye of the guest—or a sugar basket or stately swan gracefully carrying a load of sweets. For special events, gum paste may be formed into any size or shape for the creation of emblems, novelties, or even replicas of buildings.

Cakes are usually presented in their original form and decoration and are cut on the buffet. For a fast buffet luncheon, however, the cakes may be precut to facilitate service.

Fruit compote (stewed fruits) may be another item among the desserts. These are presented either singly or mixed in glass bowls. In summer, these bowls are placed on ice.

Fresh fruits and cheeses must also be considered—the fruits in a basket of interesting design and the cheeses on a clean board or marble square. A Horn of Plenty or cornucopia, woven from straw or similar material, makes an attractive corner piece when filled with colorful choice fruits.

Fresh pineapple, melon, grapefruit, papaya and others may be placed on ice carvings or so that they form a part of the center piece. Fruits light up the buffet with color when correctly placed.

Presentation to the Best Advantage

An artist would never present his painting without a suitable frame. Likewise, food must be presented in the correct dish, platter, or holder. Most silver platters are made with a border design. This border should never be covered with food since it is meant to enhance the contents of the platter.

Low-Price Buffet

This buffet may be served to as many as 150 persons. The hot entrées are served from chafing dishes by a chef or waiter. As a guest moves along (here from right to left) he helps himself to salads, fish, cold meat or whatever combination of cold food is offered. The dessert is placed at the left end of the buffet and picked up after the main course is eaten.

From left to right: Bavarian Cream; Chocolate Eclairs; Cream Puffs; Cottage Cheese and Stewed Fruits; Green Beans, Vinaigrette; Sliced Tomatoes; Pickled Beets; Spiced Watermelon Rind; Potato Salad; Ripe Olives; Quarters of Dill Pickles; Bean Salad, Marinated; Tossed Green Salad on Ice; Celery, Green Onions, and Carrot Sticks on Ice; The hot dish is Sweet Breads in a patty shell with green peas. A platter with assorted cold meats and a decorated ham topped with a Pompadour bust modeled from margarine add glamour and an air of festivity to the table.

19

The Large Functional Buffet

The chef and the garde manger inspect the Sunday Night Buffet at the Caribe Hilton Hotel in Puerto Rico. This buffet is patronized not only by the guests of the hotel but by numerous people from town. The tables placed around a hollow square hold food sufficient for 500 guests with replenishments during the evening.

This shows how the center section may become the theme for any event taking place. This particular one was dedicated to the opening of the Istanbul Hilton Hotel. Each Sunday this theme is changed and the ice carving and other decorations help make the buffet successful.

In addition to over 100 different items in the line of cold delicacies and salads, a hot beef roast is carved on the buffet. The pastry chef contributed to the centerpiece which is a true replica of the hotel made from gum paste. For such a buffet, over 1,000 petits fours should be displayed. Emphasis here is placed on tropical fruits arranged in baskets.

Food in its natural state has various shapes and forms. Modern culinary art does not violate these forms of nature as the chefs of ancient Rome and Greece did by making meat in the shape of a fish, fish in the shape of a bird, etc. Each different food now follows the pattern, style, and form of nature. Therefore, the task of the buffetier is not a light one as he must select platters, containers, and garnishes that will not clash with the food he is displaying.

Although silver greatly improves the looks of a buffet table, when it is not available chinaware, glassware, or ceramics may be used. Also plywood ovals, rounds, or squares covered with aluminum foil or thumbtacked with napkins may be used with a nice effect. Mirror plate may also be used to replace expensive silver. It may be cut in any desired shape or size. Give the desired dimensions to almost any mirror or glassware shop and with one-fourth inch mirror plate and suitable plywood, you will have the necessary serving trays and platters for the buffet. With one-inch runners under each tray they will be easy to pick up and put down. The glass edges should be protected with some sort of lining.

With an ample supply of buffet platters, half the battle is won. For large fish, a fish platter, long and narrow, is correct. For medium-size buffet pieces, use round or oval shapes. For heavy pieces, square or oblong trays with handles are used.

Salads should be presented in dishes that will not be affected by the dressings. For this reason, copper and tin are banned. Glass and wood are the most suitable ware for salads but the glass must be sparkling clean and not chipped.

No platter, bowl, or serving utensil should protrude over the edge of the table. They should be pushed far enough in so there is no danger of soiling the guests' clothing or of being accidentally pushed off.

As there is little or no actual service from the waiter to the guest at a buffet, the waiting staff should be responsible for the clean-up of the buffet. The chef, maitre d', hostess, or assistant manager should supervise this process.

Every platter should have an eye-catching decoration and the foods should be arranged in the proper order and in colorful contrast to each other. On a cold meat platter, do not place dark meats next to each other. Alternate light and dark salads. Large meat and fish items should have a presentation piece in addition to the pre-cut slices and garnitures. This presentation piece may be decorated or merely have a thin coating of aspic for brilliance.

Display the food so that the guest may easily serve himself. Do not set platters with high bases in the front row. Always place low-standing items in front.

Platters should be replaced before the first platter is completely empty. Food is never attractive in a container that is nearly empty. It is the duty of the cook in charge to have the food replaced when necessary and to insure its appetizing appearance.

On every buffet table there are food items costing more than others and these are usually used up first. This poses quite a problem but the buffet should be so planned that substitutions are not made throughout the entire meal. If some foods must be replaced, they should be of the same general type.

Additional Decorations and Edible Items

Where there is a daily buffet setup, economy must be considered. It is possible to display a few pieces that will not be actually eaten though they will have the appearance of edible food. Also they will have none of the faults of untrue coloring or bad odor. These dummy items, if carefully handled, may be used repeatedly.

Instead of filling the cut out breast of a turkey with costly food such as liver purée, when preparing it for presentation substitute mashed potatoes or shortening. A real chaudfroid sauce over this filling holds well if correctly applied. If shortening is used, be sure the sauce is almost cold.

Another example is the decorated ham. On very rare occasions is this carved on the buffet. The guest merely helps himself to the slices placed on the platter with the decorated piece. The ham need not be cooked since its primary purpose is decoration. The same thing applies to the head and tail pieces of a large salmon. Do not cook these fully for they will break into pieces when removed from the pot and this piece may be used only once since partially cooked fish will soon smell. Never present totally raw fish with cooked pieces. This violates the rules of culinary art.

Another decorative dummy is the *Faisan en Volière*. The feathers and other parts of the pheasant are constructed to give a life-like appearance. Although this feathery dummy is "tabu" among great culinarians and in international shows, it will not be condemned by the guests who see this royal bird placed near the cooked meat of the pheasant. It greatly enriches the decorations of the buffet.

The perfect masterpiece is one that is totally edible. There is controversy concerning the use of the socle (base) be it made from rice, bread, or wood. Escoffier outlawed the socle and most modern culinarians follow his example. However, the advantages of using a base in many food presentations is so great that it will be used occasionally such as the bread socle for Langouste, etc.

Cleanliness must be stressed for the buffet. Paperwork, frills, wooden picks, and laces must be used with reserve. Paper frills may be used with sandwiches but they are not suitable on a fine buffet piece. Laces of silk may be used on ham but should not touch any part except the smoked skin. The legs of poultry may be decorated with a paper manchette (ruff).

Napkin Folding

Very fine decorative effects may be achieved with folded linen napkins. The art of pressing or folding stiff starched napkins is almost forgotten although the Scandinavian chefs are still proficient in this art. Napkins may be pressed and folded to appear in different forms such as a swan's neck, a boat's bow, a fan, a boat, or as a plain napkin arranged to resemble a rose or an artichoke.

Many cold food items appear to better advantage on napkins than on metal. Also, a clean napkin folded to resemble a rose or some other object, adds tremendously to a festive and clean-looking board. Many of the very fancy folded napkin presentations are long forgotten and the practice is very little known in this country. Leading in this art are the Scandinavian countries where most of the smorgasbord items are either placed directly on napkins or in bowls and platters of glass or earthenware which are, in turn, placed on fancy-shaped napkins.

Following are the directions for making the rose or artichoke from a folded napkin.

The napkin must be square and not out of shape; also, it must be starched. If many of these are used it is well to have a quantity of them, already folded, ready for use at all times. If they can be prepared on a laundry table, it is better. Sometimes the use of pins and Scotch tape will aid in causing them to hold their shape.

The accompanying illustration (double exposure) shows the rose or artichoke napkin of great popularity.

1. Each of the four corners are bent over so they meet in the exact center of the napkin. (See illustration, upper left).
2. The four corners are again folded to the center (lower left).
3. And again folded (lower right).
4. By holding the center of the napkin with the flat left hand or with a casserole dish, pull out with the right hand the last four corners folded under. Follow with each of the other eight folds. They will assume the shape shown in the center illustration.

If more petals are desired and if the napkin is large enough, other folds may be made.

Center Piece

If a buffet is small, a single outstanding platter may be used as the main point of attraction. With large buffets, the situation may demand the building of a special scaffold to support a heavy center piece that will stand out from all other foods on the buffet. For a classical buffet, an ice carving or floral decoration is proper. More details are given in the chapter on ice carving.

Tallow sculpture is acceptable if it is kept a reasonable distance from edible food. On smaller buffets, sculptures made from butter or margarine should be used as this material is closely related to edible foods and does not violate the rules of taste and culinary art.

There are many good reasons for deviating from such rigid rules. Among these are celebrations or anniversaries for particular clubs or societies. For example, if there is a buffet for a fishing affair, an ice carving for the center piece may be used with green plants, fishing tackle and nets properly arranged. For a Christmas buffet the pastry chef may supply a colorful replica of a church window. Even a Christmas tree might be used for the center attraction. For Thanksgiving, an arrangement of pumpkins and gourds in different shapes and colors with colorful autumn leaves and baskets of local fruits may be used. For Hallowe'en use a witch on a broomstick hanging from the ceiling directly over the center of the buffet with rows of Jack-o'-lanterns made from pumpkins placed on scaffolds with lighted candles inside.

These examples could be multiplied a hundredfold. It is for the chef and the maitre d' to decide the motifs for all such occasions. Lighting systems have to be worked out as well as protective measures against water damage from the ice carvings. Colored flood lamps should be carefully located so the lights will not cause a glare in the eyes of the guests. A rotating color-slide light is very good if directed on ice carvings. It should be placed about eight feet back of the carving.

Storage space should be made available for this necessary gear and apparatus for it must be at hand when needed. Again it should be mentioned that someone must be made responsible for cleaning up after the buffet service and for putting these items back where they belong.

Layout and Carpenter's Work

The layout of a buffet depends upon many things. Architecturally, almost every dining place is different. This difference calls for a study of the space in order to locate the buffet properly. The table should be as near as possible to the kitchen for fast and easy replacement of food during the service and visible to the guests in the room from all corners and at all times.

A square room demands a broken line within the buffet. This may be accomplished by varied table setups. Half-round tables may be used to advantage here. U-shaped and L-shaped layouts are other possibilities.

  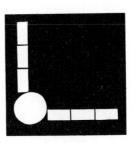

Center Square   **Long Renaissance**   **Long U-Shape**   **L-Shape**

The size and length of a buffet depends upon whether all the guests will be eating at the same time or whether the dining period stretches over two or more hours. Also, the number of people to be served must be considered. For practical purposes, the length of the buffet may be determined by allowing two and one-half feet of space per person for one fifth the number of guests.

If a party, say four hundred in number, attends a buffet including one hot food item, the serving time should be approximately one hour and twenty minutes, allowing five minutes per guest with twenty-six or thirty of them at the buffet table at one time. A buffet without hot carved food may be served in much less time. In case of a shorter table length due to limited dining room space, fast replacement from the kitchen is the answer.

For frequent buffet service, additional carpentry work may be required. A permanent platform for the centerpiece should be constructed, the size and shape varied to fit any specific need.

The foundation or underpinning of the buffet may be built of wood into two or four scaffolds or carpenters' horses on top of which is placed a wooden box-shaped top that will support up to three hundred pounds. This top should not be too high for easy placement of the ice carvings or other center pieces yet high enough for good visibility. Cloth, flowers or other decorations may be easily fixed to the wooden top of the platform with thumb tacks, staples, or small nails.

Drip pans must be available for the ice carvings. With a little ingenuity, suitable pans may be constructed with drain pipes and sufficient depth so that the floors will be properly protected.

Some buffets, such as smorgasbord, may be set up in the center of the room. To avoid a hollow center with a center piece standing alone, it is better to create one huge table of different levels. Arrange the lower tables around the outside of the square and build platforms on the inside tables, graduating the height of these up to the large center piece. This will place many more dishes within reach of the guest and leave a high space in the center decorated with flowers, foliage, or ice carving.

Buffet Selections

Following is an example of practical food selections for a large buffet that will accommodate five hundred guests:

Buffet price: $4.00
Food Cost: 33% or lower
Income: $2,000.00

Cold Food

Meat:

6 platters—small pieces of roast capon
6 platters—sliced roast loin of pork
6 platters—small pieces of roast duckling
2 large platters of turkey
4 platters—presentation piece of ham and slices
4 platters—presentation piece of ox tongue and slices
2 platters—presentation piece of roast beef and slices
2 to 4 platters—decorated chicken or turkey salad

Fish and Crustaceans:

2 platters of lobster, langouste parisienne, buffet piece
2 platters of salmon, large buffet piece and small filets
2 bowls of marinated herring
2 to 4 platters of decorated fish salad
1 to 4 platters of decorated crab meat or sea food salad
Pyramids of shrimps

Regular Salads:

Green beans with vinaigrette dressing
Sliced tomatoes, natural or with vinaigrette
Corn O'Brien with mayonnaise and cream
Beets, pickled or baby beets with oil and vinegar dressing
Cucumber salad
Tossed green salad bowl with either French, Roquefort, mustard or
    Maurice dressing
Chef's salad with garnish; French dressing
Sections of avocado dressed with mayonnaise
Asparagus, vinaigrette dressing
Potato salad

There are many other salad items such as artichokes, radishes, celery, etc., that may be exchanged with or added to the above.

Combined Salads:

Kidney bean salad	Stuffed tomatoes
Antipasto	Waldorf salad
Green salads	Fruit salads
Mixed vegetables with mayonnaise	Jockey Club salad
Artichokes, stuffed or quartered	Curried rice or macaroni salads

Fruits in gelatine

Fruits:

Fresh fruits, grapefruit, melons, papayas, and pineapples should be displayed generously throughout the length of the buffet table.

Desserts:

From 700 to 1,000 dainty French pastries
Seven fruit tarts or pies, preferably open-face
Several layer cakes

Decorations:

The buffet is a festive board and should be regarded as such when the decorations are considered. The dummy items as well as the presentation food items must be handled with taste and with creative art.

CHAPTER II

Organization of the Cold Section in the Kitchen

A well-stocked garde manger of a large kitchen has an almost uncountable number of food items within a few steps' reach. The variety is great and the risk of spoilage is ever present. With the increasing demand for cold food it has become more difficult to maintain this section of the kitchen in perfect and smooth operation. Very large establishments make further divisions in the cold section: the pantry, the cold meat room, and the butcher shop.

Refrigeration Section

The most important installation in all these departments is refrigeration. Almost all the food items are perishable and in a state of preparation. The latter must be kept in the proper temperature without losing appearance and flavor. When business fluctuates the maintenance of such a garde manger is most difficult.

The food which is to be stored and held for later use must be surveyed constantly. The orderly maintenance of this entire section and particularly of the refrigerator shelves, is a *must*. It is wise to establish rules on how the space available is to be utilized. One way of seeing that such rules are kept is to place written markers either on the doors of the reach-in refrigerators or on the shelves of the walk-in refrigerators. Once the crew is familiar with the location of each food item, the markers may be removed but the spaces must be maintained in the same way thereafter.

It is very important that all the ice boxes with their thermostats are set at the right temperature and that these installations remain in excellent working condition. Otherwise, a loss in costly merchandise is the result.

Temperatures from 2° to 8° above freezing seem to be the normal temperature—the lower for crustaceans and fish items and cold meats; the higher for garnishes, such as salads, ready vegetables, fruits, etc.

Pantry Section

In a pantry, most of the rough cleaning work of salad, lettuce, shrimp peeling, etc., should be done on one side where the sinks are located or even in the back store rooms before they reach the kitchen as the working areas for fine work should not be taken up with rough work. Inaugurate a step by step procedure from raw material to the finished product: from cold storage to the preparation station; from there to the pantry; from there to the properly prefabricated state; and finally, over the counter to the persons who serve the food.

Cold Meat Section

The garde manger or cold meat room should have a large working table placed in the center of the room. Directly opposite this table, reach-in boxes should be installed. Thus the cook has only a short distance to go in dressing up cold meat platters or appetizers. Again, an additional supply of raw material should be kept in a larger box as well as half finished products and sliced cold meats, the latter placed on trays lined with wax paper. All trays must be kept immaculately clean, their contents always set up in the same locations and daily replaced with fresh merchandise. The first duty of the person in charge of this section of the kitchen should be to remove all trays from the shelves for general inspection, rearrangement, and the replacement of sold merchandise and inventory. Only with this kind of a system will a garde manger succeed.

When it comes to more elaborate work, even artistry for buffet work, a good system of this kind is reflected in the final execution of top-grade food items. Speed is gained and even more important is the gain in the morale of the crew. There will be less bickering and more unified effort on the part of everyone. The *esprit de corps* of the crew is well worth considering and with systematic organization, the results will be rewarding.

CHAPTER III

Decorating Material

It is important that the garde manger and other cooks that work in the cold meat department have the ability to create, from decorative material, garnishes that are artistic and worthy of the dishes they embellish. Even though they may not have a natural talent for this type of work, the situation is not hopeless. With a small amount of concentration and effort through study of classical decor and guides laid down by master chefs, the cook of average intelligence should soon be able to turn out tastefully garnished buffet pieces.

Cleanliness is most essential in the decorative field and must always be kept in mind. Keep all food items in an absolutely clean condition, cool under refrigeration until the moment the decoration is added and return immediately to the refrigerator. If the decorating of one piece takes more than an hour, the chef will not be happy because other essential work will be neglected. Therefore, plan your buffet preparatory work the day before. Make some drawings, get your material ready and have it on hand ahead of time. Such preparation makes it necessary to keep the piece out of refrigeration only for a short period of time.

The decor must fit the occasion as well as the dish itself. Clumsy decoration may ruin a very fine dish. It must be in good taste and appetizing. For large platters, a clear thin mirror of jelly with no air bubbles should be poured over the bottom of cold dishes so that the garnishes are kept in place and do not get pushed about when served or placed on the buffet. This also serves the purpose of insulating the taste of metal. Large pieces are placed on the platters before pouring in the jelly; garnishes and carved meat afterwards when the jelly has set. Joints which have have been carved should always be arranged facing the guest.

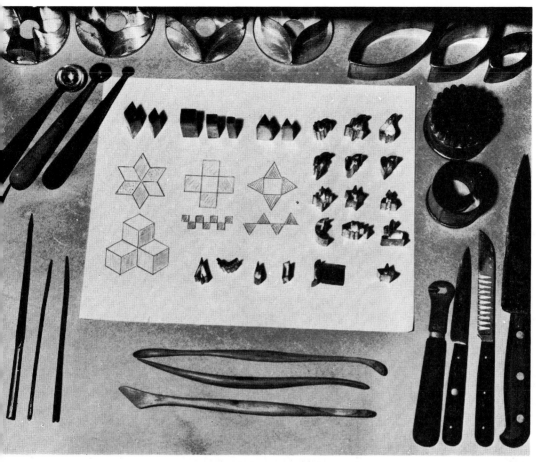

Tools for Decoration Work

Upper Row: Various cutters for sandwiches, canapés, and all other items that must be cut precisely. Counter-clockwise around center: (1) Parisienne spoons from smallest size for carrots and white turnips to medium and large size for melon balls, etc. (2) Larding and dressing needles of various sizes. (3) Wooden model tools for butter and margarine modeling. (4) Knives for different purposes: a. lemon or vegetable cutter, b. tiny knife for miniature work, c. scalloped knife for cucumbers, beets, celery roots, etc., d. a very sharp knife of medium size for most decoration cuttings. Center: These small cutters help in achieving very pleasing effects.

For the garde manger the knife is a most important tool—a large slicer for large pieces—a medium size French knife for different uses—an extremely fine and sharp knife with a six-inch blade for cutting most decoration material, and a very small stainless steel vegetable knife. Also, the electric slicer is a great help in slicing truffles, radishes, etc. Various sets of cutters with different pattern designs are a necessity in cold buffet work and will contribute toward nicely decorated show pieces. Low priced buffets demand speedy work and in such cases these cutter sets play their most important part.

31

Anchovies may be used as strips, as rings with fillings such as olives, gherkins, capers, or asparagus, or cut diagonally for salad decoration.

Top, Left to Right: Small bundle of cut asparagus spears with pimiento strips; green onion tops used to make a bundle; single spear with pimiento; hard-boiled or deviled eggs with asparagus tip and anchovy. Lower Row: One way in which asparagus may be used as decoration; slice of tomato topped with asparagus points and used with fish and meat dishes.

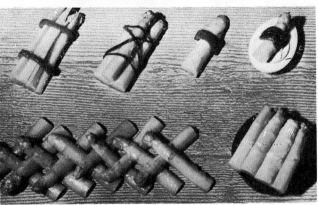

On the other hand, a professional garde manger who can slice food to perfection is able to slice and shape food in a striking decorative effect without decorating the food itself. Such presentation platters are not common but their appeal to the appetite is great. The trick is simplicity in design but many buffet platters are spoiled with overdecoration.

It is essential that one knows the kind of decorating materials that are acceptable to a given piece. Generally only edible decorations should be used. The exception to this is when a buffet is set up with dummies.

Anchovy Filets
Freed from excess oil, these filets may be cut into different shapes—tiny strips, lozenges, or formed into rings.

Apples
These may be used for game platters and water birds. If apples with brilliant red skin are used, the slices should be covered with lemon juice to retain the color. Apple slices poached and cut with a round cutter make fine garnish, the center emphasized with a cherry or plum.

Asparagus

Asparagus at any stage of growth may be used. For many things the tiny green asparagus tips are the best garnish. The larger tips may be cut to the desired length and split lengthwise for a good effect. An arrangement with small bunches of three to seven tips and crossed with strips of chives or pimientos results in attractive asparagus bundles.

Beans, Green

Cut into lozenges or arranged in little bundles, these may be included in many attractive decors.

Beets

These should be used with great care because of their color effect on surrounding food. They are not recommended for fine buffet work.

Broccoli

Little branches of intense green broccoli make a fine pickled vegetable garnish, either on top of a slice of tomato or as a bouquet arrangement with other vegetable garnishes. After boiling the broccoli to a crisp state, cool under crushed ice and transfer to a dish where it is pickled overnight in a sour marinade.

Brussels Sprouts

These may be used in a jardinière garnish for cold roast beef platters. Treat them in the same manner as broccoli.

Cauliflower

Cauliflower roses are used frequently in the cold cuisine. Boil the cauliflower to a crispness, having changed the boiling water twice. Treat the same as broccoli. If balls are desired, put some of the cooked cauliflower into a cloth and twist until the round shape is achieved. Place the balls in line on a grill and cover individually with jellied mayonnaise. After decorations have been placed on top of the balls, glaze with clear aspic.

Caviar

This is expensive but very decorative material. A simulated miniature bunch of grapes may decorate either stuffed eggs or medallions of langouste, etc.

Celery Leaves

These may be treated the same way as leeks. Parts of celery leaves give a very amazing effect when placed together around a dish covered with sauce or a fish salad.

Cherries, Sour

These may be canned and are used as garnish for game platters.

Capers

Real capers are very small and are preserved in salt water. Sometimes the larger bud of a substitute flower is merchandized for the caper. For decoration, any size may be used as long as the capers are pure in taste, firm, and of good color—a dark blue-green. Capers may be used where color is needed such as on deviled eggs.

Carrots

Carrots furnish a wonderful color, from soft orange-yellow to deepest orange-red. They are always used in a pre-cooked stage. Sliced thinly, they may be cut into any shape or form.

Chives

These make a fine green decoration, especially when the finest strips are needed. Boil the leaves for about three minutes in salt water. After removing from the water cool off immediately with crushed ice to prevent discoloration.

Corn

Tiny ears of corn are available in preserved pickled form and give a fabulous effect to many cold American dishes. If small ears of corn can be obtained, they may be pickled in the individual kitchen.

Cucumber Skin

This is used in Swedish smorgasbords largely with smoked salmon and herring platters. The fresh green skin of the cucumber is cut into strips, fringed, and arranged on the platters to give a lovely leaf effect. This garnish, of course, will not be eaten.

Cucumbers

Choose symmetrical round cucumbers with perfect green coloring that may be cut with the electric slicer in very thin slices and used in many ways, sometimes with the skin on. A slice may be cut halfway through, each side twisted, to result in a lovely shape. A peeled cucumber may be grooved with a fork to give varied slices. Cucumber peel cut into the shapes of leaves are used to decorate Swedish dishes.

Cucumbers, Pickled

Sour or sweet, sliced or cubed, pickled cucumbers are acceptable decoration for cold meat platters.

Dill

This is an aromatic herb that is harvested just before blooming. Dill is used lavishly on smorgasbords with crayfish, lobster, and such boiled cold crustaceans. Use the same as parsley.

Egg Plant Skin

This unique color is used with great success in creating scenes and emblems in decorative motifs for special buffet events.

Leeks

The tender inside leaves of leeks will furnish material for all kinds of leaves, stems of flowers, and various cut-outs where green color is needed. Leek blades come in different shades of color on the same stem. Boil the leaves for about three minutes in salt water, cool off immediately after removing from the water with crushed ice to prevent discoloration.

Lobster Eggs

These can be loosened and used like parsley—chopped and sprinkled over food.

34

Chives, the tops of green onions or scallions, and leeks supply a variation of green stems and petals for flower decorations. Parboil the choicest stems for two or three minutes in salt water and plunge at once into ice water to keep them green.

Chives are used here for the top branches and for all other designs with the thinnest stems. Green onion tops are used for the leaves of medium size and leeks for the larger type and for oblong or square leaves such as those on the bottom row.

The upper flowers are made from small outer slices of radish and a half-round of leek to form the button.

A radish or ripe olive makes the lower right-hand flower. The Lily of the Valley in this picture is cut from pimiento to contrast with the background. Use egg white on dark subjects such as mousse or dark medallions.

After blanching, keep the greens in ice water until ready to use. After forming the desired shapes, dip in aspic and place on the dish to be garnished with the help of a larding needle or toothpick. The lower ornament here is made from chives, the center one from onions, and the upper from leeks. The blossoms on the center ornament are cut from red pimiento and ripe olives. This type of design is used for items that have a coat of chaudfroid sauce or mayonnaise.

Foie Gras

This is sometimes used in different shapes as a garnish for capon and other poultry. End cuts and trimmings can be mashed together and formed into tiny balls, rolled in liquid gelée, then in finely chopped truffles. This truffle-like decor may be used in one tartlet or, slightly larger in size, as decor for a breast of Chicken Galantine or Chaudfroid.

Mushrooms

Heads or slices are very decorative whether on meat or fish. They may also be used on stuffed eggs and various salads.

Olives, Black

The sliced skin of ripe olives is very useful as well as inexpensive. It may often be used in place of truffles.

Cucumber Decorations

Cut incisions lengthwise of the cucumber with a special knife. From this, cut thin slices. From each slice cut out three-fourths as shown (upper left) and twist into an "S" shape. These twisted cucumbers may be used for canapés, on salads, cold fish, and meat items. In Scandinavia the cucumber rind is used raw to decorate smoked fish platters such as salmon and eel. In the center of this illustration, smoked salmon is made into the shape of a rose by carefully twisting the thin slices around a center bud. These pink salmon roses and the deep green of the cucumber rind make a lovely contrast on a buffet platter. Such a platter may also be decorated with a lemon border as shown at the right.

Onions, Silver
These are sometimes called "cocktail" onions. If washed and dried, they may be used effectively on many show pieces where onions are allowed as a garnish. These may be obtained in white, red, and green.

Peaches or Pears
Stewed or canned, these fruits may be used for garnish on duck, goose, or pheasant platters. A form resembling a fan may be cut from a peach half and makes an attractive garnish.

Peppers, Green
These may be used where pimientos are used though they are not so popular.

Pimientos, Red

This is a very satisfactory red decoration, just as it comes in the can. It may be cut into any shape with a knife or special cutters. It is used for all fish and meat.

Pineapples

Canned pineapple should be used because of its keeping quality and ability to hold gelatin. This fruit is used with others on game platters of various kinds. They may be cut in slices or julienned.

Pistachio Nuts

Split in halves or chopped, these may be used to garnish stuffed or sauce-covered medallions.

Radishes

Very thin slices of the radish may be used to gain a striking effect in creating flowers or other ornaments. Outside cuts of radish may be used as red dots. The usual radish rose or flower is useful. Also tiny cut-outs on the skin of a whole radish give a dotted effect for decoration.

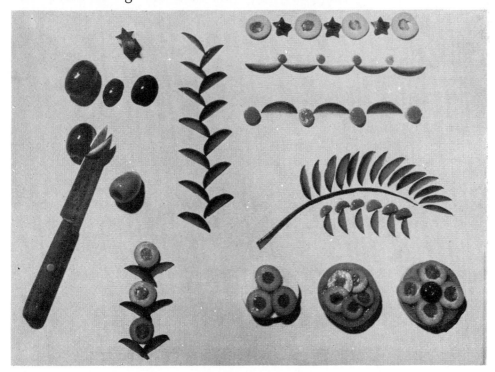

Olive Decorations

Effective borders around salad bowls when the salads have an even surface may be made from ripe and stuffed olives. This border may also be applied on salmon, turkey, and ham. Ripe olives may replace the expensive truffle where a black material is desired. Cutters such as the star may be used in cutting the thin rind of the olive. The base of the lower three decorations are tomato slices—a garnish for cold meat platters or marinated vegetables and eggs.

Salmon, Smoked

This may be cut into different shapes or twisted into rings. It makes a good decoration for canapes and fish platters.

Shrimps

This crustacean (any size) is excellent for fish platters. Tiny shrimps presented whole with the shell removed from the edible tail part make attractive garnish.

Tarragon Leaves

These make excellent green and tasty decoration for all kinds of buffet pieces and salads. Hold a branch of fresh tarragon in boiling water for one minute and cool with crushed ice. Strip only the leaves desired for garnish. Leftovers of such tarragon may be conserved in wine vinegar for months and the vinegar may be used for spicy salad sauces.

Radish Decorations

The top rows show the different ways in which radishes may be cut for the radish tray or for decoration. The third row from the top shows an effective decoration which may be used on egg slices, tomato slices, or with cold meat platters. The fourth row shows how a simple radish flower from radish halves may be used as a border. The bottoms are made from olive cut-outs. Border effects are shown in three different ways made from very thinly sliced radishes. A rosette is made the same way with a truffle or egg white for a center. In the lower left-hand corner another type of bud is shown with the stamens cut from ripe olives.

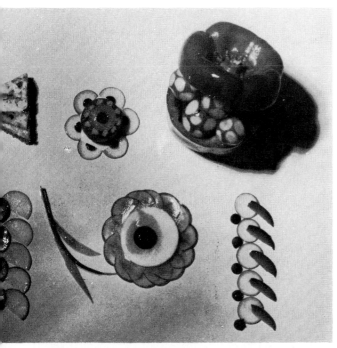

Upper Left: Radish flower is used fitting over a bleu cheese slice on a canapé. The center rosette is for decorating large salad bowls with mayonnaise-type dressing. It is made of tomato, stuffed olive ring, radish slice with truffle or ripe olive centers, and butter points. The upper right-hand corner shows the polka-dotted radish in a pepper basket—useful as a garnish on cold meat platters. Lower left and right are other suggestions for olive and radish borders. Lower center is a decoration for various aspic dishes or a large salmon slice —also for salad bowls.

Tomatoes

The meat of red ripe tomatoes as well as the skin make good red embellishment. Lovely red poppies may be simulated using five segments of the tomato as petals with chopped ripe olives as the seeds.

Tongue

For garnish this should be red salted ox tongue. It can be used to great advantage where a scarlet garnish is needed. The smallest part of the tongue yields the highest color. It should be sliced very thin on the electric slicer. Any cutter may be used to cut different designs.

Truffles

These are a very expensive imported kind of mushroom which grows beneath the surface of the ground in oak forests. Very small cans may be obtained but the quality is inferior and not of much value for decoration purposes. If large cans can be purchased and the entire contents are not used at one time, fill the remaining space with a strong sherry wine or oil so that the contents are completely covered. In refrigeration they will keep this way for more than a month.

Slice the truffles with an electric slicer, paper thin. Wash in a bowl of lukewarm water and place the slices for cutting on a thin wet cloth or napkin. Fine strips for truffle drawings are cut with a very sharp knife or a piece of thick wax paper. These strips should be laid in liquid jelly so they will not dry out before using. Any kind of drawing may be made with truffles. This is one of the most time-taking decorations and is not in common use because of the excessive labor cost. However, it is still one of the most attractive ways for expressing culinary artistry.

Watercress

This must be used very fresh. Never boil. Where a natural green leaf ornament is desired, the watercress is invaluable. This green is as edible as it is useful for a garnish.

Truffles for Large Scale Decorations

The following method of making truffles go farther means a great saving while still conserving the fine aroma and content of real truffles.

The Formula:

> 7 ozs. truffles or truffle peels with the juice
>
> 2 ozs. granulated gelatine stirred into 1½ cups of water until thoroughly blended

Mix the ingredients in a blender and let the machine run for 20 minutes. Should the truffles not be black enough, put the mixture, after the 20-minute-

Miscellaneous Decorations

Tomato skins are used for the five-petal blooms (upper left). The centers are truffles or ripe olives, chopped or sliced. At far left center, a plum tomato is stuffed with any mousse or miniature salad. The cover is replaced and decorated with egg white cut out with a tiny cutter. At upper center is a tomato slice with lobster medallion decorated with sprigs of parsley or watercress. Below this are slices of bell peppers decorated with slices of tiny tomatoes, stuffed olive rings, and a radish.

Fourth row, top left is a cucumber slice, one-fourth inch thick topped with a small tomato cut star-shape and stuffed. Below is another stuffed with an olive.

The upper right hand corner and below show quarters of artichokes. After cooking and cooling in a salt water brine to which has been added a little lemon juice to keep the artichoke white, the quarters are set upright on a rack and stuffed with any type of garnish. Lower left: tarragon leaves with chives and pimientos.

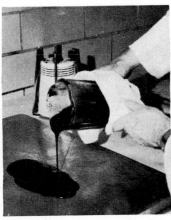

run, into a small pot and let it heat in a water bath and pour when completely black. The sheet pan, after the material is spread thin, is set to cool in the refrigerator. After cooling, any type of figure may be cut out with cutters or with a knife and transferred to the piece to be decorated. This type of truffle is edible and eliminates the need for black paper silhouettes which are not acceptable in culinary art. Red pimientos may be treated the same way.

Butter Modeling

Butter or margarine is, if properly executed, a most appropriate medium for making figures. The material is a natural for cold buffet work. It does not conflict with culinary taste because it may be eaten. Any type of human or animal figure may be modeled from margarine or butter. Since margarine stands a little more heat it is more practical for this purpose.

Method for Modeling Margarine Figures

These figures will hold in warm room temperatures if they are properly set up. Here a coat hanger is bent with the help of a pair of pliers until a skeleton of the figure is obtained. This figure is used for the shepherd below.

Nail the coat hanger to a small piece of plywood. Get all the material necessary for the modeling together first.

Knead the margarine until it is smooth but not too soft. It must have some stiffness to keep its form. If the room is too warm, the refrigerator may be the place in which to work. Hands should be cooled often in ice water. Build each bulky piece into the wiring. Wooden sticks may be used for reinforcement. When a crude outline of the figure is reached, allow it to cool under refrigeration.

Next, with the help of a knife, superfluous margarine is cut away. Now with the modeling wood, take away or add material as it is needed.

A thin layer of margarine is made by squeezing a piece of the material between two wet pieces of wax paper. With the palm of the hand the

Model of an Old Shepherd

The finishing touch here is the placing of a shellacked piece of wood—a staff —in the hands of a model of an old shepherd. This model is used for the "Salle d'Agneau"—Loin of Lamb.

The Gardener's Woman— "La Belle Jardiniere"

This is placed on a large prime rib platter. Small marinated vegetables should be arranged around the model. She is collecting radishes into a basket woven from strips of raw potatoes and deep fried, or from paste. This basket is placed in front of her.

margarine can be squeezed almost paper thin. Before removing the wax paper from the top, cover with shaved ice for a few seconds. As soon as it reaches the consistency for molding, remove the wax paper and mold it quickly in the hands to the desired shape. The top coat of the shepherd is treated in this way. Be sure that all of the wire and wooden supports are covered so that no suspicious eye could ever detect their presence.

With the model wood, further details may be added. The eyes, nose, and mouth are perhaps the most difficult parts but with some practice and several attempts, this difficulty will be overcome and the model will stand the criticism of many discriminating guests.

CHAPTER IV

Selection and Preparation of Raw Material

Selecting the right merchandise for buffet work is most important as presentation plays a greater role here than in other parts of the food section. Only the best is good enough and from an economical point of view it is wiser to buy first quality merchandise.

Comparison must be made between fresh, canned, and frozen foods. Below are listed some of the more expensive items in the cold buffet line:

Delicacies

Caviar, foie gras, smoked salmon, herring, eel, special meat cuts, imported food items, fine pickled fruits, etc., make up the list of delicacies.

Many of these specialties cost well over the average price range. Because of the high price and the character of the perishable merchandise, knowledge must be acquired on the following points:

1. Geographical origin
2. Behavior under transportation, changes in temperature, etc.
3. Quantity to purchase, methods of storing, and issuing
4. How to bring out the most desirable appearance and taste
5. How to present as originally packed and the garnish to serve with each.

Caviar

Caviar is considered one of the finest delicacies. It is the salted roe of the sturgeon, sterlet, and great sturgeon. The best fish from which the caviar comes are Beluga, Sevruga, Ship, and Osceter. Beluga comes from the big fish in the river Volga and its tributaries; Sevruga and Osceter from the Caspian and Black seas; Ship caviar from the ship sturgeon found in the Ural area. The main trading center for caviar is the Russian port of

Astrakhan. Preference should not be given to any of the above kinds without examining the size of grain, salt content, taste, and color.

Signs of quality are the lighter and larger grain. Silver gray caviar comes from Beluga. Light grey grains of about one-eighth inch and with a slight brownish tinge are more likely to come from the Sevruga. Caviar should be shiny, not dull. The coarsest grained light transparent kinds are the most expensive. The price decreases as the commodity grows darker.

The term *malossol* describing the finest grades means slightly salted and refers to the method of preparation. *Beluga malossol* means "slightly salted great sturgeon caviar." Caviar is shipped either in barrels or, more often, in tight fitting cans which contain from four to six pounds. The original cans bear the trade marks on top. It is therefore advisable to serve caviar in this original container. It must be served on ice, preferably on a lovely ice carving.

On a separate tray, garnishes prepared to eat with this delicacy should be near at hand. These may be hot Blinis and sour cream, melba toast, lemon wedges, and finely chopped onions. Blinis are small buckwheat cakes kept warm in a chafing dish.

Suitable drinks are champagne, white dry wines, vodka, aquavite, or sherry.

If caviar is served on toast, great care must be taken in spreading the grains so that the eggs are not bruised. Garnish the edge with a fine border of butter and serve lemon wedges with it.

Several countries can the roe of fish other than sturgeon calling it the caviar of such and such a fish—for example, "salmon caviar."

Herring

The Scandinavian countries, as well as Holland and Germany are famous for their herring specialties. The herring are packed in barrels or are canned. Different sauces and brines are used to pickle the herring filets to exquisite taste. Holland, Belgium, and Germany export fine herring products such as "Rollmops" (rolled herring in sour marinade); Bismarck herring (sour type herring, boned and in a fine marinade); and Matjes herring (still with the milk or the roe inside and either marinated or plain salted. In the Scandinavian manner the brine is slightly sugary and contains condiments and aromatics).

All these specialties must be very cold when served. Matjes herring filets should be placed in a glass container resting on crushed ice.

The restaurant Krog in Copenhagen is famous for its fish specialties and among them are two fine herring dishes. The first one is creamed herring. It is made of salted fish, boned and cut in appropriate diagonal pieces. Next, layer after layer is placed in a large glass bowl, with a layer of sliced onions between each. The creamy herring is finished with the sieved roe or milk of the herring and thinned with sour cream.

The second herring dish served at the Krog combines the herring with a special clear marinade of purple color and onions. Dill twigs garnish the top.

Herrings in different brines and marinades are imported in cans. It is therefore, a treat for connoisseurs to see the original can presented on the buffet. With such specialties, it is recommended that the top be removed and placed beside the can so everyone may see and read what is offered.

Sardines and Anchovies

The best sardines come from Portugal and France. American clientele, in most instances, ask for skinless and boneless sardines but for some reason, the plain sardine, dipped in hot oil, head removed and then baked results in a much tastier product. Sardines from Portugal and France should be presented in their original can with the cover removed. Raw onion rings in one side dish and capers in another are proper garnishes.

Very small sardines are called Brissling. They are obtained from the Baltic Sea by Denmark, Sweden, and Norway and from the Atlantic by Canada.

Even smaller than the foregoing are the anchovies, but this tiny sardine is treated quite differently. Anchovies are first salted with sea salt and placed in barrels where they stay for a long period of time. Finally they are taken out of the developing brine, cleaned of scales, head, insides, and bones and laid separately, one after the other in a can and pure olive oil poured over them before they are sealed up. They are useful as a tasty garnish for many fish dishes on the hors d'oeuvre table. They make decorative toppings for fish salads and, at the same time, bring out the flavor of the salad. Anchovy paste may be used in cold and hot sauces.

Smoked Salmon

Smoked fish of any kind may be purchased either preserved for a limited time by its smoky treatment, or canned. Of course, the former is the gourmet's delight. Because of the limited time smoked salmon can be preserved and the risk involved by the packer in not disposing of his goods within that time, this delicacy is rather expensive.

All salmon are not suitable for smoking. The first of the season's catch is usually best for this purpose since the fish is fat and the meat firm. Later in the season the fish sometimes become lean and stringy. Today much smoked salmon is canned but even in the can the product is not immune to bacteria. For this reason, canned smoked fish should be kept refrigerated and purchased in small quantities.

The proper treatment of fresh salmon to be smoked is also essential. The way it is salted, the grade of smoking, and what wood is used are very important factors. The Norwegian fisherman perhaps has the best method since he turns out some of the finest smoked fish in the world market. Norwegian salmon turns up only during a specific season and when the catch is made, the salmon is cured for a few days in the cellar before being cold smoked.

In the Scandinavian countries, salmon is eaten raw after a brief pickling of the raw filets in brine after the meat has been sprinkled with salt, sugar, placed on a bed of fresh dill sprigs and covered with the same herb. After pickling overnight, thick slices are eaten with boiled potatoes.

This raw salmon, in Sweden, is called *Graved Lax* and is one of the finest delicacies on the rich smorgasbord. Smoked salmon is almost a must at any Scandinavian table. On the American continent, Nova Scotia produces a counterpart of this Scandinavian dish. The old Scotch immigrants back in the 17th Century must have brought the recipe for this from Scotland. In England, fine smoked salmon is sent to the tables of the royalty and the Savoy Hotel in London.

On the Atlantic coast, the Nova Scotia salmon is on the market almost the whole year. Out-of-season markets are in the early spring. New York's leading delicatessen stores handle smoked salmon along with other canned fish. On the west coast smoked salmon is found in the British Columbia area and around Seattle. There are few places, however, where the gourmet can get the real, mild, perfectly smoked salmon. Many food stores handle smoked salmon in glass jars but this type does not have the original flavor. However, it is worth mentioning for use in cold buffet work such as flavoring for purées and fillings for stuffing eggs, making canapes for less expensive affairs, decorating strips over vegetables, etc.

The finest smoked salmon comes in sides, the outer skin on, without head but with fins. If stored in a cool place enveloped in an oily wax paper, the product will keep for weeks. If the merchandise is too soft, it has not the preserving capacity and should be used soon. Salmon should be cut in thin slices. This can only be done with a long, thin knife. Any remaining bones should be pulled out with a pair of pliers before cutting. There is a difference in the method of slicing smoked salmon in front of the guest or when it is done by the garde manger. In front of the guest the whole side is resting on a napkin-covered plank and the maitre d' carves the fish in thin slices, resting his left hand on a folded napkin over the broad side of the fish and cutting from left to right. A few slices should be removed first, beginning with the tail end of the fish. Have lemon, onion slices, and capers ready in small glass bowls. Thin toast and butter is demanded with smoked salmon of extra quality.

Fresh Fish

The most appropriate fresh fish for cold presentation is salmon, lake trout, trout, chicken halibut, or turbot. These fish may be presented whole. Filets, medallions, and suprèmes of various fish may be used to a certain extent. The best for this purpose are Dover sole, wall-eyed pike, or carp other than the filets of trout and salmon.

Fresh fish, of course, taste best but are not always available. Frozen merchandise is only a substitute because it lacks the fine flavor and juiciness found in the fresh item.

The most economical fish is the salmon weighing about 12 to 18 pounds. The season for this fish differs in various locations. The same is true of lake trout and trout. Rainbow trout from the hatcheries may be purchased the year around.

Fresh fish break very easily during cooking. It is recommended, therefore, that they be kept on shaved ice about twenty-four hours before cooking.

In the waters around Florida, the Hawaiian Islands, and in the Caribbean, famous game fish are available. Though they may not be suitable for the guest's plate they often make important decoration pieces. After this purpose has been served, they may be used for salads or chowders.

Meat

Of all the meats, beef and pork are used most for the cold buffet. Cold roasts from different parts of the animal are always popular items. In a well-scheduled kitchen, many roasted items which are leftovers from hot meals may be used to great advantage, thus lessening the food cost.

Any prime or choice grade roasts used in hot cuisine may be adapted for the cold buffet. An economical but still fine offering is the sirloin strip of the *good* grade if one understands how to choose this type of meat. This "good" sirloin strip makes excellent roast beef platters and offers more lean meat than any prime rib does. Beef for low-priced buffets is sometimes chosen from thoroughly aged top sirloin, shoulder cloth, or rib-eye roast. Top round is not recommended as it is not as tasty as the others.

From oxen, the salted and smoked tongue is one of the most preferred special pieces. A fine specialty salad may be made from the snout by going through the same process as for corned beef. The well-cooked snout (Museau de Boeuf), after cooling, is sliced into very thin slivers, put into a stone vessel and marinated with vinegar, salt, pepper, onions, and other condiments. This type of meat salad is finished with oil just before serving.

The loin of pork is another favored roast. When cut into small slices and mixed with other cold meat items and sausages, it makes a low-cost roast platter. Trim the fat well from the pork before roasting and it can be presented with its natural outside roasting color of golden brown. This same advice is true of any roast that needs trimming. All fine roasts must be butchered correctly and tied to some extent.

Poultry

Poultry must be of top grade for the buffet. It is necessary that the raw bird be well dressed and tied so that it will roast in perfect shape. Sometimes for certain game birds, the feet of the bird are left on. In this way, the hunter and connoisseur may realize the origin of the bird.

Game

Furred and feathered game is used with great effect in fall and winter. Wonderful buffet pieces may be created with a saddle of deer, elk, or wild boar.

Vegetables

Vegetables for cold buffets must be colorfully prepared. The merchandise must be mature, of good color, and fresh. Vegetables should be cooked in salted boiling water and cooled immediately in cold water or on shaved ice so they will keep their color. When cold, marinate with vinegar, lemon juice, and sometimes with wine, oil, herbs, and salt. Green salads are mentioned in a special chapter.

<h1 style="text-align:center">CHAPTER V</h1>

Hot Hors d'Oeuvre Selections for Cocktail Buffets

From the scores of variations for hot hors d'oeuvre, there is room in this book to publish only a few. The following is a selection of the most popular ones and, with the variations given, an assortment may readily be chosen.

 *Bacon-Wrapped Hors d'Oeuvre*

These are very popular and may be made with meat, fish, seafood, or vegetables—the latter precooked. Keep the food to very small portions and broil or pan-fry just before serving time.

Variations:
All of the following items may be wrapped in bacon and prepared as above:

Chicken Livers	Oysters
Scallops	Artichoke heart quarters
Shrimps	Beef tenderloin tips, cubed
Shashlik type of cubed lamb, seasoned with thyme or marjoram	Zucchini
	Cocktail sausage
	Mushroom heads

 *Barquettes*

These are made either from pie crust or puff paste in tartlet mold shaped to resemble a boat, filled just before serving, usually topped with a very fine sauce.

Variations:
Shrimp barquettes—small cooked shrimps placed in a row in the barquette, covered with Hollandaise, supreme, curry, or Newburgh sauce.

Fill the barquette with small cubes of foie gras, covered with concentrated Madeira sauce. Chicken liver sauté may also be used. A slice of truffle forms the decoration.

Crab meat may receive the same treatment as shrimp. Caviar may also be used.

Barquette au Fromage—the same as a cheese tartlet.

 *Batons*

These are oblongs of puff paste, filled, covered with the same dough and cut into narrow strips. They are tied around the sides with the filling in, so that they puff up rather than spread out when baked.

Variations in Filling:
Very popular when filled with anchovies, skinless sardines, cheese of any type, or a spicy purée.

 *Bouchées*

These are puff paste patties. For hors d'ouvre they are made in miniature, about one and one-half to two inches in diameter. The cover may be used or not; if not, a decoration of some sort should top the filling. The bouchées are baked ahead of time and filled at the last minute so that the crust remains crisp.

Variations in Filling:
A paste made from Strasbourg foie gras. Top with a drop of Glace de Viande and a truffle slice.

> Chopped chicken and mushrooms in cream
> Chopped ham and green peppers in cream or Creole sauce
> Chopped chicken liver purée
> Calf's brain with Hollandaise sauce
> Sweetbreads with suprème sauce topped with mushroom slice
> Cheese fondue

 *Beurrecks*

These are Turkish specialties. Fill crèpes or pancakes with a thick cheese Mornay, roll and cut in small rectangular pieces; bread and fry. These may also be crescent shaped.

Blinis

These are buckwheat cakes, served hot, usually with caviar in a folded napkin in a chafing dish.

Ingredients:
- ½ cup of warm milk
- ½ oz. of yeast
- 3 tablespoons of flour

Mix and allow these ingredients to rise. Add:
- 2 cups of buckwheat flour
- 1 cup of hard flour
- 2 egg whites

Mix as much heavy cream as necessary to obtain a thick cream sauce. Flavor with salt and nutmeg and put in a warm place for one hour. Shortly before serving, beat the whites of two eggs and add it with the same amount of whipped cream to the blinis dough. From this dough make dollar-size pancakes, if possible in a special blinis pan with hollows. A bowl of sour cream is usually served with the caviar and blinis.

Canapé Lorenzo

This hot hors d'oeuvre is very popular and may also be served with green salad.

Ingredients:

2 lbs. crabmeat	½ cup Sauterne
½ lb. fresh chopped mushrooms	1 cup cream sauce
½ diced green pepper	4 egg yolks
½ red pimiento	4 shallots
1 teaspoon English mustard	2 tablespoons butter

Pinch of cayenne

Preparation: Heat butter in a sauce pan and add chopped shallots, mushrooms, and green peppers. Sauté for a few minutes and add remaining ingredients. Heat and season to taste. Put the crabmeat mixture on small rounds of toast and sprinkle generously with Parmesan cheese or cover with Welsh rarebit sauce. Bake just before serving.

Cheese Balls

Variations: 1. Mix a generous amount of grated Swiss or Gruyère cheese with hot thick cream sauce (two parts cheese to one part sauce). Allow the cheese to melt in the sauce, stir well and add salt, paprika, or cayenne and a few drops of Worcestershire sauce. Pour this mixture into a pan and cool. Make balls with the aid of two teaspoons and dredge them in flour, dip in beaten egg and bread them. Fry to a golden brown shortly before serving. Place a toothpick into each cheese ball and serve hot from a chafing dish.

2. Mix the grated cheese with the same amount of bread crumbs. Season with salt, nutmeg, mustard, and Worcestershire sauce. Add a beaten egg and a little cream to the mix so it may be formed into balls. Bread the cheese balls and fry just before serving.

3. Dip balls the size of teaspoons from the same cold mixture as described in Variation No. 1. Then dip in beer dough and fry.

Clam Fritters

Dip clams in a beer batter and fry in hot fat or oil. Use hot sauce or Remoulade sauce for dip.

 ### Croissants

These are made from Vienna dough, filled with cold stuffing and baked.

Variations in Filling: Swiss Gruyère cheese and ham, diced very small and mixed with a little heavy cream sauce.
Chopped mushrooms, Swiss Gruyère cheese and cream sauce.
Fine creamed chicken.
Chopped olives (ripe or green), tomatoes, peppers and blue cheese mixed to a purée.

 ### Croûtes

These are made from bread or special rolls on which a food item is baked to a crust. Sometimes the bread is fried to a crust in butter and topped with a creamy meat item.

Variations in Filling: Use as a spread a cooked paste made of Parmesan cheese, eggs, a little flour, salt, paprika, a little white wine or white sauce to make a paste of medium consistency.

Deviled Sardines: Mix butter with English mustard and spread on buttered toast same size as sardine. Top with sardine and bake just before serving.

Mushroom Toast: Cook fresh sliced mushrooms with heavy cream, shallots, cayenne, and salt to a tangy thick sauce. Place on buttered croutons cut in small pieces, and bake with a little Parmesan cheese and butter.

 ### Croquettes and Cromesquis

Croquettes are made of cooked meat or fish, diced very fine and mixed with thick cream or veloute sauce. When cold, cut into small sausage shapes the size of a small bottle cork. Croquettes are breaded.

Cromesquis are wrapped in a single slice of fat bacon, dipped in beer dough and fried in deep fat.

Variations in Filling:

Minced or diced chicken

Chicken and ham, mixed

Salmon

Cromesquis a l'escarlate with finely diced smoked ox tongue

Fondue Bruxelloise: Emmenthal cheese, diced very fine, mixed with thick Béchamel sauce poured finger thick into a pan. When cold and stiff, cut into small squares, bread, and fry just before serving.

Dartoise

These are made from pie crust and puff paste, half and half. The bottom crust is filled, a cover of the same paste is laid over it, closed tightly on both sides, baked, and then cut into small tidbits.

Variations in Filling: Nicoise: Make a purée from chopped onions, olives, garlic, tomatoes, and spice (marjoram, thyme, or oregano). Crisscross anchovy filets over the purée. Close with dough and bake.

Chop mushrooms, green peppers, onions, garlic, and olives very fine and sauté to a purée. Season spicily, fill paste and bake.

Tomato purée, spiced with oregano and black pepper. Fill and cover with Mozzarella cheese, blue cheese, or leftover cheese from the cheese board. Bake and garnish with a sprig of parsley.

Eggs Benedict

This very popular dish for Brunch or other buffets where a light dish is required is made with poached eggs. These are placed on toasted and buttered English muffin halves with a slice of grilled ham the same size as the muffin. Cover the eggs with a spoonful of Hollandaise sauce and brown quickly under a salamander. Decorate with a slice of truffle or ripe olive and serve from a chafing dish.

Eggs Foo Yong

Mix equal amounts of bean sprouts, sliced fresh mushrooms, finely sliced onions, small shrimp, crabmeat, and julienned ham. Add small cuttings or scallions or green onion tops, salt, and pepper. To this mixture add enough beaten eggs to barely cover. Do not add soy sauce as it darkens the mixture.

Place one-quarter inch of peanut oil in a sauté pan. Heat and pour small portions of the mixture (like corn fritters) into the hot oil. Cook to a golden brown, turning over once while cooking.

Make a sauce of chicken broth to which soy sauce has been added, bring to a boil, thickening slightly with cornstarch. This may be served as a hot chafing dish item with the sauce and rice on the side.

Fish and Meat Balls

These are easy to make and if well seasoned or served with a tasty dip or sauce they make excellent hot hors d'oeuvre.

Variations: Prepare meat balls in the regular way. They may be made from beef, veal, lamb, or pork or any combination of meats. With various seasonings, many tasty hors d'oeuvre will result. Use such seasonings as curry powder, paprika, liquid smoke flavor, marjoram, oregano, garlic, chili peppers, Parisian pâté seasoning, and many others. For dips use barbecue sauce, cheese sauce, hot sauce, or horse radish sauce.

Fish balls are made from cooked fish. The most popular are made from dry cod which has to be soaked first, then cooked and mixed with dry mashed potatoes, a little egg yolk, and salt and pepper for seasoning. After this has cooled, form small balls, dip in flour and beaten eggs, bread, and fry shortly before serving.

Crabmeat balls: Mix crabmeat with thick veloute or cream sauce, seasoned and cooked for a few minutes. Spread out in a pan and cool. Form balls which may be served breaded or dipped in beer batter and deep-fried.

Sausage Cake Meat Balls: These are made from sausage mixed with a generous amount of bread crumbs for binding, and pan-fried.

Kidney Stew

Sauté finely chopped onions in butter and add a few peeled and seeded tomato cubes and veal kidneys, cleaned and cubed. Sprinkle a little flour over the kidneys, mix well and deglaze with a small amount of sherry. To this add enough brown sauce to cover the kidneys. Bring to the boiling point but do not cook the kidneys as they will get tough. Fresh mushrooms in quarters may be added.

Orlys

This is the name given to hors d'oeuvre made from fish or meat, coated with batter and fried in deep fat. They are usually accompanied by sauces used as a dip.

Variations in Filling:
    Shrimp wrapped in bacon
    Crab meat or crab legs
    Cooked artichoke quarters
    Tomato quarters
    Zucchini cut in slices one-fourth inch thick
    Fondue Emmenthal or Emmenthal cheese sticks

 *Oysters*

Oysters on the half-shell, served hot, are very fine delicacies for the cocktail party or the buffet table. The shell is filled with the selected recipe and shortly before serving it is baked or heated.

Variations: Kirkpatrick: Place a spoonful of hot sauce in the shell, the raw oyster on it. Cover with a small slice of lean bacon, sprinkle with cheese and a few drops of butter. Bake for about eight minutes.

Casino: Make a mix of chopped green peppers, crisp bacon, parsley, lemon juice, and Worcestershire sauce mixed with soft butter. Place the raw oyster in the shell, a half slice of thin bacon on it and top with the teaspoonful of the mix. Bake about eight minutes just before serving.

Oysters a la Ridglea: Chop fine equal amounts of the following: ham, green peppers, mushrooms, and shallots or onions. Sauté shallots in butter; add peppers, then the other ingredients and sauté with a small amount of Sauterne. Make a coarse purée which is seasoned with chopped parsley, chives, oregano, and a touch of garlic. Place a teaspoon of this purée in a shell, set a poached oyster on it and cover with a little Mornay sauce. Sprinkle with cheese and butter, bake 10 minutes and serve hot.

Oysters Rockefeller (modified recipe): Poach oysters in their own liquid. Place in their shells and cover with a very fine mash of spinach to which a few tarragon leaves have been added. Season with Anisette or Pernot or Louisiana absinthe, salt, pepper, and a sprinkle of Accent. Top the spinach purée with Hollandaise sauce and bake until brown.

Oysters Mornay: Cover slightly poached oysters with Mornay sauce and finish au gratin.

Pizza alla Napoletana

Pizza is a very popular hot hors d'oeuvre. Since it is so well known, only a brief mention will be necessary.

A common bread dough into which a small amount of oil has been added is used as the base on which the ingredients are placed. The dough is rolled out to about one-fourth inch thickness, round in shape. On this is placed various items according to recipes and taste: filets of anchovies or fresh sardines, mozzarella, tomato paste or flakes, a small amount of garlic, oregano, salt and pepper. Sprinkle a small amount of olive oil over this and place in a hot oven.

Miniature pizzas may be made two or three inches in diameter. They should be served hot in a chafing dish with a flat surface or directly from the baking sheet.

Quiche Lorraine

This is a cheese tart of great popularity. Line a nine-inch pie dish with puff paste trimmings and prick with a fork. Fill the bottom evenly with finely diced Gruyère or Swiss cheese—about 10 ounces. Add one medium-size onion finely chopped and sautéed in butter to a white glaze, one-half cup of julienned bacon also sautéed, and one soupspoon full of chives. Over this pour a Royal mix from three pints of milk, five eggs, two tablespoons of flour, and one-half teaspoon salt, one pinch each of nutmeg, white pepper, paprika, and three tablespoons of grated Parmesan cheese.

Bake about 45 minutes before serving. Cut on the buffet table into 10 to 14 portions and serve hot.

 *Rissoles*

These are miniature turnovers, half-moon in shape. They may be filled the same as tartlets.

Scotch Woodcock

This famous hot hors d'oeuvre is made with scrambled eggs, cooked with heavy cream and served on anchovy-buttered toast. Pile the scrambled eggs on the warm toast and decorate with strips of anchovy filets.

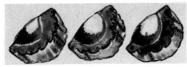 *Tartlets*

These are miniature tarts—small pie dough shells baked either filled or empty. If baked empty fill them with uncooked Navy beans so the bottom will not buckle. When the crust is crisp, empty the beans and refill with any chosen filling.

Variations in Filling: Swiss Gruyère and Emmenthal cheese give the best results. Dice the cheese very small and fill the tartlet half full. Cover with Royal mix and bake slowly until a golden brown on top. This is easily reheated in case of early preparation. *Royal Mix:* 1 quart of milk, 8 eggs, 1 soup spoon of flour, salt, pepper, paprika, and nutmeg.

Use Gruyère cheese and finely diced bacon browned to a crisp, and chives. Cover with Royal mix and proceed as with above recipe.

Dice chicken livers very fine and add to concentrated Madeira sauce. Top with truffle or mushrooms. Bake empty and fill with the following:

> Sweetbreads a la Reine.
> Calves' brains with Hollandaise sauce.
> Chicken liver purée.
> Lobster Newburgh (very small pieces of lobster).
> Tiny curried shrimp.
> Crabmeat on wild rice with Hollandaise sauce covering.
> Oysters after poaching, cut in pieces and mix with white wine sauce.
> Small mushrooms, sliced, mixed with Hollandaise sauce and glazed under the salamander.

CHAPTER VI

Cold Hors d'Oeuvre for the Buffet

The word *hors d'oeuvre* is French and means work outside the regular cuisine. Hors d'oeuvre are relishes and appetizers made from scores of different combinations of delicacies and tidbits that delight the lovers of fine foods. There are hot as well as cold hors d'oeuvre but this chapter will take up only the cold ones.

Similar to the French hors d'oeuvre are the Scandinavian smorgasbords, the Italian antipasto, and the zakouska of Russia. In the beginning, the Western World probably got them from ancient China. At any rate, every nation with a culinary culture to speak of has created specialties of this kind. They all have a similar duty—to enchant the eye with attractiveness and to please the palate and stimulate the appetite with exciting flavors.

On many occasions, hors d'oeuvre accompany cocktails before dinner. The size must, therefore, be small. Making a meal out of such spicy food is not recommended as a steady diet despite the fact that in France and other middle-European countries, mainly during the hot summer months, guests of hotels and restaurants enjoy them as a complete meal. In these cases, delicacies and strongly spiced items will be eaten with milder foods such as salads of fruit, melons, tomatoes, asparagus, potato salad, etc.

The American cuisine, with leading chefs from all parts of the world, has contributed an enormous variety of hors d'oeuvre to our menus, and there will be further contributions from this part of the kitchen.

Of whatever origin, these specialties are mostly prepared from smoked, pickled, or marinated fish; crustaceans; mollusks; meats of special treatment; eggs; marinated vegetables; tiny tartlets; duchesses; éclairs; and bouchées with fine fillings. Many good leftovers from the hot kitchen can be transferred into a fine hors d'oeuvre with the right kind of culinary approach in creating something new.

Hors d'oeuvre in the classical menu language means also that all finer type cold foods should be included whether as a single item or as a group of variations. Therefore an assortment of canapes, caviar on ice, foie gras medallions on toast, oysters on half shell, shrimps, shrimp cocktail, fruit supreme or melon on ice, galantine, pâté, salami, and other fine cold cooked meats are hors d'oeuvre. Of course there is also a possibility of serving the galantine, the pâté, or other substantial meat or fish items, as an entrée. The difference here is the size of the portion and the way it is presented.

The hors d'oeuvre we present on the following pages may be served also as appetizers, either on the daily menu or any festive menu. You will find a few which figure on almost every a la carte menu of the finer hotels. We group them into items which have similarity among themselves.

A good hors d'oeuvre selection will consist of about twelve different items. If high priced delicacies are used the platter is called the "Hors d'Oeuvre Riche." As the illustrations show, the various items are put into glass dishes which are not large enough in most instances to hold more than one portion. The larger containers hold about six.

In fine restaurants, hors d'oeuvre are often served from a wagon. Containers here are somewhat larger and hold up to 10 portions each. The wagon is rolled to the guest's table for selection and service is given by the waiter or cook. These hors d'oeuvre are served as a first course in a full course meal.

In some first class establishments hors d'oeuvre are displayed on a buffet near the entrance of the dining room, the display usually consisting of a

Styles of Cocktail Glasses

From Left to Right: 1. Large fruit cup. 2. Silver supreme cup with glass insert. 3. Cocktail forks. 4. Small dinner-size cocktail glass. 5. Stemmed cocktail glass. 6. Supreme glass of more recent design. 7. Supreme cocktail glass, entirely of glass except the metal ring. The cup may be used for grapefruit and melon cocktails. 8. At extreme right, economy-size insert of glass with ring and cup.

fine ham presented in a hamholder of silver ready to carve, a side of smoked salmon, some herring specialties in original barrels or cans, a towering fruit basket with tropical and local fruits, little wooden boxes containing select peaches, figs, strawberries etc.

Cocktails

Cocktails served from the kitchen are entirely different from those in the bar but the effect of a cocktail should be the same—to whet the appetite. The American cuisine has developed an attractive way of serving cocktails. In a picture series the most popular are shown.

Sea food cocktails are served with cocktail sauce mix. The recipes are among the dressings, Chapter VII. Fruits and fruit sections may be marinated in Sherry, Port, or brandy-type spirits; also liqueurs such as Maraschino, Anisette, etc. Plain tomato juice is valued as a cocktail also.

Fresh Fruit Supreme

Supremes are the finest of fruit cocktails—citrus fruit sections, melon balls, berries, and other fruits. If raw apples or pears are used the fruits should be marinated for hours before using because they are too solid when used fresh. Often such fruit mixes are put into the glass with a top decoration of fresh fruit sections, berries, and fresh mint. A fruit cocktail mix from the can may do in some instances but is not considered adequate for this purpose.

Above: Fruit Cocktail Supreme

Melon balls, strawberries, raspberries, and pineapple chunks.

Above, Left: Fruit Cocktail Supreme

Pineapple, grapefruit, and orange sections topped with a melon ball.

Below, Left: Melon Ball Cocktail

Left: Preparation for Fruit Cocktail Supreme in Melon Basket

Below: Stewed fruits and fresh fruit combined, presented in a cut-out watermelon basket. The fruits should be marinated with wine or spirits of liqueur.

Melon Cocktail Supreme

Supreme of fruit has to be served very cold. In order to keep the fruits ice cold, the supreme container has been designed. This ice container keeps the inserts looking frosty and fresh. All fruits for such service must be cut, the seeds removed, then cooled to refrigeration temperature. For the melon cocktail, any ripe melon may be used. Crenshaw Melon Supreme or a mixture of cantaloupe, honey dew, and watermelon is a colorful creation. A small sprig of mint on top is good decoration and has a lovely odor. The melon should be marinated for a few hours in order to make a tasty cocktail. Sprinkle granulated sugar over the melon balls which are kept in an earthenware bowl, then pour a dessert wine over the fruit. Cover with a lid or wax paper and the odor of the wine will stay with the fruit.

Pineapple Tropical

First, cut the pineapple in quarters as shown. Cut away the inedible woody part and cut the meat from the shell so the latter resembles a boat. Cut the fruit into small sections and arrange on the pineapple shell as shown at the bottom of the illustration. In the empty spaces place berries or melon balls or citrus sections. Sprinkle rum over the surface, top with a sprig of mint and serve on ice.

Here papaya slices, pineapple sections, oranges, boysenberries, melon balls, and peeled grapes are used. With a little imagination, many artistic arrangements may be created.

Fruits

Fruit sections or pieces of different fruits may be used on hors d'oeuvre arrangements. These fruits should be served on ice. Melons and pineapple are the most popular in this line. Melons must be ripe to give the full flavor. This is true of all fruits. An additional melon ball of a different color or a mixture of strawberries or raspberries makes an attractive decoration.

Pineapple may be cut into thick slices with the skin still on but the meat cut at the edge for easier eating.

The Hawaiian way of cutting a pineapple boat is very attractive. Ripe figs are delicate items for this occasion also, in some instances with the skin removed.

Mango is a rather difficult fruit but is occasionally used fresh as a ripe fruit. It is peeled, the meat is cut off the seed in thick cuts and served in glass. Philadelphia cream cheese, formed in small round balls, goes well with mangoes.

Grapefruit or oranges make fine hors d'oeuvre when cut into baskets and filled either with fruit sections, jello, chicken salad or Waldorf salad.

A Meal from Fruit

With a grapefruit knife, remove center of the pineapple and cut the fruit from the shell. Cut the two pieces of pineapple removed from the shell lengthwise and reserve for later use. Additional fruits—grapefruit, papaya, grapes, bananas, oranges, apples, peaches, pears, and figs—may be cut in sections and mixed with the cubed pineapple from the remaining half. Put all fruits into a china bowl and sprinkle a little sugar over them. Add dessert wine—Sherry or Port—and liqueurs—Grand Marnier, Maraschino, or Curacao—and spirits—Kirsch, Brandy, or Drambuie—to this sugared fruit. Blend gently and place in a cooler for a couple of hours with a tight wax paper covering. Shortly before serving time, fill the pineapple shell with these fruits and decorate the top as shown.

Fruit Platter

Such platters do much to lighten up a buffet table. Smaller platters of china or pottery may be placed the length of the buffet table or individual dessert plates may be arranged to fill up all empty spaces. It gives the buffet a most colorful and appetizing look. In this illustration the grapefruit is sectioned and decorated with thin apple slices, each section filled with a berry or melon ball. Maraschino or Creme de Menthe dripped over the top adds to the flavor.

Papaya

Hawaii is exporting a small portion-size papaya but as this fruit is perishable, it is not available in all parts of the country. The meat is golden yellow and resembles the melon but is much finer. Serve papaya in halves or sections on ice with a wedge of lime. The seeds resemble caviar and may be eaten but they are usually removed before serving.

Shrimp Cocktail

From the tiny Alaskan or Island shrimps to the jumbo shrimps of the Gulf, a great variety may be served for cocktails. Frozen shrimps of any size and popularity can be obtained today on the American seafood market.

Shrimps must be treated correctly or they are a dangerous food item. Handled correctly they are a delight. The cooking time depends upon the size. A medium size shrimp should not be cooked longer than eight minutes. Plunge them into boiling court bouillon and after cooking, drain them immediately. Quick cooling is important, especially if they are not served the same day they are cooked. Shaved ice is recommended during storage in the refrigerator, and they should be covered generously with it. After this they must be peeled and deveined. Sometimes shrimp still show a black streak after being deveined. If this is the case, wash them thoroughly and after draining, add a little salt so they will regain their natural salt taste.

Small shrimps are heaped in a little mound; larger ones are grouped in fours and fives, depending upon the size and price of the cocktail.

A lettuce leaf tucked into the side of the container will garnish favorably. Pour the sauce over the shrimp at the last moment or pass sauce separately if there are two sauces on the menu.

Oyster Cocktail

Four regular size oysters make a dinner cocktail. If fresh oysters in the shell are not available, shucked oysters will serve. Before putting seafood into a cocktail glass a little bedding of chiffonade of lettuce is made in order to fill the bottom and make the seafood stand out more attractively. A crisp piece of lettuce placed daintily on the side of the cocktail glass adds to the cocktail's appeal. Sometimes a sprig of watercress will do the same. Then the oysters are set in the middle and the cocktail sauce poured over it at the last moment. A little cognac in the cocktail sauce adds to the flavor. Lemon tips are served with all seafood cocktails.

Olympia Oyster Cocktail

This is a special kind of oyster and is merchandised on the Pacific coast. Olympia oysters average 100 to the pint. Preparation and set up are the same as for regular oysters.

Marinated Fish

Leftovers of cooked fish may be marinated. Take off skin and remove bones carefully. Do not mash but break into small bits. Spread this out in a pan, chop a little onion, parsley and, if you like, julienned or small dices of green peppers, celery, tomatoes, or all of them. Sprinkle this over the fish, and add salt, pepper, a little Worcestershire sauce, and lemon juice. Finish with vinegar and oil. Decorate with egg slices. If desired, mayonnaise instead of vinaigrette may be used to finish the salad.

Pickled Fish

Herring, either in marinade or in sour cream or only salted are very acceptable hors d'oeuvre. Some of these specialties are served in the original can so the guest may see the brand. See also information about smoked fish.

Shrimp Cocktail

Olympia Oyster Cocktail

Lobster Cocktail

Seafood Cocktail

Shrimp Cocktail

Crableg Cocktail

Mixed Hors d'Oeuvre, European Style

A choice of vegetables, fruits, fish, eggs, meat, and other delicacies are assembled in glass-partitioned containers and placed on neatly folded napkins. In the right-hand dish are asparagus spears, vinaigrette; in the left-hand dish, antipasto and sardines. The center dish contains, beginning at the top and moving clockwise: caviar-stuffed eggs, avocado sections with mango chutney, shrimps, cantaloup with Prosciutto ham. The center section contains various types of olives. Placed on the napkins at the side are green onions and celery stocks with sprigs of parsley for garnish.

Hors d'Oeuvre Riche

This is a selection of different appetizing hors d'oeuvre with Langouste Parisienne in the center. The other dishes contain shrimp-filled barquettes, sardines, goose liver mousse, stuffed eggs, Greek salad, and game pâté. Melba toast and mayonnaise dressing are served on the side.

Meat Hors d'Oeuvre

Among these should first be mentioned the different sausage specialties. *Charcuterie fine* is the French word for a great many kinds of sausages such as Italian salami, sausage de Lyon, Bologna, Mortadella, Kosher Salami made from beef, Head Cheese, Braunschweiger Liverwurst, and others.

Ham

Air dried or smoked ham, of which Westphalian ham, Prosciutto, or Virginia ham are well known make, when properly prepared, excellent hors d'oeuvre. Also tasty country ham, of which almost any state has outstanding specialties, may be used. Any raw ham must be cut very thin and not too far ahead of serving time. Cones or rolls may be formed. Rolls stuffed with asparagus, pickles, olives or with vegetable salads, are other ways of presenting ham slices.

Ox Tongue Salted and Smoked

Ox tongue sliced thin may be used either plain or stuffed with piccalilli. Julienne of tongue with pickles makes a good vinaigrette hors d'oeuvre.

Meat Salads

Any type of leftover roast or boiled meat may be made into a tangy meat salad by cutting the meat either julienne style or into neat cubes. Cut off any fat first. Meat salads may be combined with different colorful vegetable items such as red pimiento, green peppers, radish slices, strips of cucumbers, sliced or quartered mushrooms. The meat salad tastes best when mixed with a vinaigrette sauce with chives sprinkled over it.

Beef Rolls

Medium rare roast sirloin may be cut into slices, stuffed with a spread of suitable choice and rolled. The finger-thick rolls are then cut into the desired lengths and glazed with aspic.

Canapés

Canapés belong to the same group as hors d'oeuvre but they should not be called such. It is confusing to do so. "Canapé" is a French word and means "something which is raised." In culinary language this means something that is set on toast or bread or even crackers.

The treatment of canapes may vary with the bread base which should be crisp but not hard. The bread should be toasted, cooled, and spread with a thin layer of foamy beaten butter. This butter spread will protect the toast from getting soaked from juicy toppings.

On the following pages are illustrations of many canapés. The captions list the fillings and decorations used.

Smoked Salmon

On buttered toast topped with egg and pimiento.

Bismarck Herring

Wrapped around a dill pickle and topped with an onion ring.

Sardine or Brisling

On garlic or mustard buttered toast, topped with onion ring, topped with chopped eggs and chives.

Sardine

On buttered toast topped with butter applied with bag.

Salmon Caviar

Buttered toast topped with cream cheese nest filled with caviar and topped with chopped chives.

Tuna Fish Purée

Buttered toast topped with tuna fish purée with butter border and thin strip of anchovies.

Lobster

Lobster spread on toast, thin slice of lobster tail, chopped white and yolk of egg on corners.

Caviar

On butter toast with butter border. Cocktail onion in center.

Herring

Rectangular filet of herring on lettuce leaf topped with pickles, onion ring, and pimiento.

Ecrevisse

On butter toast and decorated with egg yolk purée.

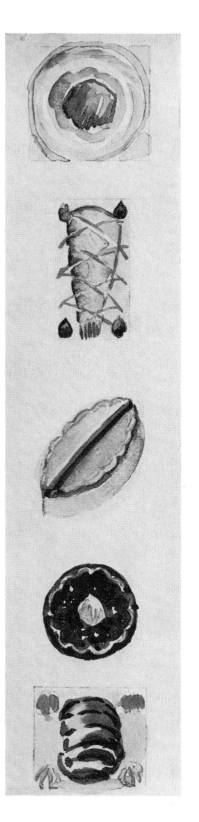

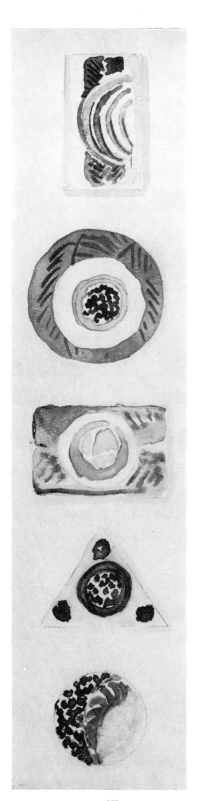

Anchovies

Anchovy butter on toast with anchovy filet topped with section of Bermuda onion.

Caviar

Buttered toast topped with egg slice, caviar, and Bermuda onion.

Smoked Salmon

Topped with egg slice and caviar.

Egg Spread

On toast topped with slices of stuffed olives.

Sardine

Two half filets of sardine on buttered toast top with egg and mushroom slice.

Shrimp

Shrimp spread on toast topped with half of a shrimp.

Anchovies

On toast. Anchovy roll filled with caviar. Decorate corners with capers.

Anchovies

On toast. Fine slices of anchovy with butter border. Cocktail onion in center.

Caviar and Shrimp

On one side of toast round place caviar, other side egg white chopped. Top with shrimp.

Crab Leg

On buttered toast place lettuce leaf, egg slice, and crab leg. Decorate with pimiento.

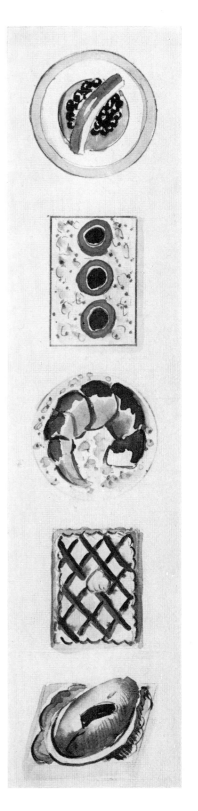

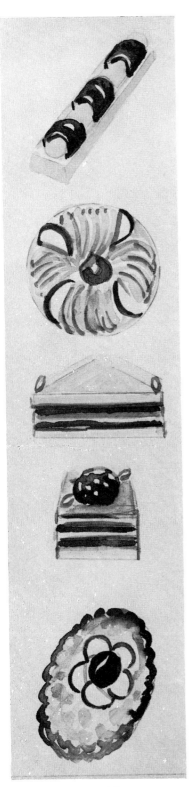

Roquefort and Anchovies

On toast, roquefort cheese paste decorated with anchovies.

Midinette

Pumpernickel bread spread with Camembert cheese and chopped truffles.

Roquefort

On toast, roquefort cream cheese spread decorated with radish slices. Caper in center.

Cream Cheese

On saltine cracker decorated with pimiento or radish and chopped chives.

Cheese

Any cream cheese variously colored on pumpernickel bread decorated with pistachio nut.

Anchovy

On buttered toast, decorated with egg and mushroom slice.

Cheese

Same as above topped with radish and pistachio.

Ham

Cooked ham on buttered toast topped with half asparagus spear decorated with pimiento.

Bacon and Cheese

Cream cheese mixed with bacon and chives topped with radish slices and ripe olive slice.

Ham Mousse

Rippled on toast with ripe olive sections.

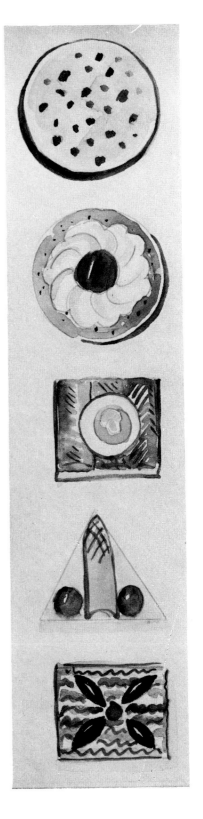

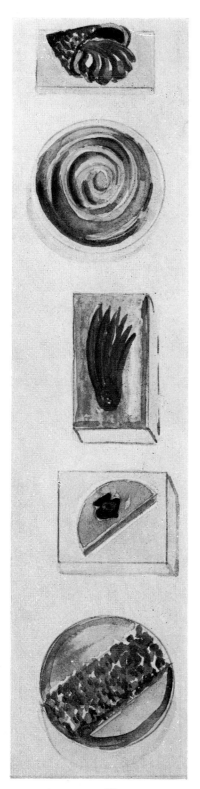

Salami

Cornet of salami on buttered toast filled with tiny gherkins.

Bouchere

Tongue on buttered toast with foi gras roll decorated with truffle and aspic.

Roast Beef Roll

Slice of thin roast beef and maitre butter on toast, cooled and sliced. Brush with aspic.

Liverwurst

On toast, heaped in mound shape with butter border and truffle slice.

Roast Beef

On buttered toast, thin slice of roast beef brushed with aspic, decorated with gherkins.

Ham

On buttered toast with asparagus. spear.

Foie Gras

On buttered toast with truffle cut-out.

Gauloise

Poultry mousse enclosed in ham roll with asparagus.

Alsacienne

Foie gras paste and chopped ox tongue on toast.

Bohemienne

Ham purée on pumpernickel bread decorated with paprika and gherkins.

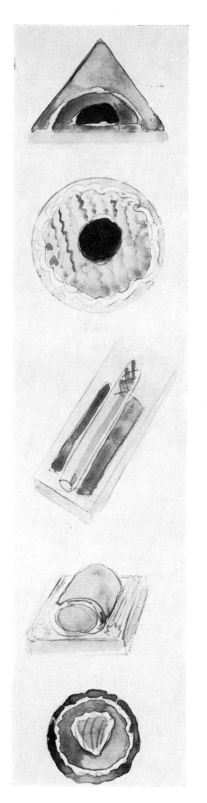

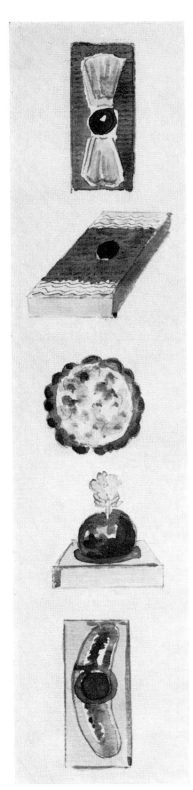

Tongue

Thin slice of tongue on buttered toast with thin wedges of pineapple topped with half of cherry.

Antoine

Buttered brown bread with lettuce leaf and tomato topped with chopped eggs and radishes.

Tongue Spread

On toast trimmed with butter and truffle slice.

Charley

Roquefort cream cheese between thin slices of pumpernickel.

Bacon-Cheese Spread

Bacon chopped with cream or any cheese on cracker.

Clermont

On toast thin tomato slice, cucumber slice, egg slice. Aspic over top. Cool and cut.

Meat Ball

On buttered toast place a small meat ball on pickle slice held with toothpick.

Massena

Parsley buttered toast on tomato slice topped with asparagus spear and chopped egg.

Sausage

Cocktail sausage on mustard buttered toast with ring of stuffed olive.

Rose Marie

Cream cheese on brown bread topped with radish slices and gherkins.

Such toasted canapes should be served as fresh as possible. However, many times hundreds of canapes have to be prepared for a single party without adequate time to prepare them at the last minute. In such instances the bread base is not toasted, and the topping, for better appearance, is coated with a thin layer of aspic. This enables the canapes to be kept in perfect condition for the same day or even into the second day.

Besides toasted breads, special breads such as pumpernickel, rye bread, or crackers of different kinds and shapes may be used. Assorted breads and crackers add to the attractiveness of the canape plates.

To organize the preparation of an unusual amount of canapes the following steps are necessary:

1. Secure sandwich loaves which are three or four days old. Fresh bread cannot be cut evenly nor be spread properly.
2. Soften the butter by allowing it to stay at kitchen temperature the necessary length of time. Whip it thoroughly to achieve a fluffy paste. Only butter prepared in this way will spread evenly over the bread.
3. Cut the bread into slices one quarter inch thick. For mass production, cut the bread the long way from end to end. Cutting and placing each canape individually takes on enormous amount of time and it is doubtful if they will look as well trimmed as when cut the long way. The outer crust may be saved for the purpose of protecting the cut bread from drying out. Wrap a few strings around the sliced loaf, cover with a napkin, and place in the refrigerator. This way the bread may be kept for two or three days.

Canapés in Preparation for Service

To speed up preparation of a large number of canapés, first cut the bread the long way of the loaf. Butter the bread and place on it whatever topping belongs there. Place it on a pastry rack and cool well in the refrigerator before cutting it into the desired shape.

Just before serving the canapés, place the bread strips with topping along the edge of the cutting board. Place the knife frequently in hot water so it will cut through the bread easily. Oblong or square-shaped canapés may be cut in this fashion very speedily. Round canapés will have to be made singly.

Canapés Arranged for Service

The arrangement of the canapés on the large tray is left to the judgment of the person in charge of the buffet table. Above, Left: Here the canapés are not arranged symmetrically. This type of arrangement really demands a centerpiece.

Below, Left: Here the same types of canapés are placed in easily distinguishable rows.

Below: Contents of Canapé Tray

From Left to Right: 1. Roquefort cheese on round pieces of toast garnished with a dot of pimiento. 2. Anchovies in strips. 3. Smoked salmon garnished with egg and mushroom slices. 4. Asparagus spears on mustard butter garnished with strips of pimiento. 5. Cheese squares. 6. Liver purée on oval-shaped toast, butter border with star-shaped truffle. 7. Salami cornet with stuffed olive held in place with frill. 8. Half skinned sardine with butter decoration and capers. 9. Egg spread topped with egg and tomato slices with butter points. 10. Herring filets decorated with mustard butter.

Canapés Arranged with Center Piece

From Left to Right: 1. Asparagus spears wrapped in thin slices of ham decorated with mustard butter. 2. Smoked salmon with ripe olive meat. 3. Anchovy purée decorated with anchovy filet and pickled onion. 4. Egg slice on round toast with egg purée border stuffed with red caviar. 5. Caviar triangle with split shrimp on top garnished with chopped parsley. 6. Toast oval with spooned foie gras and truffles. 7. Smoked salmon with ripe olive meat. 8. Crab legs with maitre d'hotel butter topped with caper. The centerpiece is a pineapple decorated with shrimp.

4. If spreads of different ingredients are used, they should be prepared ahead of time and set aside for later use.

5. Canned stuffs should be opened and taken out of the can, and placed neatly in lines on trays.

6. Place watery ingredients on racks or elevations so the juice can run off. Otherwise the canape will be soggy.

7. Decorating items have to be cut ahead and placed either in jelly, oil, or water, depending upon the nature of the material, to keep until needed.

8. Sometimes a small centerpiece is set in the center of the platter. These must be made ahead of time and space provided for them. Attractive centerpieces may be made of models from butter, wax, or margarine; from fresh pineapple, the top cut off to be replaced later, cored and the center replaced with a small supreme glass to hold sauce. Shrimp may be attached to the edge of the pineapple with fancy picks. A melon or grapefruit basket is another attractive centerpiece.

9. Platters for canape service must be laid out with sparkling white linen napkins or lace doilies. Emphasis must be laid upon a good setup and correct tools. Accuracy in cutting is most essential. A little smoothed butter in a cornucopia-shaped holder can be dressed into a line or frill around the topping. Colored butter, if used, must be a pale pastel shade.

There are scores of possibilities for making canapes. The usual assortment should have about 10 or 12 varieties. The flavor of each must be different: smoked fish, eggs, crustaceans, cheeses, butter spreads, vegetables, sausages or ham, and many others.

Italian Antipasto

"Antipasto" is a typical Italian hors d'oeuvre. Despite the fact it is prepared almost entirely from vegetables, it is not a salad. Prepared in accordance with the following recipe it will keep in good condition for almost a month if refrigerated.

Following are the ingredients:

1 plate chopped onions	1 quart stuffed olives
1 plate diced carrots	1 pint small peppers
3 stalks diced celery	1 plate small buds, cauliflower
1 plate strips of green peppers	1 gallon pearl onions
1 plate fresh artichoke quarters	4 pounds small mushrooms

capers

2 quarts olive or peanut oil	1 gallon tomato paste
2 quarts wine vinegar	½ gallon chili sauce

1 soupspoon chopped garlic

Juice of 8 lemons

Tie in a cheesecloth bag:

2 teaspoons white pepper	1 soupspoon oregano leaves
6 bay leaves	1 teaspoon marjoram powder

12 cloves

1 bundle of parsley tied together

Heat the oil in a large sauté pan. Sauté the onions first until they have a glossy appearance. Add carrots, celery, pimientos, artichokes, cauliflower, mushrooms, stirring often. When these vegetables are sufficiently steamed, add lemon juice and vinegar. Blend in the tomato paste. Add condiments and two soupspoons of salt. Stir well and bring to a boil; then allow to simmer for one hour. Add other ingredients—olives, peppers, capers, pearl onions and mix gently. Bring again to a boil while stirring and remove from the heat. Adjust salt content. Put in an earthen crock. When cool, place in refrigerator. Serve cold with a few anchovy filets or pieces of tuna fish or sardines on top. Glass or earthenware bowls are used as containers for service on the buffet.

Top row, left to right: chopped onions, diced carrots, diced celery, strips of green peppers, fresh artichoke quarters, stuffed olives, small peppers.
Bottom row, right to left: small buds of cauliflower, pearl onions, diced mushrooms, capers.

CHAPTER VII

Cold Sauces and Dressings

The basis of nearly all cold sauces is mayonnaise. If treated properly many delicious variations result. These are achieved by adding ingredients such as pickles, anchovies, tomato ketchup, chili sauce, relish, kitchen herbs, and seasoning, the latter carefully measured.

Fine mayonnaise is made only with olive oil. A second choice is peanut oil. Dietetic measures, as well as economy, call for a more digestible mayonnaise when the basic preparation is changed somewhat and cornstarch sauce is used.

A few important recipes which vary in quantity and oil content are as follows:

Finest Mayonnaise—Small Quantity

Ingredients:
> 1 quart oil, preferably fresh olive or peanut oil
> 3 or 4 egg yolks
> Juice of 1 lemon
> 1 oz. vinegar
> Salt and pepper
> ½ teaspoon mustard, dry or French
> Few drops of seasoning (Worcestershire or Maggi)

Preparation:
Mix egg yolks, mustard, seasoning and vinegar in a round earthenware bowl and gradually add slightly warmed oil, stirring constantly. Salt and pepper last.

Finest Mayonnaise—Large Quantity

Ingredients:
15 gallons olive or peanut oil
100 egg yolks
1½ gallons vinegar
20 oz. salt
8 oz. mustard
Salt, pepper and Worcestershire sauce

Preparation:
Same as for preceding mayonnaise

Mayonnaise with 30% Oil Content—Large Quantity

1. Boil 1 gallon vinegar, 6 gallons water, 1 lb. salt
2. Mix 8 lbs. cornstarch, 1½ gallons cold water
3. When Step 1 is boiling, mix it with Step 2, and bring back to the boiling point.
4. Pour in a mixing bowl and cover the surface with a layer of crushed ice to prevent crusting over while cooling.
5. When cool, which takes a few hours, place in mixing bowl and rotate slowly for five minutes.
6. Gradually add:

100 egg yolks
1 small bottle Worcestershire sauce
3 to 5 gallons oil
4 soupspoons Accent powder
5 oz. Maggi seasoning
10 soupspoons of mustard

7. Color with egg coloring to right tint.
This economical mayonnaise may be kept in refrigerator for weeks.

Mayonnaise—Yields 12 Gallons

Ingredients:

20 oz. salt	2½ quarts vinegar
5 oz. English mustard	10 gallons salad oil
2½ quarts egg yolks	1 pint hot water

Preparation:
1. Weigh and sift dry ingredients.
2. Pour in large mixing bowl, add egg yolks and beat at No. 2 speed until blended.
3. Add oil slowly until the mixture is well emulsified and quite stiff.
4. Add vinegar, a small quantity at a time; add more oil and continue adding oil and vinegar until all has been incorporated.
5. Add hot water slowly at the last. This binds sauce for better storage up to two or three weeks.

76

Variations of Mayonnaise Dressing

Thousand Island Dressing:

Amount:
5 gallons

Ingredients:

4 gallons mayonnaise
3 pints chili sauce
3 pints green peppers, finely chopped

1½ pints pimentos, chopped
1 pint chopped ripe olives
¾ pint Worcestershire sauce

1½ dozen hard boiled eggs, chopped

Preparation:
Combine all ingredients and blend thoroughly.

Remoulade Sauce:

Amount:
3 gallons

Ingredients:

¾ pint parsley, chopped
¾ pint dill pickles, chopped
½ cup prepared mustard
½ cup tarragon vinegar

¼ cup anchovy filets, chopped
¼ cup capers, squeezed and chopped

3 gallons mayonnaise

Preparation:
Combine all ingredients and add to mayonnaise.

Tartare Sauce:

Amount:
1 gallon

Ingredients:

½ pint parsley, chopped
½ pint sweet pickles, chopped
¼ cup chopped onions
3 hard boiled eggs passed through fine sieve

1 tablespoon lemon juice
1 tablespoon prepared mustard
1 tablespoon chopped capers
Dash of tabasco, salt, and pepper

1 gallon mayonnaise

Preparation:
Add all ingredients to mayonnaise and blend well.

Ravigote Sauce:

Amount:
1 gallon

Ingredients:

4 tablespoons chopped kitchen herbs
1 gallon mayonnaise

Preparation:
Blend both ingredients.

Plaza Dressing:

Amount:
1 gallon

Ingredients:
1 gallon mayonnaise
8 tablespoons Worcestershire sauce
8 tablespoons chutney

Preparation:
Blend well.

Mousseline or Chantilly Sauce:

Amount:
1 gallon

Ingredients:
1 gallon mayonnaise
1 gallon whipped cream

Preparation:
Blend.

Lorenzo Dressing:

Amount:
1 gallon

Ingredients:
1 gallon mayonnaise
1 cup fine julienned hearts of celery
1 cup of pineapple
½ cup of watercress

Preparation:
Blend all ingredients. Sometimes Lorenzo dressing is built up with a French dressing base. In this case, chili sauce and watercress are used and pineapple is omitted.

Garde Manger Dressing:

Amount:
1 gallon

Ingredients:
Essence of 2 cloves of garlic
4 tablespoons horseradish
4 tablespoons chopped parsley
1 gallon mayonnaise

Preparation:
Blend all ingredients.

Green Dressing:

Add blanched herbs and spinach, which have been strained through a sieve, to mayonnaise so that sauce acquires green color and flavor.

Vincent Sauce:

Remoulade Sauce with same spinach and herbs as for Green Dressing.

Tyrolienne Sauce:

Amount:
1 gallon

Ingredients:
1 gallon mayonnaise
2 grated onions
1 cup of tomato ketchup

Preparation:
Blend mayonnaise with tomato ketchup and grate 2 medium size onions directly into the sauce; mix.

Russian Dressing:

Amount:
3 gallons

Ingredients:
2 gallons mayonnaise
2 quarts chili sauce
3 cups chopped green peppers
2 cups chopped pimientos
3 cups chopped parsley
5 tablespoons Worcestershire sauce
5 tablespoons tarragon vinegar
3 teaspoons salt
1 teaspoon pepper
6 tablespoons imported caviar

Preparation:
Combine ingredients and stir until well blended.

California Dressing:

Amount:
1 gallon

Ingredients:
6 oz. small white seedless grapes
1 cup chopped pimiento
1 gallon mayonnaise

Preparation:
Blend.

Green Goddess Dressing:

Amount:
2 gallons

Ingredients:
8 cloves garlic, minced
1 lb. anchovies well drained
   and mashed to a paste
2 cups green onions finely
   chopped
1 cup lemon juice
2 cups tarragon vinegar
5 pints sour cream
4 quarts mayonnaise
2 cups chopped parsley
Salt, and freshly ground pepper
   to taste

Preparation:
Combine all ingredients, stir well until blended. Chill thoroughly and use with mixed green salads. If dressing is too thick, depending on consistency of mayonnaise and sour cream used, it may be thinned down with a little water.

Mayonnaise Collée: (Jellied Mayonnaise)

(Used as a covering sauce on which decorations are placed—for salmon, vegetables, eggs, etc.)

Amount:
3 quarts

Ingredients:
2 parts mayonnaise
1 part liquid aspic

Preparation:
Let the meat gelée cool to a sirupy consistency and blend with a spoon, into the mayonnaise. This sauce is used for covering different cold food items; fish, eggs, vegetables, etc., and must have the right consistency when used. When too cold the sauce will get lumpy. Therefore hold bowl, with contents, in warm water to get sauce smooth again.

Gribiche Sauce:

Amount:
1 gallon

Ingredients:
1 gallon mayonnaise
1 cup finely chopped egg yolk
2 tablespoons of chopped chervil, parsley, and chives

Preparation:
Blend all ingredients.

Andalouse Sauce:

Amount:
1 gallon

Ingredients:
1 gallon mayonnaise
2 lbs. peeled ripe tomatoes with seeds and juice removed and julienne of red pimientos.

Preparation:
Chop tomato meat fine and, with julienne of pimientos, add to the mayonnaise.

Lime, Lemon, or Orange Cream Dressing:

Amount:
2 quarts

Ingredients:

1 quart mayonnaise
⅓ to ½ cup fresh lime, lemon
or orange juice

1 quart whipped cream
Add a little sugar.

Preparation:

Mix mayonnaise with lemon, lime or orange juice. Fold in whipped cream. Add sugar if needed. Keep salad dressing on ice, not in refrigerator, and make up as needed.

Roquefort Cream Dressing or Bleu Cheese Dressing:

Amount:

1½ gallons

Ingredients:

1½ lbs. Roquefort or for bleu
cheese cream dressing, substitute bleu cheese
½ oz. garlic
½ cup chopped onions
1 quart mayonnaise

3½ quarts sour cream, commercial
½ cup lemon juice
½ tablespoon white pepper
1 cup cider vinegar
about ¼ cup salt

Preparation:

Grind cheese, garlic and onion and add to mayonnaise. Mix on low speed for two minutes. Add remaining ingredients and mix two more minutes.

Chaudfroid Sauces

White Chaudfroid Sauce I:

Amount:

½ gallon

Ingredients:

6 lbs. veal bones
2 lbs. chicken bones, wings, etc.
2 onions, 1 carrot and some
celery, all diced
2 pints white wine

Juice of 4 lemons
Crushed peppercorns and salt
1 quart heavy cream
2 egg yolks
Water

Preparation:

Cut bones into pieces and blanch with water, bringing to a good boil. Cool under running water until clear. Then put into a casserole with a little butter and sauté with the vegetables without browning. Pour white wine over the sautéed mass and cover with water. Add salt and peppercorns. Boil slowly for about three to four hours. If it cooks too rapidly, additional water has to be added, which is not recommended. Be sure to remove all scum from the surface from time to time so the liquid remains clean. Strain stock and cook it down to about one quart, then add one quart heavy cream and bring to a boil.

Flavor the sauce with a little cayenne and add salt if necessary. Finish with two egg yolks and strain sauce through cloth.

Notice: This sauce is made entirely without flour or gelatine added. The gelatine content comes from good veal bones and the correct cooking process.

White Chaudfroid Sauce II:

This is a preparation of chaudfroid sauce with gelatine and flour sauce added. This is a short cut and not recommended for finer work but for covering large buffet pieces or center pieces. Of course this sauce must also be prepared for taste and flavor in event the piece will be eaten. This type sauce is also used for dummies.

Amount:
   3 gallons

Ingredients:
   2¼ gallons thin white sauce made from butter, flour and chicken stock
   12 soupspoons of granulated gelatin
   3 quarts heavy cream

Preparation:
First prepare a thin white sauce (Supreme) and while still hot sprinkle the powdered or granulated gelatine in small quantities into the sauce while stirring with a whip. When all visible gelatine grains are completely dissolved in the sauce, add heavy cream and bring it quickly to a boil, always stirring with the whip so gelatine does not burn on the bottom. Strain through cloth and add salt and cayenne pepper to taste. Put sauce into a stainless steel container on crushed ice and by stirring frequently but gently bring chaudfroid sauce to the right covering consistency. Cold chaudfroid sauce may be desolved by putting container, with sauce, in bainmarie. Start over in cooling down to the right consistency.

Pink Chaudfroid:

Prepare a small amount of strong tomato sauce, omitting fat if possible. Mix tomato sauce with adequate amount of white chaudfroid sauce in order to get the desired color. Do not use artificial coloring for it may ruin the appetizing appearance.

Green Chaudfroid:

Use white chaudfroid as the base. Preparation of a green coloring of natural appearance may be made with green herbs, spinach, and parsley. The greens have to be run through the grinder. The resulting liquid mash must be pressed through a towel into a bowl. The mash in the towel is useless. Place the bowl containing the green liquid, full of small green particles, into a bainmarie and shake it until the liquid begins to separate. At this moment, take from the heat and after a few minutes strain through a napkin. The small amount of green left in the napkin is intensive enough to color chaudfroid sauce a natural green.

82

Brown Chaudfroid:

To one quart heated *Glace de Viande* add three-fourths quart of tomato sauce and two quarts of diluted aspic. Mix well and add one-half glass of madeira or sherry. If the color is too red, add caramel coloring.

Cumberland Sauce—a sweet sauce served mostly with game.

Ingredients:

6 oranges	1 soup spoon English mustard
1 lemon	1 lb. currant jelly
2 pints red wine	Orange and lemon juice

Cayenne

Preparation:

Take off a thin layer of the rind of the oranges and lemons. Julienne rind and boil it for 10 minutes in the red wine. Mix English mustard with a little red wine—just enough to make a paste. Mix this in the currant jelly. Squeeze the juice from the oranges and lemons into the sauce; also the julienned rinds with the cooking liquid. Add a little cayenne to taste.

Vinaigrette Sauce

Amount:

2 quarts

Ingredients:

1 quart salad oil	3 tablespoons chopped capers
1¾ pints vinegar	2 tablespoons chopped chives
¼ pint water	or green onion tops
3 hard boiled eggs, chopped fine	1½ tablespoons prepared mustard
½ cup parsley	½ tablespoon Worcestershire sauce
½ cup finely chopped onions	

Salt, pepper, Accent

Preparation:

Combine all ingredients. Mix thoroughly each time before serving. Add a few fine cubes of red pimientos if color is desired.

CHAPTER VIII

Preparation of Fish, Crustaceans and Mollusks

On the cold buffet, the salmon, the crab, the lobster, and the shrimp along with other delicacies of the sea have such an established place of honor that without them the cold buffet would scarcely be worthy of the name. Their color and variety are indispensable when it comes to the organization of a proper cold buffet, not only because of eye appeal but also the important factor of tasty nutrition. Salt water fish contain iodine, iron, calcium, and phosphorus along with many other necessary food elements.

Fish are divided into two classes, fresh water and salt water fish. For culinary purposes, crustaceans and mollusks are also grouped with fish. The majority live in water and vary in quality. This variation, even in the same species, is usually determined by local conditions. Also, two pertinent facts must be remembered in the preparation of fish:

1. Spawning uses up a great deal of energy, especially in the female. During the spawning season and for some time afterward, the fish is lean and tasteless. Such fish should be banned for buffet work.

2. Because of their high water content, fish decay easily forming a dangerous fish poison.

Fish for buffets should be fresh, not frozen. However, there are a great many fresh-frozen filets of fish which are very useful in the preparation of salads. Fresh trout and salmon must remain under refrigeration for 24 hours. Otherwise, the body will break up and fall apart while cooking.

For buffet work, salmon is the favorite. Also useful among the large salt water group are small halibut, turbot, and to some extent, large game fish such as marlin and albacore, a species of tuna fish. Buy salmon and trout intact as they lose their identity without the head. Do not remove the head. Any kind of fish may be used in buffets just so they are presented as naturally as possible.

Basic methods of preparing fish for the cold buffet are (1) boiling in a "court bouillon"; (2) au bleu; (3) steaming; and (4) braising.

Boiling

Fish are boiled in plain salt water or in a specially-seasoned liquid known as "court bouillon." The fish loses less flavor if placed in well-salted hot water, brought to a boil, and allowed to simmer without actually boiling.

Court Bouillon for Fresh Water Fish

To make one gallon:

7 pints of water	8 ozs. finely sliced onions
1 pint of vinegar	1 laurel leaf
2 ozs. of salt	1 small bunch of parsley stems
14 ozs. of diced carrots	¾ oz. of peppercorns

Parboil this court bouillon for about 40 minutes, strain and use for cooking fish.

Court Bouillon with White Wine

½ gal. California Sauterne   ½ gal. water

Add other ingredients as used for court bouillon above. This is particularly suitable for cold fish dishes—both salt and fresh water fish. The liquid may be used for preparing fish jelly.

Liquid for Salt Water Fish

1 gal. of water   2 ozs. of salt

Add a generous portion of lemon juice.

Rules for Cooking

Use only enough water or liquid to cover the fish. Use, if available, a fish kettle large enough to accommodate the length and width of the fish. Never let the water in which the fish is cooked boil—only simmer.

If the fish must be cooked in pieces, the liquid must be at the boiling point when the fish is placed in it. If the fish is whole, the skin may easily break when it is placed in boiling liquid.

Au Bleu

Only fish freshly killed and with unbroken skin can be cooked in this manner. The fish should not be scaled and the fins must be left on. Trout and carp are most suitable for this method of cooking.

Prepare strong salt water and add five ounces of vinegar to each gallon of water. Finely sliced root vegetables, leeks, laurel, peppercorns, and some sprigs of parsley may be added if desired. The fish must be killed only a short time before using, and carefully cleaned. They are then laid on a plate and a little vinegar is poured over them before they are placed in the hot, not boiling, liquid. They must only be allowed to simmer or otherwise they will fall apart.

Cool the fish in the same liquid. Be careful in handling them after they are cooked because the skin slips easily and gives the fish a scratched appearance.

Steaming (*Filets and Portion Sizes*)

For this method of preparation, use shallow pans. Fish filets lose much albumin if wrongly treated. This albumin lies directly under the skin. Therefore, make sure that the liquid into which the filets or slices are placed comes quickly to a steaming boil so that this albumin thickens immediately and is not lost.

The pan must be brushed over with a layer of butter before the liquid is added so that the filets will not stick. Also, each filet must be brushed with butter where it touches the next one. Otherwise, they will stick together and break when separated. Cool in the same pan.

For buffet work, the fish filets should be placed on a rack, carefully covered with the sauce indicated, decorated, and covered with a fine film of fish jelly prepared from the court bouillon.

Braising

The fish is usually larded and steamed on a base of diced vegetables in a little wine. There are many varieties of fish galantines.

Salmon

Salmon, always a welcome culinary treat, is an appealing decorative piece and lends grandeur to any cold buffet. This delectable fish is part of the daily fare in Scandinavian countries and it is small wonder that they have found many ways to serve salmon tastefully and attractively. To give credit where it is due, the series of pictures herewith demonstrates the Scandinavian method of preparing salmon. Needless to say, the culinary expert will have many possibilities for variations in presentation such as *en Bellevue, à la Norvegienne, à la Parisienne,* etc. The basic procedure for all of these is the same; only the decorations are different.

Preparation of a Cold Whole Salmon

As with all other buffet pieces, special attention is required in preparing and cooking the fish. The meat of the fish is particularly tender and great care must be taken that the salmon maintains its natural appearance. To accomplish a better effect, it should be presented on its belly, not on one side.

1

2

3

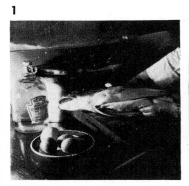

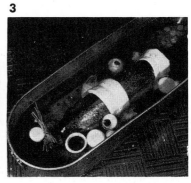

1. Preparation of a Cold Whole Salmon

After the fish is thoroughly cleaned, care should be taken in arranging the wadding in order to regain the graceful shape of the salmon.

2. The tail fin and back fin, if not needed for the finished piece, is trimmed. The fish is then placed on the inset of the fish kettle and securely tied. Since the string may cut into the flesh during the cooking, a cloth should be wound around the fish before the string is loosely tied to the rack.

3. The fish is seen in the partly filled fish kettle. In order to make the onions, carrots, parsley, and bay leaves more visible they appear here to be floating on the surface of the water. For the actual cooking process they should be placed on the bottom of the kettle before the fish is arranged on the rack. If preferred, a fish stock (court bouillon) may be cooked ahead, the vegetables and spices removed, then cooled before the fish is added for boiling. If the first method of cooking is used, the necessary amounts of salt and vinegar are added and the fish is then covered with *cold* water. For best results, bring the water to a full boil and then *simmer slowly* until the salmon is cooked. The approximate cooking time for a salmon of 15 to 20 pounds is 40 minutes. After the fish has cooled *in the cooking water* (fish bouillon) allow it to dry completely on the rack.

4. The salmon may be presented with or without its skin but it is best not to place the garnishings directly on the skin. In this illustration, the skin has been partially removed in the center of the fish, the surface evened out with a knife, superfluous fat and gelatin removed, and small openings filled.

5. For suitable garnishes use shrimps, cucumbers, stuffed deviled eggs, stuffed baby beets, small cones of smoked salmon, and small filled tomatoes. A slicing machine is a great aid in preparing radishes, cucumbers, and truffles for decorations as they should be paper-thin.

6. After the salmon has been thoroughly cooled in the refrigerator it should receive a coat of thick jelly. Next the decorations, also dipped in jelly, should be arranged in place. Shrimps, previously sized and dipped in jelly, are placed on the back of the salmon stuffed with small radish slices. Small balls, formed from cucumbers, truffles, and ripe black olives are also used in the decoration. The eye of the salmon may be effectively emphasized by the use of a slice of egg white and a piece of truffle.

On the platter use stuffed eggs, tomatoes, asparagus, cucumbers, shrimps, artichoke bottoms, vegetable timbales, etc. For sauce, use mayonnaise and mayonnaise variations.

4

5

6

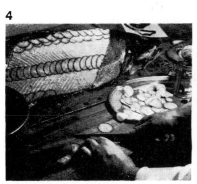
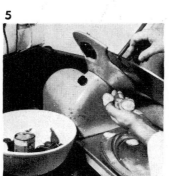
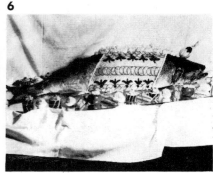

To achieve this, in dressing the salmon, not eviscerated, use a wadding of napkins or other clean cloths. First, the fish is split open in two places, the viscera taken out through these openings. Fish that are purchased eviscerated may be treated the same way if carefully wadded.

A 12 to 15-pound salmon yields approximately 30 to 40 servings. When buying, always order the fish intact, with the head still on the body. If frozen fish must be purchased, be sure they are not old fish from the past season. Usually fresh salmon keep very well for two or three days in refrigeration.

Fish Jelly

To prepare fish jelly use two pints of fish stock, four ounces of gelatine powder, and the beaten whites of three eggs. Bring these ingredients to a boil and strain through a napkin. This will yield sufficient fish jelly to dress a 12-pound salmon.

Additional Presentations of Cold Whole Salmon

Salmon a la Parisienne

Remove a piece of the skin from the salmon in the shape of a saddle and cover the exposed surface with mayonnaise collée or paste. Decorate along the edges of the saddle with butter, slightly rose colored. Dress with a cornucopia, chervil, lobster coral, truffles, and mushroom buttons. Garnish the platter with artichoke bottoms filled with vegetable salad. Serve mayonnaise on the side.

Salmon a la Norvegienne

This is a skinned salmon garnished with tiny shrimps. An additional garnish may be cucumber barrels filled with purée of smoked salmon and tartlets with crab mayonnaise. Serve with sauce Russe and tiny stuffed tomatoes.

Miramichi Salmon, New Brunswick Style

This is fresh salmon from the Miramichi River in New Brunswick, Canada, garnished with lobster claws and tails and served with potato salad, hard boiled eggs, and additionally garnished with fiddle heads, a local vegetable specialty. Serve with mayonnaise and ketchup on the side.

Fresh Gaspé Salmon, Laurentian Style

Prepare as directed in any basic recipe. Garnish the partly skinned salmon with shrimps. Decorate the middle part of the salmon with truffles—perhaps a design of a sail boat.

Fresh Chinook Salmon, Fantasia

Sever the head from the body of a fresh Chinook salmon about four inches behind the breast fins. Cut the tail from the body about 10 inches above the tail fins. Cut evenly so that the tail part will stand erect later for decorative purposes. Cook both the head and the tail upright in a kettle of court bouillon for five minutes. Cool over night.

The body of the salmon is cut in two lengthwise filets and the skin removed. Make small slices about one inch wide from the filet in order to get about

24 to 30 nice portions. Take these pieces of filet from the cutting board, place them in a shallow pan and poach them in the steamer for about 10 minutes. Cool them on a rack and decorate each filet individually with select truffles, radishes, olives, etc.

Finally, place the fish on a large silver tray, head in front and tail at the end. Between, place the filets in an exact arrangement, leaving an open space in the mid section. Fill this space with crisp green lettuce hearts. Garnish the remaining space with hard boiled eggs stuffed with caviar, either Russian or salmon, asparagus tips, cucumbers, and tomatoes stuffed with adequate fillings. With this salmon, serve Sauce Chantilly.

To Prepare a Salmon Masterpiece

For this presentation, choose a particularly fine salmon. Any size may be used but one weighing from 16 to 20 pounds makes a particularly good display.

Step 1.

Shorten the tail fin somewhat and cut off all other fins. Start an incision about two inches behind the head and run it along the back to within three or four inches from the tail fin. Guide the knife straight down the back bone and through it to the hollow space of the belly. Remove backbone and bones on the flanks. This allows the fish to be poached with both flanks still intact. The fish should be placed on a board with both cleaned filets neatly placed apart on a sheet of aluminum foil. The court bouillon in which the fish is cooked should never be brought to a full boil. This permits the filets to remain in place. Merely bring it near the boiling point and poach for one-half hour.

After the necessary cooking time, take the board with the fish out of the liquid and let it set so the surplus stock can run off. Then place it in the refrigerator for proper cooling.

The aluminum foil is used under the fish in order to slide it from the board to the presentation platter without the danger of breaking it. After the fish is on the platter, cut the excess foil around the fish away with scissors, leaving the foil under the fish on the platter.

Step 2.

It is not usual to garnish the fish on the presentation platter but in this case there is no other choice. In order to keep the platter clean, cover it all around the salmon with waxed paper, sticking the ends of the paper under the fish to hold it in place.

Step 3.

Fill the center of the body with a solid Italian vegetable or salmon salad. Be sure the ingredients are not wet. The mayonnaise mixture must make a smooth, solid salad. When these ingredients reach the proper temperature, the salad with gelatin content will stiffen enough to be molded with a spatula to the proper fish form.

Step 4.

Keep in mind that both filets must be presented as naturally as possible. Be careful not to smear any salad or sauce on them. Protect them with cut-out wax paper. Next, prepare a chaudfroid sauce. Proper handling of this sauce or of mayonnaise should be practiced. Applications that are too cold result in a covering resembling tapioca pudding—full of small lumps. To get the right consistency, chaudfroid must be easily stirred with a ladle, rotating the ladle in the same direction in a clean china bowl which stands in crushed ice. As soon as the sauce begins to cool, take it out of the ice and stir slowly until the sauce begins to adhere to the upturned bottom of the ladle. This is the moment to apply the coating to the fish. Let this first cover cool before applying a second. Should the first and second coating be too thin, it is well to apply a third, making a smooth even surface about ⅕ inch thick.

Step 5.

As soon as the fish is properly treated with the sauce covering, take off the surplus with the point of a small knife. Remove the wax paper from the filets and clean them spotlessly.

Step 6.

Next comes the decoration of the piece. Any adequate decoration may be applied but the culinary artist should bear in mind that he is decorating a fish and not an animal that lives on land. The decorations should be suitable and suggestive of the sea.

A seascape made from truffles and put on free hand is an appropriate decoration. A drawing will help in giving the proper proportions. All decorations must be placed on the fish by dipping first in aspic. Next comes the application of the fish jelly. This is difficult as the fish is not on a rack and the drippings will fall unevenly unless a brush is used. Dip the jelly brush in aspic which has become syrupy and stroke gently over the surface. Allow the first layer to cool before making a second and be careful that brush marks do not show. After the entire surface including decorations has that fresh and sparkling look, a line of shrimps may be placed along the back of the fish and sized mushroom caps over the head. Now remove the wax paper from the platter, clean the platter and place other garnishes around the fish.

Sometimes it is not practical to place all of the garnishes on the fish tray. When there is a large number to be served, a separate platter should be used for such garnishes. However, on the salmon described above, the platter and garnish were prepared as follows:

For this huge fish, no suitable silver tray was available. A large wooden plank of sufficient size was fitted with mirror glass to the exact size and shape of the plank and fastened with clamps. The border was lined with the flat shells of oysters that had been smoothed and shaped to uniformity with a grindstone and shellacked to make them glossy. Each shell had a hole drilled through it so it could be nailed to the edge of the wooden plank. To prevent the thin coating of aspic on the plank from escaping, a thin butter border was placed around the very edge of the mirror. The aspic may be applied either before or after the garnishes have been placed. However, it is better to pour the aspic after placement to prevent disarrangement in moving.

The garnishes for this piece consisted of the following:

1. Halves of hard boiled eggs stuffed with salmon-egg caviar.
2. Jumbo artichokes properly cut and cooked. When cold, these were set on a rack and filled with salmon mousse. When the mousse is stiff enough to cut, slice the artichokes into six or eight sections (like a pie). Dip the knife for each cut into boiling hot water which assures clean cutting.
3. Small peeled tomatoes in the shape of a basket stuffed with marinated cucumber balls.

Serve with mayonnaise or sauces of mayonnaise derivation.

The piece described above won the first prize at the Fort Worth Culinary Exhibition in 1956.

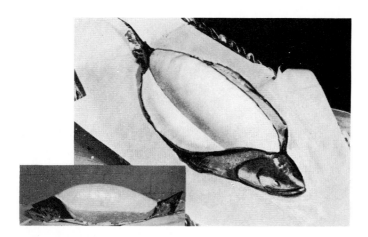

To Prepare a Salmon Masterpiece

Shorten the tail fin somewhat and remove all other fins. Start an incision about two inches back of the head and run it along the back to within three or four inches from the tail fin. For further directions see Step 1 in the text.

The center of the body is filled with a solid Italian or salmon salad. For directions, see Step 3 in the text.

The finished salmon platter with all its garnishings is explained in detail in Step 6 in the text. The garnishes include halves of hard boiled eggs, stuffed with salmon caviar; jumbo artichokes properly cooked, cooled, filled with salmon mousse and cut into six or eight sections; small peeled tomatoes made into the shape of a basket and stuffed with cucumber balls. On the corners are the shells of choice Maine lobsters from which the meat has been removed and made into medallions placed on the back of each shell. All garnishes are glazed with a thin layer of fish aspic. Oyster shells decorate the edge of the platter.

Salmon Medallions, Sauce Verte

One method of serving portion-size salmon is achieved by first cutting the fish into filets, leaving the tail section whole. Shorten the tail fin with scissors. Take off the skin and remove any bones from both filets. Make two-ounce slices from the filets. If they are formed into round shapes, almost exact medallions result. Tie a thin butcher's twine around each medallion to keep it in shape while poaching 10 minutes in court bouillon. Remove the fish kettle from the fire and let the fish remain over night and cool in the same liquid.

The next day, place the medallions on a rack. In the center of each place an egg slice. Fill a paper piping bag with creamy mixed butter and garnish a thin border of butter around the edge of each medallion. After cooling thoroughly, fill in this petal-shaped butter border with a mixture of ketchup aspic. Decorate the middle of the egg slice with a slice of ripe olive. Glaze the medallions with fish aspic.

These medallions may be arranged in any way the garde manger wishes. The fish tail may be placed on the platter and other garnishes arranged around the medallions. Salmon delivered without the head may be decorated in this manner.

Serve Sauce Verte with this dish—cucumber or tomato and stuffed egg with asparagus tips.

Center Cut of Salmon Oregon

From a very large fish, cut out about 10 inches from the broad middle section. Boil this center cut as you would prepare the entire fish.

Once it is cooled and placed on a rack for decoration, remove the skin and replace it with an adequate layer of mayonnaise collee. When the jellied mayonnaise is stiff enough, a decoration made from truffles or other suitable decorative material may be added.

Oregon is a place where fine salmon as well as crabs and oysters are available. Therefore, on both ends of the salmon middle piece, place a crab on its back, stuffed with Crab Louie or an Italian salad, topped with crab legs. These crab legs are also decorated and jellied. Decorate with bouquets of green asparagus tips and garnished eggs. Oysters may be added. Poach them and place them in small scallop or clam shells and fill with fish jelly. Serve with mayonnaise.

Filets of Salmon, Italienne

Filet and skin a 12-pound salmon. Poach or steam the filets and allow them to cool on a rack. For decoration, use a good quality of fine garnish—cucumbers, radishes, truffles, mushroom slices, etc.

Prepare an Italian vegetable salad in which little shrimps should be mixed. Make a flat cake from this salad on a platter and place a filet on top. Around this arrange stuffed tomatoes or stuffed eggs, or both.

Salmon Medallions, Sauce Verte

Here small filets from salmon have been shaped into medallions. The round shape is created by using a butcher's twine, tying it around the raw filets. They are then poached in court bouillon. Notice the varied decorations. Mayonnaise collee or butter of the right consistency has been placed on each medallion with a paper cornucopia in the shape of a flower. Tomato ketchup thickened with one third thick aspic or gelatine powder is then piped into the petals of the design. The same type of garnish is used on the fish tails. Pimiento on halves of boiled eggs and fish aspic cut-outs complete the platter.

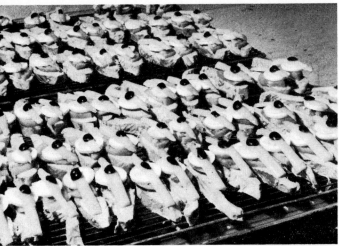

Preparation of Salmon Filets

From the practical point of view, most buffets demand small portions of food items. In order to keep the guest line moving at the desired pace, it is advisable to have the portions ready-cut rather than carve the fish in front of the guests. To gain this result the raw salmon should be cut into boneless filets of desired size and poached. Also, whole slices may be poached and after cooling in the fish brine, lifted out, the skin and bones removed and arranged on racks as shown in this illustration. The garnishes are placed on each slice and the whole glazed with a thin layer of fish jelly.

This illustration shows a method of presenting portion-size salmon filets. The head and tail of the salmon are cooked separately, decorated appropriately, and glazed. An Italian salad in aspic is placed in the center and the filets are arranged symmetrically.

93

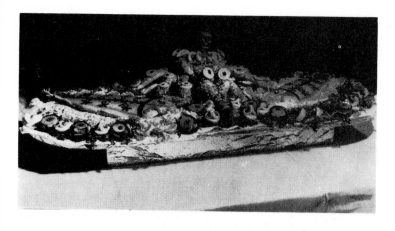

Filets of salmon Italienne may be arranged with a huge King Crab in the center. In this presentation the two filets of the salmon are not sliced into portions. The skin is removed before cooking and the bones are taken from the belly. The filets are then poached in court bouillon and allowed to cool over night in the same liquid. The next morning the filets are carefully removed from the shallow casserole and placed on racks. In this illustration the broad end of the fish has been decorated with truffles to resemble a fish's head. Other decorating materials may be substituted for truffles with equally good effect.

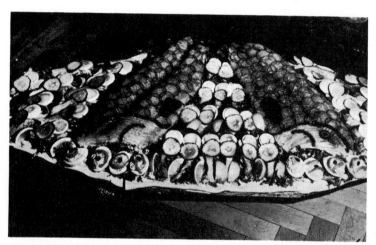

This shows the same preparation as above but the sides of the filets are decorated with very thin slices of cucumbers or dill pickles.

Here is another practical way of arranging filets around an artificial salmon made from vegetable salad Italienne. The head and tail of the salmon are placed at opposite ends of the platter and the space between is molded with a vegetable mayonnaise which has been slightly stiffened with gelatine. Be sure that the vegetables are thoroughly drained before mixing with the mayonnaise and the liquified gelatine. Cool in a refrigerator before applying a thin layer of mayonnaise over the body part. Decorate with thinly sliced cucumbers.

Salmon Aspic

Trim pieces of salmon to form medallions and simmer. When cooked and cold, coat with mayonnaise or chaudfroid sauce. Decorate appropriately, arrange on a flat glass dish, and pour on aspic.

Preparation of Salmon Mousse

The following recipe is used in preparing salmon mousse:

> 4 lbs. precooked salmon without bones or skin
> 6 cups cream sauce
> 2 cups heavy cream
> 6 soupspoons of gelatin powder
> Seasoning: salt, pepper, Accent, cognac, cayenne, Maggi seasoning, Worcestershire sauce—all to taste.

A mousse is a fine creamy dish which is prepared mainly from the cooked fish to which is added cream sauce or veloute, whipped cream, and jelly. It presents a substance somewhat like a fluffy chiffon pie. A mousse should have just the right consistency to keep its shape but it should melt in the mouth—not be solid enough to require chewing.

Because of its consistency, a mousse is seldom presented without a container of some sort—glass bowl, paper cup, tartlet, patty shell, or in tomatoes or artichokes. Tomatoes or artichokes are usually cut into sections.

The cooked salmon should have the consistency similar to that of a purée. To gain this result, in the absence of a mortar, use a chopper. In mixing, add gradually the cream sauce and the gelatin or fish jelly. Flavor sparingly. When all ingredients have been thoroughly mixed and the desired consistency reached, it should be strained through a fine sieve. The resulting paste is placed in a china bowl and whipped until it shows the needed smoothness. Whip the cream until it is *almost* stiff and add it to the soft paste. This combination will stiffen quickly so the selected molds must be filled *at once*. Place in the refrigerator for two hours. The top of the mousse may be decorated with truffles or any appropriate decoration. This dish may be called *Cold Salmon Soufflé* or *Mousse de Salmon*.

Halibut—Sole—Trout

Halibut Moderne

For this beautiful buffet piece a chicken halibut of about 15 to 20 pounds should be purchased, preferably freshly caught. Frozen halibut becomes very dry when cooked and lacks much of its distinctive flavor. If possible, purchase the fish with its head on so it may present its own special appearance. Since most kitchens do not have the facilities to poach a fish of this size, one of the large bainmaries may be used.

With the dark skin side down and the light skin side up, make incisions along the back bone and on the sides. Take out the two filets from the light side and cut them into equal portions. These are poached separately from the remainder of the halibut. After cooking, place them on a rack and cover each with a spoon of mayonnaise collée.

Preparation of Salmon Mousse

The first step: carefully flake the cooked salmon and see that it is completely free of bones and skin. The cold cream sauce should be ready for use and the gelatin powder dissolved in hot cream.

Place the flaked salmon into a rotating chopper and gradually add the cream sauce. Finally add the heavy cream in which the gelatin powder has been dissolved. Add seasoning and before the mass becomes too stiff, remove from the chopper.

Using an edging knife, carve the sides of cucumbers and cut them into equal half-inch pieces. Blanch them in a boiling mixture of salt and vinegar until slightly tender but still crisp—about five minutes—and place on a rack to cool. Decorate with half slices of egg and small shrimps. Glaze with aspic.

Place the stiffening mousse in a mound shape on a larger platter and mold it into the shape of a fish. This can be done with a spatula dipped frequently in hot water. Other garnishings are seen in this illustration—very thin cucumber slices, radish slices, and gherkins enveloped in smoked salmon and cut in slices as they appear on the top of the mousse.

A very fine fish-shaped china platter was used for the presentation of this salmon mousse. The life-like eye is cut from a slice of ripe olives and the sides of the fish decorated with radish, cucumber, and olive slices. Finally the mousse is glazed entirely with fish aspic.

Spread cheesecloth on the bottom of the bainmarie. Place the remaining fish on the cloth and fill the pan with salted water and lemon juice. Bring the water to the boiling point and allow the fish to simmer about 40 minutes. Drain off the liquid, remove the fish and place it on a large board or rack overnight to cool.

In the meantime, prepare mousseline of salmon or carp the same as for Gefuellte fish. Shape this mousseline with two spoons, egg shaped, and decorate with truffles. Small fresh mushrooms must be prepared also for further decorations. These mushroom heads are set on a fine slice of lobster meat and glazed with fish jelly.

On top of the remaining part of the halibut which has been placed on a large oval tray and covered with mayonnaise, arrange the portions of halibut and mousseline and the medallions of lobster. Beside the head, place the carcass of langouste or lobster for decoration.

It is advisable to serve salads on the side—asparagus tips vinaigrette, stuffed artichokes, avocado, etc., with mayonnaise.

Filet of Sole Calypso
Roll the filet on a wooden stick, one inch in diameter. Simmer and remove the stick. Place the rolls on marinated tomato halves. Fill the hollow with crab mousse or salad. Place crab legs on top and arrange with jelly croutons. Serve with Calypso sauce (Mayonnaise and chili sauce mixed).

Filet of Sole Cecilia
Coat the filets with white chaudfroid. Place shrimp mousse on top. Group tiny shrimp on egg slices between the filets. Serve sauce with caviar on the side.

Rainbow Trout in Sauterne Aspic
Large Rainbow trout and even portion-size trout may be used for a fine buffet tray. Simmer the fish slowly in a court bouillon with white wine, preferably California Sauterne. If the fish are freshly caught they will break up easily. To prevent this they should be placed in a basin and covered generously with crushed ice three hours before cooking. This gives the flesh more structure. The court bouillon should be only lukewarm when the fish are put into the kettle. After simmering the necessary length of time, cool the trout in the same liquid before removing and place on a rack.

The liquid is then carefully strained through a napkin. Add granulated gelatin powder to this fish stock and heat it to a lukewarm temperature in a water bainmarie. One quart of stock requires 10 ounces of gelatin. As soon as the gelatin has dissolved in the warm fish stock the clearing process may be completed. Add the whites of four eggs to this stock and with a whip beat the liquid over a fire until it comes to the boiling point. Add the juice of one lemon, mix well, and again bring to a boil. Cover the pot and set aside. After 15 minutes the egg white will have gathered in all the foreign particles and the fish aspic is ready to be strained through a napkin. If it lacks strength, add a little Accent powder.

For dressing the trout, take adequate trays or Escoffier dishes, deep enough to allow a finger-thick layer of aspic to be poured on. The skin of the fish should be removed because it is rather leathery on cold trout. Small decorations may be added such as truffles, whites of eggs, or red pimientos. Next, give the fish a coating of aspic, cool thoroughly in the refrigerator, and place the trout side by side on a tray which has already been covered with fish jelly. No other garnish is necessary because the impression of the clear aspic would be disturbed. Any salad served with the trout should be on the side in a special salad bowl as well as any additional dressing.

Trout—Rainbow or Others

Small-portion trout which are kept on ice more than one day should be cooked and skinned before decorating. Young trout, fresh from the river may be prepared *au bleu*. Be careful not to scratch the surface of the skin as the scratches will turn out black. Bring the trout, completely covered by liquid, to a boil and cool in the same stock. Sometimes it is desirable to tie the trout in a ring shape. In this case, take a small butcher's needle threaded with twine and pass it through the tail and mouth of the trout, tying the ends of the thread together. Allow the fish to cool and proceed with the decorations.

Trout Royal

Simmer the trout tied into ring shape and allow to cool. Remove skin and place on glass. Fill the inside of the ring with crab salad and garnish with shrimp and tarragon leaves. The back of the fish is garnished with truffles and some rounds cut from the whites of eggs. Glaze the whole fish with jelly and surround with cucumber and tomato slices.

Lobster—Langouste—Crab—Ecrevisse—Shrimp

These crustaceans are attractive contributions to a buffet. A great many ways of using them have been developed throughout the years—"Langouste à la Parisienne," "Buisson d'Ecrevisse," "Pyramide de Crevettes," and "Cracked Crabs" to name only a few.

Cold Maine Lobster Parisienne

Two empty shells from very large lobsters are used for the center in this presentation, placed on a wooden triangle as a base and covered with aluminum foil. Neatly sliced meat from the lobsters is arranged on top of the empty shells, readily available for service. The slices are held in place by softly kneaded butter. The claws are arranged around the side. Mayonnaise or a derivative may be served separately.

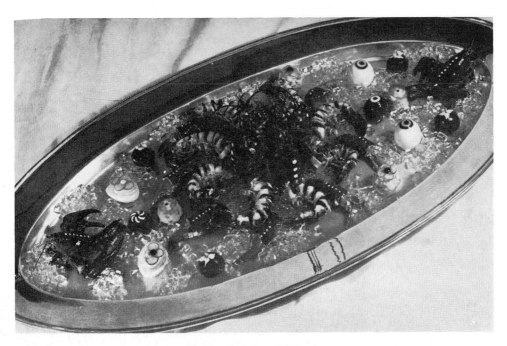

Maine Lobster Victoria

This dish carries the name "Victoria" because of the crown arrangement of lobsters in the center. The tails of the lobsters are extracted and several bodies fastened together with skewers or toothpicks so they stand upright. The tail meat is cut into slices and arranged with alternate slices of truffles in one half of the empty tail shell. The claws are broken in the middle so that the meat protrudes from the broken end and is easily extracted. The balance of the claw shells are decorated with small points of egg white and truffles. The lobster meat and shells are brushed with aspic. On each end of the platter a crayfish is placed with claws bent backward and fastened under the tail, also decorated. Stuffed eggs, stuffed tomatoes, and small aspic cubes are arranged about the platter. Serve mayonnaise or a derivative with additional garnishes.

The Maine lobster found along the Atlantic coast is the most delicious of all and they are found in great abundance as far north as Nova Scotia.

The langouste is found in the Caribbean and the crabs along the California coast of the Pacific and the Maryland coast of the Atlantic.

Shrimp from the Gulf of Mexico are of fine quality and color. There are also many tasty shrimp caught along the coast extending from California to Alaska. These vary in size from the tiny San Francisco Bay shrimp to those giants that number only a few to a pound.

These crustaceans should be placed in court bouillon. In Scandinavia a few caraway seeds or dill flowers are added. Lobsters weighing about a pound should be boiled for about 20 minutes; langouste for about 25 to 30 minutes.

Lobsters

For buffet show pieces, the jumbo sized lobsters should be selected. The larger ones, however, are not so tender and it is advisable to use the flesh of these in a salad. Usually lobster is served on a buffet in halves. As it is a very expensive item, more often small lobsters are chosen. From 1¼ to 1½-pound lobsters, very nice portions are possible and the meat at this weight is the best.

As lobsters are sometimes fished in excessive amounts they are protected by law and during many months they are difficult to secure. The Fish and Game Commission rechecks year after year and limits the total catch to a certain amount. There are a few commercially operated lobster pounds which are not bound to these laws because they care for the lobsters from the time they are hatched until they are grown. Penobscot in Maine and St. Andrews in the Bay of Fundy in New Brunswick, Canada, are two in particular which send lobsters to all parts of the United States and Canada in special containers. Sent air freight, they arrive at their destination as fresh as when they left the lobster plant. Open lobster fishing seasons, though varying with locality, usually run through June and July. Small lobsters that measure less than three inches from nose to end of body, tail not included, are illegal to keep and must be put back into the sea.

There are many ways to cook lobster. Gourmets say they taste better when cooked in plain salt water, preferably sea water. They claim this permits the lobsters to retain their natural flavor. Make sure that only live lobsters are used. Dead ones are dangerous as the meat may be poisonous; also, it may be dry and broken into small pieces. To offset delay in transportation it is sometimes wise to order the lobsters cooked and frozen in dry ice.

Make sure the liquid in which the lobster is cooked is boiling so that the creature is killed instantly. Otherwise, the flavor is changed unfavorably. For a lobster weighing one and one-half pounds, allow about 15 minutes cooking time. After cooking, hang those which are to be presented whole for decoration by a string where they will cool and drain at the same time. This draining of the excess liquid will prevent a wet tray on the buffet. After cooling, keep the cooked lobsters under refrigeration until time to prepare them for service. Under good refrigeration, they will keep well for two or three days.

Lobster Victoria

Cut the cold lobster in half and remove the intestines and stomach. The meat from the tail and claws is taken out of the shell, cut into finger-thick slices and arranged in the opposite shell. Alternately between every lobster slice, put a slice of truffle. The claw is placed in the front part of the lobster. Arrange nicely on a platter. Serve mayonnaise sauce on the side. Also serve a vegetable salad with egg slices.

Aspic of Lobster

Use a tasty fish stock and white wine to build an aspic. Decorate the bottom of a mold with green and black olive cut-outs. Cut the meat from the tail

Aspic of Shrimp and Maine Lobster

Remove the meat from the tails from the underside with the aid of scissors.

In lieu of a silver tray, a round mirror attached to plywood is used.

The build-up of the platter. Note the use of the glass plates.

Opposite Page: The finished presentation. For complete instructions see text page 105.

Aspic of Lobster with Truffles

For a centerpiece, place an empty bowl or styrofoam base in the center of a large glass or silver platter. This is to hold the glass plate on which the aspic or lobster salad is placed and should be the same size as the lower part of the aspic. The empty lobster tails are placed against the base, hollow side out. The lobster meat is then placed on a rack, glazed with aspic, decorated with truffles and placed inside each hollow shell, decorated side out, making them easy to remove when service starts. The aspic is then taken out of the mold, carefully placed on the glass plate, and the plate put in its place topping the entire presentation. The contrast of the white meat against the red shells is very striking. This is an excellent set-up for lobster when a fast-moving buffet is required.

of a large lobster into medallions and arrange them, dipped in aspic, into the aspic mold. Fill with aspic and cool under refrigeration.

After unmolding on a flat glass platter, decorate with additional jelly croutons and deviled eggs. Serve with mayonnaise or Louis dressing.

Aspic of Lobster with Caviar

Use the same treatment as for *Aspic of Lobster* above. Put the caviar on halves of hard boiled eggs from which the yolks have been removed and arrange them around the aspic. It is advisable to serve this platter on crushed ice.

Lobster Parisienne

Tie the lobster to a flat plank of wood. After boiling and cooling, remove the meat from the tail. After removing intestines, cut the meat into medallions, garnish and coat with jelly. Put the lobster shell together again and skewer to a sloping base. The typical arrangement for "à la Parisienne" demands the placing of the medallions on the back of the lobster shell and the usual garnish of artichoke bottoms filled with pyramids of vegetables.

Lobster Mousse, New England

First, a mousse of all the tail meat from the lobster must be prepared consisting of the following:

1 quart lobster meat	2 to 3 ounces brandy
2 pints cream sauce	Worcestershire sauce
1½ pints fish aspic	cayenne pepper
lemon juice	

Grind the lobster meat and work into a fine purée in a chopper. Strain through a fine mesh wire sieve and place in a bowl. Add strained cold cream sauce, mixing it in a little at a time. Also add a cool aspic. When the mixture begins to show the first signs of thickening, fold in semi-stiff whipped cream. Next, place it in a glass bowl immediately before it begins to stiffen too much. A correct mousse is a delicate thing and should never be "chewy" but should melt in the mouth. This is the reason why it is better to present it on ice as the room temperature may cause it to melt.

When the mousse has sufficiently cooled, a decoration may be applied. On top of the decoration a thin layer of fish aspic should be placed and the whole placed in the refrigerator for cooling.

The meat from the claws is removed and decorated with truffles. The empty and cleaned bodies of the lobsters are filled with mousse, decorated, and glazed with aspic. This buffet platter received maximum points at the International Culinary Show in Switzerland in 1954.

Aspic of Shrimp and Maine Lobster

Live lobsters of uniform size are tied together in pairs so that they will retain their proper shape when cooked. The legs and claws are cut off and cooked with the bodies. Work fast to prevent loss of juice and to lessen the suffering of the crustacean. After they have cooked and cooled in the broth, dry the bodies and claws on a rack. Cut the strings and remove the meat from the tails from the underside with the help of scissors. The meat from the tails has to be cleaned in salt water and evened off slightly on the sides. The decoration may begin with the tails placed side by side on a rack. If a whole lobster tail is too much for one portion, cut it in two, lengthwise.

A set of adequate cutters are used on very thin slices of truffles to make these decorations. Dip them first in aspic before applying. When this work is finished, put the lobster in refrigeration. When thoroughly cooled, give the surface of the tails a glaze of aspic.

For the foundation of this piece *styrofoam* may be used. The acceptability of this material remains to be established. However, it is very useful in buffet work for lettering, etc. For this particular platter the styrofoam was cut into a cylindrical form with a knife. The food is not placed directly on this material—it is merely used to maintain the form.

The empty lobster shells are placed, head down, around the styrofoam cylinder and fastened with tooth picks. In the illustration, in lieu of a silver tray, a round mirror attached to plywood was used and the extra lobster shells were used for covering the edge of the platter. The styrofoam cylinder is pasted to the center of the glass and on top a glass plate is fastened which supports a second cylinder against which the decorated lobster tails are placed. A second glass plate on the very top holds the aspic of shrimps.

An adequate dressing such as mayonnaise or its variations is served with Italian or Russian salad. The aspic should be tasty and crystal clear prepared from a fresh fish bouillon and a good gelatine.

Langouste.

These are among the most attractive of the crustaceans. Their long antennae add a note of weird marine charm to the buffet. To add to this effect, thumb tacks may be used to create spirals with the antennae. After the spirals have been formed by tacking to a small board, place the langouste in the refrigerator for 24 hours and the antennae will remain in spirals. Careful handling is necessary as the ends are dry and break easily.

Langouste à la Parisienne
Prepared in the same manner as Lobster à la Parisienne.

Aspic of Langouste
Selected slices of langouste are decorated with truffles which are attached to them with liquid jelly. The truffles may be cut in the shape of stars, half-moons, or rounds. Take a mold which is bathed in jelly and arrange these truffle slices in it. Fill the inside with pieces of lobster, celery or asparagus tips and fill up with jelly.

When the aspic is stiff enough, unmold upon a platter that has been covered with a thin layer of jelly. Garnish with caviar-stuffed halves of eggs. Serve with mayonnaise.

Maine Lobster en Bellevue

This is an amusing arrangement, the center made the same way as for Aspic of Shrimps and Maine Lobster. The lobster man topping the presentation is made with very fine pliable wire and the cleaned and dried shells of the lobster. The shoes and nose are made from the claws. The figure is attached to a wooden platform covered with foil. A miniature chef's hat is placed on its head. "Lobster en Bellevue" means a well decorated lobster. The original recipe is: split a cooked lobster in half and remove stomach, intestines, and meat. A delicate vegetable salad with mayonnaise is filled into the front part of the shell, the edge lined with chopped clear fish aspic and the claws, without the shell, placed in the center of the salad. The tail-meat is sliced into four sections, the meat from the right half slices in the left shell and vice versa. The lobster meat is decorated with sliced mushrooms and truffles.

Here a Maine Lobster is treated the same way as for "Bellevue" except that it is shown without the shells to gain space. Center piece is a lobster salad decorated with truffle.

Langouste à la Parisienne

Unlike other lobsters, the langouste has no heavy claws but the tail part has more meat. In order that uniform medallions may be cut from the extracted tail, precautions must be taken in cooking. The live langouste, weighing from 8 to 18 pounds, must be tied to a board of equal length so that it will remain in the desired shape before and after cooking. Also, care must be taken that the long graceful antennae are not broken.

The white meat of the tail is removed with the aid of scissors. In this picture, the upper part of the shell is cut into and broken out, section by section. The inside of the tail should be filled with shredded lettuce so the medallions will stay in place and be visible. On the rack is seen the meaty part of the whole langouste tail. To the right the medallions are garnished with a slice of truffle. A second method of presentation is more difficult but very effective. In cutting out the inside part of the shell to remove the meat, leave the outside intact and place the medallions on the hard shell keeping them in place with the aid of kneaded butter.

Garnishes that accompany the crustacean are stuffed eggs with caviar, slices of peeled tomatoes, asparagus tips, etc. To give these added appeal, cooling aspic may be brushed over them. A thin film makes the garnishes bright and shining. After cooling in the refrigerator, the platter may be assembled.

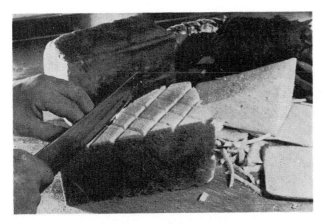

Since the classical presentation of a crustacean demands an upright position, a base must be made. This illustration shows how to cut a bread base. A stale loaf of bread is cut into a triangular shape. After making a few incisions in both sides of the base for decorations, immerse the bread in a deep fat fryer and leave until crisp and brown. When completely cool, dip the bottom of the base in egg white and place on a heated platter where it will adhere firmly. The langouste may be held in place with a skewer if the base is at too steep an angle.

A very thin layer of aspic is poured over the silver tray on which the langouste has already been placed with its bread base underneath. Be careful in pouring the aspic to avoid bubbles. Allow it to set until stiff and on this surface place the garnishes.

Shrimp

Shrimp comes in varying sizes and qualities. The Pacific coast shrimp are preferred by some people over those from the Gulf of Mexico because of variation in iodine content. This is a matter of individual preference.

Shrimp are highly perishable and should never be left out of refrigeration after they are cooked. Shrimp and crab, at summer temperatures, develop a food poisoning within an hour's time. But if they are kept refrigerated there is little need for worry on this score. Frozen shrimp should never be thawed and re-frozen.

Along the California coast are found the large shrimp known as *prawns*. In the Mediterranean and Adriatic, they become the size of small lobsters and are called *scampis*. Wherever they are, these crustaceans are accepted as very fine seafood.

The smallest shrimp known are the San Francisco Bay Shrimp, 350 or more to the pound. The cost is high because of the time required to shell these miniatures. Although these small creatures may be found anywhere from San Diego to Alaska, San Francisco Bay is the only place where they are fished for commercially. The next in size on the Pacific coast are the firm-fleshed Alaska shrimp. These run about 150 to 180 to the pound. They are found plentifully along the California coast.

Langouste à la Parisienne with assorted hors d'oeuvres. The medallions on the langouste are decorated with pimiento, truffle, and leek. The border is made from chopped aspic and chopped truffle lined on with a pastry bag. The hors d'oeuvres are canapés of foie gras, asparagus vinaigrette, batons of anchovies, stuffed eggs, stuffed peeled and marinated tomatoes with shrimps, ham mousselines, celery, and radishes. Mayonnaise dressing or a derivative, and Melba toast are served on the side.

The buffet may be greatly enhanced at times by displaying the shrimp intact in all its shining armor plate. In this way, fine effects may be achieved as garnish for salads, aspics, or fish platters. When used in this way, the hard shell covering of the shrimp's tail should be removed without breaking the fleshy part from the body.

There are many different species of the large Baya California shrimp, especially the prawns. These are purchased by the count—45 to 65, 31 to 42, 21 to 25, and 15 to 20 to the pound.

Shrimp usually are shipped uncooked, frozen, and headed. If a slight odor of ammonia is detected, the shrimp are fresh. When fresh, they are dry and firm. Avoid any slippery or soft shrimp.

They are at their best when cooked in sea water. This preserves the natural flavor. Usually a court bouillon with salt water, whole black pepper, and a choice of onion, garlic, celery, parsley, bay leaf, or pickling spices may be used. It is important not to overcook shrimp. Bring them to a boil, then simmer—the small ones for about five minutes; the larger ones up to 10 minutes. If they are cooked too long, the shrinkage is 25 per cent or more. From the larger shrimp, remove the back so the intestines may be washed out under a good stream of water. Salt slightly after washing.

Crabs

There are two varieties of crabs: (1) hardshell crabs, available throughout the year (frozen during the closed season), restricted to the Pacific Coast and (2) softshell crabs, available from May until October when the crab throws off its shell.

The hardshell crab is used to some extent on the cold buffet, served more often as a salad than as a whole piece. Occasionally it may be dressed up as "Cracked Crab" and served on a platter with ice or on a bed of lettuce.

The body shell must be thoroughly cleaned, then filled with a salad and topped with a colorful garnish. Miniature cocktail glasses may be filled with crab meat and placed around a quantity of cracked legs, garnished with lemon wedges.

111

Cracked Crab

A Dungeness Crab from the Pacific coast weighing two pounds.

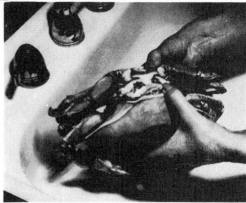

Clean the cooked crab thoroughly with a brush. To separate the shell from the body, put your right thumb on the base of the back leg, your left thumb on the base of the shell. Then twist and pull open the shell which comes off easily.

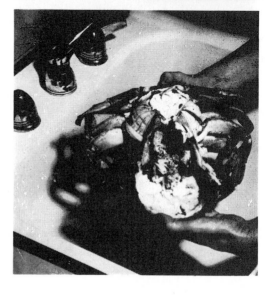

Break off the tail and the head and wash the legs of the crab to remove any remaining scum. Hold the body cavity under a strong stream of cold water to remove the inedible parts.

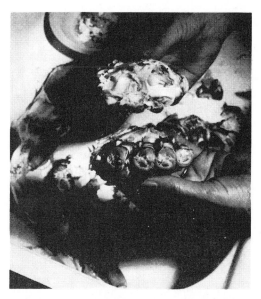

Twist off all the legs from the body. Holding the body, break the shell in half at the center seam. These body parts contain most of the meat.

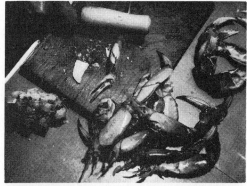

Here are all the cleaned parts of the crab. Save the yellow or green and white crab butter—also called the marrow. This may be seen in the dish at the top of the picture. Gently wash all the other parts. The lungs and tail, seen center right, are of no use.

Crab legs are best cracked with a round wooden mallet. With the curved side down, hit the legs sharply and quickly so the meat will not crush.

Crushed ice is placed on a lining of green leaves and the cracked legs placed neatly in the shape of the crab around the center which is taken from the two body parts. Plenty of lemon and either Mayonnaise, Louis or Thousand Island Dressing are usually served with Cracked Crab with garlic French bread well toasted. A Cracked Crab luncheon is simplicity itself.

The Dungeness crab of the Pacific coast is a fine delicacy and Crab Louis, a San Francisco special, is famous the country over.

The same precautions of preparation and refrigeration must be observed for the crab as for the lobster. Crab legs, free of shell, may be purchased either fresh or frozen. They make good items for combinations with artichoke bottoms, tomatoes, or other vegetables. With some imagination, wonderful buffet platters may be created.

Crab Louis

Arrange lettuce leaves around the inside of a salad bowl with a few shredded leaves on the bottom. Heap crab meat on top of the shredded lettuce and pour Louis dressing over the salad. Sprinkle the top with chopped egg, and decorate with tomato wedges, asparagus tips, and ripe olive.

Monterey Crab Delight

Mix the shredded meat of a large crab and the green and white marrow with two spoonsful of fine mayonnaise and the juice of one lemon. Use a thoroughly cleaned abalone shell for this dish. The abalone is a mollusk with a handsome shell and lined with beautiful mother of pearl. For further description of *Monterey Crab Delight,* see the illustration herewith.

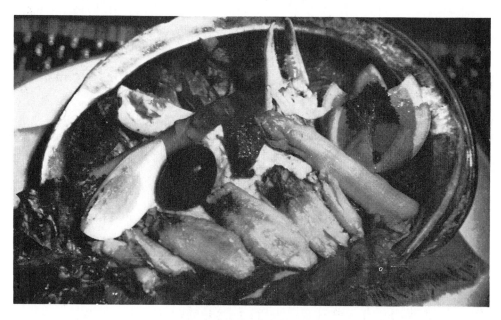

Monterey Crab Delight

A decorative abalone shell has been used here as a container for this truly Western dish. The shell is lined with brown limestone lettuce and chiffonade. On top of this is a mound of crab salad. Garnish with asparagus tips, pimiento, ripe olive, egg quarters, tomato, crab legs, one cracked claw with shell on for decoration, and lemon. Usually the crab salad for this dish is made with Louis dressing.

Dressed Crab Irlandaise

Here is a dressed crab, Dublin style. The crab meat, including the crab butter (marrow) is chopped and mixed with mayonnaise. Season with salt, lemon juice, cayenne, or a few drops of Tabasco sauce. Place the purée into a thoroughly cleaned crab shell. Decorate the top to represent the Irish flag—green on the left made from finely chopped parsley, white in the center made with egg white, on the right paprika-dusted egg yolk from hard boiled eggs. Place on a lettuce leaf and serve with lemon.

Dressed Crab Irlandaise

Two- and three-pound crabs make lovely show pieces but for this particular dish smaller crabs are more often used. The crab meat, including the marrow is chopped and mixed with mayonnaise and a few drops of Tabasco sauce. Decorate with parsley, egg whites, and paprika, green, white, and red—the colors in the Irish flag. For further directions, see the illustration.

Certainly there are a great many ways to combine this type of crab preparation. It is left to the imagination of a good cook to contrive different fillings with crab meat as well as the top decoration in order to produce appealing variations.

Aspic of Crab Legs, San Francisco Style

For this, use choice crab legs readily found on the market. Combine with a good fish jelly and prepare an aspic in the usual manner.

Clean the shells of two three-pound crabs and fill them with a fine salad of artichokes. Sprinkle the top with finely sliced ripe olives, green onions, and chopped radishes. Place deviled eggs along the sides of the molded aspic. Serve mayonnaise or Louis dressing on the side.

115

Cracked Hardshell Crabs

Crabs weighing two or three pounds are preferable for this. Clean the crabs in the usual way, breaking the body part out of the shell. Crack this body in half and remove all legs. Wash the body under cold water and cut each half in two pieces. Do not rinse the flesh too much or the characteristic crab flavor will be lost. The legs should be cracked with a wooden hammer or similar instrument.

By using several crab bodies, a nice centerpiece may be arranged on a platter. Place the legs on a lettuce bed in an attractive arrangement around this center piece. If the crab bodies are cooled they may be placed on broken ice on top of lettuce leaves. Use generous lots of lemon and parsley as additional garnish. Serve the popular Louis dressing with this preparation.

King Crab

The tender meat from the large legs of the Alaskan or Japanese King Crab may be treated the same way as the smaller species. A very attractive buffet platter may be created if the purveyor supplies the body of this unusually large crab.

Ecrevisses (Crayfish)

These sweet water crabs are considered outstanding delicacies. They are more abundant in European rivers than in those of America. There are many enemies in the life of a crayfish and epidemics also sometimes erase all of them in one area.

Sweden celebrates the opening of the ecrevisse season in August with great fervor. A good Scandinavian will eat a dozen of them and with every tail of ecrivisse he will take one little glass of Brantwin or Aquavit in celebration. Each year, with traditional pleasure, the Swedes consume them by the million. In France they are prepared in the hot cuisine in a great many ways but no cold buffet is served without them. The French chef twists the claws of these living ecrivesses toward the back and the pointed part of the claw he sticks into the tail part and throws it, at the same moment, into the boiling court bouillon. This is the way the crab gets its unique appearance and as a garnish for large salmon and other center pieces appears very well as a little fiery red monster.

It is sometimes advisable to take the intestines out of the living crayfish, which kills him instantly. To do this, take the middle fin of the tail between the forefinger and thumb, twist it once around and carefully pull the stomach out, then plunge the crayfish into the boiling court bouillon. This procedure is used as a safeguard against any poison that might remain in the tail part. However, if crayfish are kept in clear running water for quite some time before preparation, it will not be necessary to extract the intestines first.

Ecrevisse à la Nage

This classical way of serving crayfish (ecrevisse) demands nothing more than court bouillon in which they are cooked. Medium size ecrevisses call for a ten-minute cooking time. Serve them in the liquid in which they have been cooked, in a bowl of generous size. They may be eaten in the fingers with no further garnish. Crayfish bibs and fingerbowls are used.

Ecrevisse, Swedish Style

Prepare a bouillon of saltwater, add a little sugar, and a bunch of fresh green dillheads. Boil the ecrevisses in this aromatic bouillon for about ten minutes and drain. There is no need for refrigeration as these ecrevisses should be served the same day.

Cover a large platter with a colored napkin. Put one to three cocktail glasses in the center and hang as many ecrevisses as possible by the tail on the glasses. Garnish between with fresh dill blossoms and place more ecrevisses on the platter. It is an appetizing sight with the red ecrevisses mixed in with the green of the dill, excellent for buffets especially those attended by Scandinavian people.

Crown of Ecrevisses or Buisson d'Ecrevisses

For this attractive presentation a 15- to 20-inch wire stand is necessary. About eight round wire shelves are attached to a center pole, each shelf graduated in size toward the top. The boiled ecrevisses are hung by the tail on this rack and garnished with either dill or parsley.

Aspic of Ecrevisses

The tail part of the ecrevisses are used for this since the claws do not have enough meat. Preparation of the aspic is the same as for lobster.

Mollusks

Oysters

On all American coasts we find a great variety of shellfish, some of great delicacy. Among the commercially-handled shellfish are oysters, scallops, and clams. These are headless creatures with strong shells, top and bottom, deeply convex at the back and connected by a projection which forms the hinge by which they may be opened. The creature may withdraw entirely into the shell which it may open or close at will. Inside the shell, the viscera are surrounded by a mantle which leaves two openings at the back. Through the lower opening the breathing water is taken in; through the upper the used water is ejected together with the excreta. The bottom of the mantle is left open for the fleshy foot to come through. This is the usual means of propulsion for most shell fish though some swim by opening and closing their shells.

Most shellfish live in the sea where some species attach their shell to rocks. Others live in sand, still others in mud, and some bore their way into the rock. Most of them are edible.

Some oysters reach a size of from six to ten inches but the largest oysters are seldom the best. Choice oysters of fine taste are usually selected from the smaller sizes. Location and the condition of the beds largely determine their delicacy of flavor.

Oysters in great abundance and finest quality are found along the Atlantic coast, the Gulf of Mexico, and the Pacific coast. There are certain spots such as Chesapeake Bay, Bouctouche in Northumberland, and the Olympia oyster habitats of the Pacific North West which deserve special mention. Blue Point and Cape Cod oysters are used in the New York area and are very fine. New Orleans consumes its local oysters which are very similar to the famous Marenne of France. Most Pacific coast oysters are too large and the taste is not so fine because of muddy water. But a great specialty is the Olympia oyster, the tiniest one on the market. One hundred shelled Olympia oysters will scarcely fill a ten-ounce glass. In the market they come shelled and are served mostly in cocktails and chowders.

The buyer must be sure to see that only live oysters (those with firmly closed shells) are bought. Dead oysters which should never be eaten, have a widely gaping shell. Eating them may lead to serious poisoning.

Oysters on the Buffet

Though not used frequently on the buffet, oysters may be used with excellent effect for cocktail parties. In this case an ice carving may be used for the base in the shape of a slender Venetian gondola or a graceful ship of the style of the old Vikings would be highly appropriate as a receptacle for the shellfish. If this is not possible, use a large shallow dish filled with crushed ice garnished with seaweed, salad leaves, parsley, lemon stars or wedges, and gain a very attractive effect.

When opening oysters, one must be careful not to pierce the oyster itself as much of the natural juice would be lost weakening the characteristic flavor. Lemon juice takes away the natural taste but is often used, as well as the common cocktail sauce used for most seafoods.

Do not place the oysters on the buffet until service is ready to begin.

Clams

Little Neck clams and Cherrystone clams are occasionally used on the cold buffet. Presentation of clams is similar to that of oysters—served on a base of ice or on crushed ice. They are fine for mixed salads.

CHAPTER IX

Eggs

No cold buffet is complete without decorated eggs. Deviled eggs are the most commonly used but there are many other kinds, each filled with a flavored purée and great originality may be shown in the decorations.

The filling of a deviled egg is made from the hard boiled egg yolk, strained through a fine sieve, worked over with a spatula, and flavored with salt, pepper, mustard and a few drops of tabasco sauce. A little mayonnaise or soft butter may also be added. Put this purée into a piping bag with a star insert and dress it nicely on halved or quartered eggs from which, of course, the egg yolk has been taken to make the purée.

For various buffet pieces a decorated quarter or half egg is needed. In such cases add only a little softened butter to the purée and garnish with a caper or a slice of stuffed olive.

The egg yolk purée may be replaced with other flavorful pastes such as mixtures of egg yolk with anchovies, with smoked salmon, with tongue, with goose liver, with chicken liver purée, with tuna fish purée, with sardines or ham. Decorate the top and coat with jelly.

Eggs Cardinal
Prepare an aspic of crab salad and asparagus. After unmolding, arrange halves with crab legs and surround with stuffed deviled eggs.

Eggs with Caviar
Cut boiled eggs in halves with notched edges. Remove the yolks and fill with caviar. Arrange on flat toasted caviar rounds.

Eggs with Shrimps
Halves of deviled eggs with a shrimp and a slice of truffle or black olive on top, glazed with jelly.

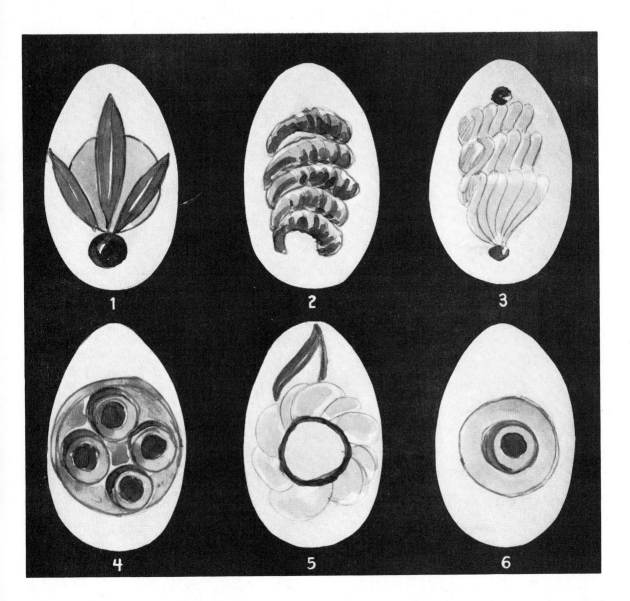

1. Egg either stuffed or plain, decorated with three tarragon leaves and a round truffle slice.

2. Stuffing of salmon mousse decorated with a row of tiny shrimps.

3. Egg yolk filling applied with bag with star-shaped insert, decorated with capers.

4. Slice of tomato on hard boiled egg decorated with stuffed olive slices.

5. Egg yolk purée applied with the flat insert of a pastry bag. Radish slice forms center. Stem is made with chives and the leaf from tarragon.

6. Egg yolk mixed with mousse of ham, tongue, or salmon and decorated with slice of stuffed olive.

7. Stuffed egg with caper in center.

8. Egg either stuffed or plain decorated with avocado and rounds of pimiento.

9. Deviled egg-half decorated with strips of anchovies and circled with radish slices.

10. Large star insert of pastry bag dresses egg purée into this shape. Decorate with stuffed olive slice.

11. Fill egg-half with mousse of tongue and decorate with piece of string bean.

12. Half boiled egg topped with short asparagus tip banded with a strip of smoked salmon.

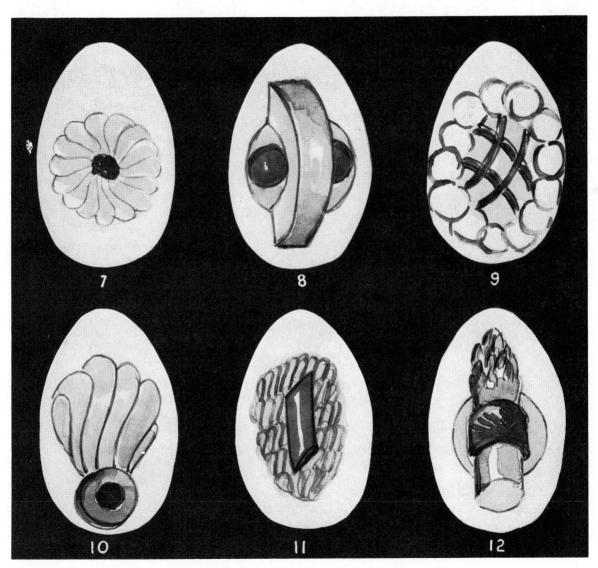

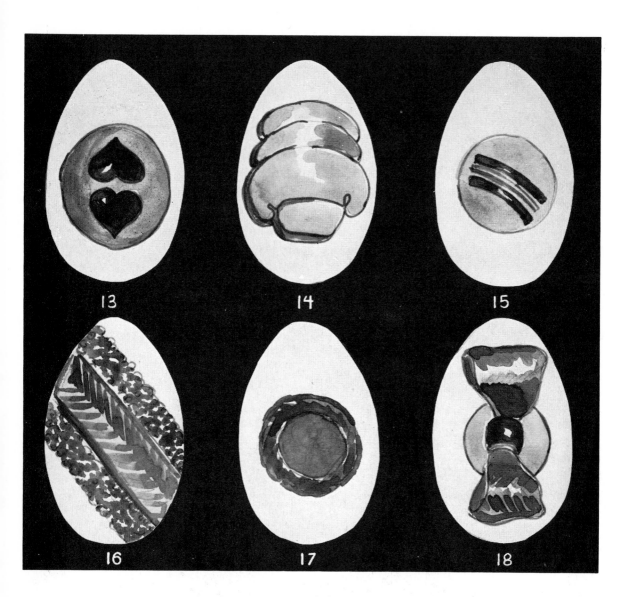

13. Stuffed mushroom head is placed on half of boiled egg and decorated with truffle.

14. Row of mushroom slices topping stuffed egg.

15. Ham mousse stuffing, decorated with strips of truffle and egg white.

16. Hard boiled egg topped with smoked salmon banded with caviar.

17. Place anchovies around gherkins or small dills, cut rolls in one-fourth inch slices and place on boiled eggs.

18. Form miniature bow tie from ribbons of smoked salmon. Use ripe olive half for center and place on boiled egg.

Eggs, Danish Style

Halves of hard boiled eggs stuffed with miniature lobster salad.

Eggs Jardiniere

Prepare a fine cosmopolitan salad (mixed vegetables and lobster, crabs, and shrimp). Place it in the center of a glass platter, cover with asparagus tips and surround with deviled eggs. Serve mayonnaise on the side.

Eggs Gourmet

Roll a slice of smoked salmon around Russian caviar. Cut this roll into smaller rolls and place on top of deviled eggs.

Eggs, Italian Style

Prepare from mixed vegetables with thick mayonnaise a salad which is shaped to a dome on a large glass platter. Cover this dome with a layer of mayonnaise and decorate with a grill of thinly sliced anchovies. Place around this an arrangement of deviled eggs with caper on top of each and a border of very thinly sliced salami.

Eggs, Russian Style

This is the same as Eggs, Italian Style except caviar is used for filling the eggs.

Soft Boiled Eggs Bristol

Cook the eggs six to seven minutes so that the yolks are still soft. Cool immediately under cold running water and peel carefully. Place the eggs in rolls of raw ham (preferably Prosciutto) and garnish with truffles and tarragon leaf. Serve with cubes or timbales of ham mousse.

Soft Boiled Eggs San Francisco

Cover soft boiled eggs with half white and half pink chaudfroid sauce and place on a tartlet filled with Crab Louis.

CHAPTER X

Aspic

Aspic is a savory jelly used to garnish meat or fish or to make a mold of meat, fish, or other edibles. It is made by boiling the flesh and bones of most animals, straining to get a clear broth, and cooling to a gelatinous solid. The best sources for such aspic are calves' heads and feet, pig rinds, halibut, and carp.

For those broths that do not congeal sufficiently, commercial gelatine in the form of leaves or powder is used. Almost completely free of any foreign odor, these gelatines are on the market, either with a natural flavor or with meat extracts, fruit extracts, or various flavors.

A requisite in the professional handling of aspic is to obtain crystal clearness. Also the gelatine content must not be so great as to destroy the flavor. To get a product which is perfect, a laborious process must be followed.

1. Prepare a fine broth with enough raw material used to get the necessary strength, color, and aroma. Correctly measure any additional gelatine used.
2. The gelatine is, of course, dissolved in the broth and both must go through a clarifying process.

For the cold cuisine many different aspics have to be prepared, the most popular being meat and fish aspics. Next come aspics from poultry, game, and game birds.

Aspic is clearly affected by temperature. At high temperature it will melt like snow. Keep in mind that the aspic for all dishes for which it is used must have just the right degree of stiffness in order to hold its shape. On the other hand, it must not be so stiff that it will not melt in the mouth without chewing. Two primary considerations are the degree of room temperature and the length of time the aspic dish must hold its shape at that temperature. Make the aspic a bit stiffer during the warm months. Good garde mangers continually taste the aspic during the cooking process to see that the flavor is right. Another test is made by ladling a small amount into a dish and placing it in the refrigerator for 10 minutes. In this way the flavor as well as the gelatin content is tested before the aspic is completed. If a gelatin stock is used there is no question how much is to be added as our recipes give the exact quantity.

In the older recipes veal stock from the head and feet of calves was used as a base for aspic but for some time now this was considered to complicated and regular beef broth or consommé is used. The older recipes also recommended chopped beef for the clearing of the broth. Modern recipes call for fresh beef blood which is much more efficient for this purpose than egg white or chopped beef.

The process of making aspic is similar to that of consommé except for the addition of gelatin which will stick to the bottom of the pan and burn if it is not stirred constantly. For this reason it is best not to cook the aspic at full heat unless a flat stirring spatula is used constantly until the liquid is brought to the boiling point. Once this is reached do not stir briskly but shift the pot to the side of the stove and allow the liquid to boil very slowly for an hour.

It is best to add all the ingredients while the aspic is cooking. Adding the salt or wine later may cause a cloudiness and spoil an otherwise perfect aspic. Even the best Sandeman Port may cloud an aspic when added after the cooking.

Straining the aspic is very important for a completely clear aspic may be ruined by straining through a greasy cloth or a napkin containing a minute amount of soap. Stainless steel or stone bowls are best suited for holding aspic in reserve. Make sure that all utensils for straining and storing are scrupulously clean. A napkin does very well for straining because of the tightly woven material.

If a strainer which may be purchased for this purpose is not available, turn a kitchen stool upside down and tie the corners of the napkin securely to each of the four legs of the stool. Underneath the cloth place a bowl for catching the strained aspic with a second bowl near by for use when the first one is filled. First, pour a few ladles of the thick substance into the cloth so it will act as a filtering bag. Take particular care that the liquid is free of egg white particles that may cloud the finished aspic.

Aspic is extremely vulnerable to bacteria and should never be touched with the fingers. Use a silver spoon to taste and test. After it is cold, use a clean ladle or knife to cut out the quantity needed. Never use the hands as germs might cause the aspic to spoil within a few hours. If it is handled correctly, aspic may be stored in the cooler for more than two weeks. Do not freeze.

The color of the aspic depends upon the raw material used. A meat aspic is dark, a fish aspic light, and a poultry aspic medium in color. For culinary

Top: The wall of the mold is built up with decorated slices of stuffed breast of chicken. This is a left-over that helps lessen the food cost. Only the center slices receive a decoration before being placed in the mold.

Center: The same process as above but with decorated outside slices.

Bottom: The unmolded aspic is accompanied by more sliced and glazed breast of chicken. Aspic cubes are placed between the neat rows of sliced chicken. If a further design is desired, either from truffles, egg whites or other material, this must first be built into the mold. It cannot be applied after unmolding. The aspic must be crystal clear as this decoration should be plainly visible to be effective.

correctness, a meat aspic must be served with meat, fish aspic with fish, etc. Never mix them. If the color is not quite right a few drops of caramel coloring may be added after straining.

The use of aspic is not limited to molded dishes but may be used for many decorative purposes. On the cold buffet it is a must. It may be used as a garnish for cold roasts and for giving the buffet that clean sparkling appearance that is so necessary.

Recipes for Aspic

Recipe for 1 Gallon Regular Aspic

Prepare ingredients for clarification two hours before it is to be used. Mix all ingredients in a pot of about three gallon capacity and leave in refrigeration.

Ingredients for clarification:
    2 lbs. raw coarse ground beef shank or lead beef—no fat
    ¾ quart cold water
    5 egg whites
    1 diced onion
    1 diced carrot
    1 soup spoon of salt
    1 sprig each of tarragon and thyme
    Juice of 5 lemons

With the ingredients of "reduction" make a strong concentrate, reducing the liquid by cooking to half the volume.

Ingredients for reduction:
    5 ozs. vinegar
    Parsley sprigs and shallots chopped fine
    Peppercorns, crushed
    Dried mushrooms

Add the above ingredients for reduction to the stock which should be luke-warm. Stir the gelatin in slowly so that it will dissolve properly and not form lumps. If gelatin leaves are used (preferable) soak them first in cold water until soft. Then add to the lukewarm broth for dissolving.

Ingredients for stock:
    1 gallon beef or poultry broth
    8 to 10 ozs. of gelatin powder

Next, take the clarification solution from the refrigerator and mix it with the stock. Place it on the stove and use a flat wood spatula in moving it about on the bottom of the pot so the gelatine will not burn. At the first sign of boiling, reduce the heat to a very low boiling point and boil for one hour or until clear. The aspic is now ready for straining through several folds of cheesecloth or a closely woven napkin. Any grease spots floating on the surface must be removed with absorbent paper. If the color is too light, add a few drops of caramel coloring. Some prefer the light colored aspic because of its brilliance.

Some old recipes recommend the use of Madeira or Sherry wine for flavoring. Test this out first as it may cloud the aspic.

Place the finished aspic in the refrigerator as soon as it is cold.

Recipe for 1 Gallon Regular Fish Aspic
For this aspic use the heads, bones, and trimmings of fish, preferably halibut, sole, or carp.

Ingredients:
>   2 to 5 lbs. of bones, heads, and trimmings
>   1 diced onion
>   1 diced carrot
>   Parsley and thyme
>   ½ teaspoon of peppercorns
>   2 bay leaves
>   1 large glass of Sauterne wine
>   1½ gallons of water
>   Juice of 4 lemons

Put these ingredients into a pot and boil slowly for 30 minutes. Strain and salt to taste. Cool until lukewarm and measure exactly one gallon of this broth. For summer consumption add 8 ounces of gelatin a little at a time. For winter consumption, add 6 ounces.

Aspic of Filet of Dover Sole

The filets of several Dover soles are flattened out with a heavy knife blade. Some of the smaller ones are reserved for the fish filling made as follows: Bone fish completely and add the same amount of white bread which has been soaked in milk and pressed out. Flavor with chopped onions slightly sautéed, salt, pepper, cayenne, and nutmeg. Put all this through a chopper, adding a few raw egg whites for better binding. This mixture is then driven through a fine wire mesh. Place it next in a bowl on ice and add a small amount of whipped cream so a very smooth paste results. For color, add fine cubed smoked salmon and chopped truffles.

Spread each filet flat with the help of a spatula and top them evenly with the filling—the same thickness as the filets. Roll compactly and poach in white wine and fish stock for 10 minutes. Cool in the same liquid. Cut in small slices and use in an aspic as illustrated.

On the bottom of a large mold place a layer of aspic about one-fourth inch thick. When it is completely stiff, place on it the decoration—in this case, a slice of truffle. Supporting the aspic are empty lobster bodies, cut straight so they will stand erect. They are strung together with invisible wire which gives them more strength to support the plate containing the aspic.

On the front of the platter are barrels made from blanched and pickled cucumbers filled with caviar and decorated with truffles. The four corners are taken up with the shells of lobster tails filled with *Lobster Victoria* and cubed fish aspic. Deviled egg quarters complete this culinary masterpiece which is served with Sauce Chantilly or some sauce derived from mayonnaise.

128

In a large bowl put ½ pint of egg whites and whip slightly. Still whipping, add the fish broth slowly until the egg whites are completely mixed in with the broth. Put this liquid back into the pot and still using the whip from time to time, bring it to the boiling point. Reduce the heat and simmer for 30 or 40 minutes until clear. Strain and add very little caramel coloring because fish aspic is meant to be light.

Gelee au Porto (Aspic for Foie Gras and Similar Delicacies)

This aspic of top quality is prepared with old Port wine. The basic recipe may be used but instead of using all broth, divide the broth and the Port wine: 1 quart of Sandeman Port and 3 quarts of consomme or good beef or chicken broth. This aspic is darker than any of the other varieties because of the Port wine.

Shrimp Aspic

It is seldom possible to purchase shrimp with their bodies intact. Here the empty shells are used only for decoration. The presentation is made on a silver platter with a glass insert because metal might influence the flavor of the food. Decorations are small stuffed tomatoes, peeled and decorated with green tinted butter, and stuffed artichoke bottoms. The empty spaces are decorated with small aspic cubes. Sauce is served on the side.

The build-up of a shrimp aspic. Lobster or crab aspic may be made the same way.

Artificial Aspic

There are a few products of ready-mixed granulated aspic powders which are very good in taste and appearance. The product given preference depends upon the choice of the individual.

Use of Aspic

There are two major ways of presenting an aspic with: (1) unmolded on a platter and (2), in a glass container.

The first way makes the better presentation; the second has its place when very little gelatine content is desired or when the aspic is served on an ice base.

In general, specially designed aspic molds are used. They have the advantage of proper cooling and the unmolding is more easily accomplished than from other types of molds because the sides of the mold are thinner and it takes just one moment to hold the mold in a bowl of warm water to loosen the aspic.

The professional word for preparing a mold to be filled is *chemisér*. It comes from the word shirt and in this case means to put a coating or lining of aspic on the walls of the mold. This chemisér procedure is difficult but with practice a perfect coat of desirable even thickness may be applied. The mold must be placed in a bowl of ice and water for thorough cooling. Be sure the ice water reaches the upper edge of the bowl but do not let it run in. Do not hold the mold down with warm fingers as this spot will remain warm and will not take the aspic.

The aspic must be cooled to a sirupy consistency before being applied to the mold. Fill it up to the very edge and turn the mold constantly in the ice water until the aspic begins to take hold on the walls of the mold. As soon as a thin layer of aspic about one-fourth inch thick has solidified, the mold is removed swiftly and the still liquid part of the aspic remaining in the bottom of the mold is poured out. Continue to roll the mold in the hands so the last remaining drops of aspic are evened off. In case it does not turn out satisfactorily, melt it and start over again until a perfect lining is obtained.

Never freeze an aspic. Freezing tends to give the dish a milky look. Always reserve some of the same aspic used for croutons as a last decoration of the unmolded aspic. Glass is first choice as a receptacle for aspic although other ware may be used to advantage.

CHAPTER XI

The Galantine—Pâté—Terrine—Mousse

Galantine is the culinary word for a delicate filling containing boned poultry, game birds, or meat. This filling is placed carefully in the center of the raw, boned meat, rolled and enveloped in a towel, tied, and poached in adequate stock.

The filling or stuffing is the most important part. From the classical galantine, other galatines have been developed such as shoulder of lamb, breast of veal and pork, and others.

Large capons are the best known base for a galantine. As America is abundant in good turkeys, this type of poultry may be used with even more economy than capon. Pheasant and partridge also make a delicate galantine.

The preparation demands a skillful boning of the bird. The skin should not be lacerated. If this happens, the openings must be sewed up. The cooking process is also important as over-cooking dries the galantine. Never use old fowl as it must be cooked too long which destroys the appearance as well as the taste. The filling must be seasoned carefully.

A galantine is a very expensive buffet item—even more so when foie gras and truffles are used.

Preparation of a Capon Galantine
First, singe the remaining feathers. Next, cut the wings above the first joint and the legs between the first and second joint. If the poultry is delivered eviscerated this makes the preparation complicated because the openings have to be sewed together before filling.

Place the bird on its breast, make an incision from the neck back to the tail, and begin to bone with a sharp pointed knife, first on the left side, then on the right, cutting close to the bones. Cut loose the body from the bony structure, lay it flat on the cutting board and take one leg bone after

132

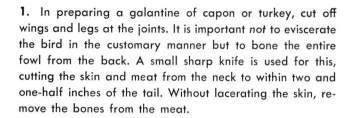

1. In preparing a galantine of capon or turkey, cut off wings and legs at the joints. It is important *not* to eviscerate the bird in the customary manner but to bone the entire fowl from the back. A small sharp knife is used for this, cutting the skin and meat from the neck to within two and one-half inches of the tail. Without lacerating the skin, remove the bones from the meat.

2. The meat-shell is spread on the table; the drumsticks are separated and also boned. The deboning of drumsticks and breast should be done in a manner that makes it possible to distribute the meat evenly over the shell. As the illustration shows, the tough sinews must be removed from the breast filets.

3. The stuffing is now prepared with these ingredients: 20 ozs. lean veal; 20 ozs. lean pork; 40 ozs. fresh, unsalted bacon fat. The seasoning consists of four ozs. of Cognac or Sherry, three ozs. of salt mixed with finely ground mixed herbs, and three eggs. The stuffing must be finely ground and it may be necessary to run it two or three times through the grinder followed by about a minute's run through the chopper. As the percentage of fat is rather high in this kind of stuffing, do not allow it to become warm in the working process. In addition to the stuffing, prepare the garnishes—evenly cut strips of unsalted back fat, tongue, truffles, foie gras or chicken livers, pistachios, and red peppers.

4. The stuffing is now spread one-half inch thick over the meat shell. It is topped through the center with thick strips of foie gras or chicken livers, interchanged with tongue and bacon fat. Truffles and pistachios and red pimientos are also placed on the meat shell. Another layer of stuffing and garnishes follow and the galantine is now ready to be closed. This is done by sewing the back shut with strong yarn. Care should be taken that the galantine is smooth and even all around.

5. After galantine has been sewed shut it is placed on a napkin or cloth which is heavily buttered, rolled in the cloth and tied at the ends and in the middle.

6. In this cooking pan are two galantines of different sizes, ready for cooking. Celery, carrots, and leek have been added to the bones and the galantines are covered with chicken stock. The cooking takes about one and one-quarter hours after which the galantine is cooled in the fluid. After cooling, the fluid is squeezed out, the galantine is removed from the cloth and placed in another one which is kept tight so the even form of the galantine is maintained. It is then returned to the same fluid and weighted down. This also helps to preserve the shape.

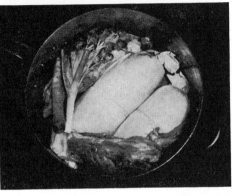

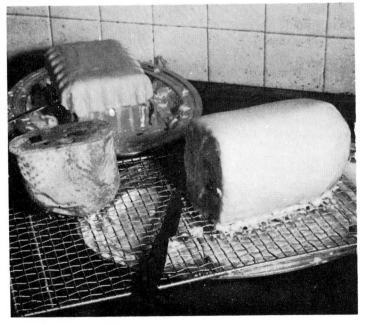

7. The following day the galantine is taken out and is now ready for use. It is only necessary to cut it evenly and garnish it with aspic.

Should a more elaborate presentation be required, part of the galantine is covered with chaudfroid sauce; the other part remains plain and is cut in even slices. The chaudfroid-covered piece may now be decorated with truffles, olives, or other ingredients in any desired motif. After the decoration is completed, the piece is covered with a thin layer of aspic. In some instances, a base of cream of wheat is used which is also covered with chaudfroid sauce.

The galantine, in this case with an Hawaiian motif, is now ready for service. On the model the decor was accomplished with outlines made of truffles and the solid parts painted in with delicately colored jelly of rose, brown, and yellow hues. Aspic painting is extremely difficult and should be practiced before it is done on the galantine itself. An arrangement of raspberry gelatine on orange slices has been used here to garnish the edges of the platter. Mango squares with papaya balls are used as additional garnishes with the Hula dancer on the galantine emphasizing the Hawaiian motif. Pineapple slices or peaches may also be used as garnishes. Waldorf salad is also a suitable garnish.

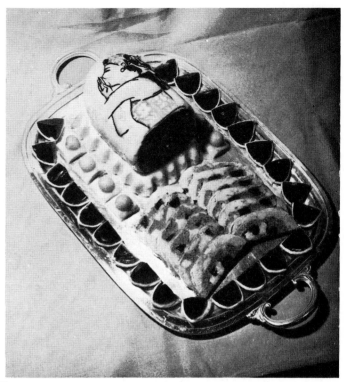

Left Above: Galantine of Capon and Foie Gras

On this beautiful and delicate piece, notice the block of foie gras imbedded in the center of the filling. Also the inserts are neatly set in a circular arrangement to give the most effective appearance. The butterfly decoration is explained in Chapter XII. A few round aspic cut-outs give the platter sparkle.

Left Below: Galantine of Capon Argenteuil

This is a classical presentation of the galantine. Argenteuil is a French locality where asparagus is cultivated.

the other from the legs—also the bones from the wings. The inside part of the breast meat must be freed from the tough sinews found there. If some of the meat should come loose from the outside skin, place it back so that an even layer of meat is distributed over the whole skin. A little spiced salt should be sprinkled over this. A few finely chopped shallots, sautéed slightly in butter, will flavor the galantine splendidly. Now the galantine is ready for filling. The entire procedure used in preparing a galantine is shown in the illustrations.

Galantine of a Suckling Pig

At the International Culinary Exhibit in Switzerland (1954) the American Team presented the only exhibit of an entirely boned and stuffed suckling pig. The piece won maximum points. The chef who looks for a different and attractive piece for the buffet will find in this unusual galantine the outstanding center piece. Step-by-step pictures explain the process.

Galantine of Pheasant

The basic preparation for the pheasant is the same as explained in the series of illustrations for capon or turkey. The stuffing, however, is different and contains the following ingredients:

1 lb. pheasant meat free of skin and sinews	2 lbs. fresh back fat
1 lb. lean pork	3 ozs. mushrooms

Filling: Add truffles, back fat strips, foie gras, pistachios, and seasoning.

Galantine of Veal

The veal galantine is made from a small breast of veal. Following are the ingredients for the stuffing:

1 lb. lean veal	1 lb. chicken or pork liver
1 lb. lean pork	1 lb. fresh back fat

Filling: Cubes of fresh back fat, ox tongue, ham, and if desired, truffles and pistachios. Seasoning.

After the galantine has sufficiently cooled in its own stock, take it out of the liquid and roll it again in another towel as tightly as possible. Put it back into the liquid, press slightly, and leave it in until the liquid has completely cooled. Decoration and further treatment is as indicated for turkey or capon galantine.

The Pâté

Pâté is the French word for paste and in this instance means a pie of delicate meat paste. The pâté is one of the oldest buffet pieces found in the ancient cook books. The French cuisine has always cultivated this specialty and from there comes the finest of all pâtés, the gooseliver pâté. Garde mangers put a supreme effort into turning out a pâté par excellence and with an inspired creative touch.

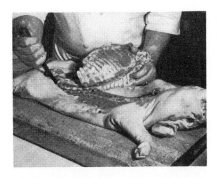

A small suckling pig, not over 15 pounds, should be correctly opened. Be sure the skin is not punctured except where the incision is made. Otherwise, such punctures must be sewed up or the filling will burst through. Bone the animal from the inside leaving the skin and meat intact, cutting as close as possible to the bones. After the belly is boned and the meat scratched from the breast bones, the shoulder comes next. Only the front feet remain with bones. The shoulder blade and second joint must be removed. Near the neck, cut the back bone between two vertbras and follow the backbone the entire length of the body to the place where the hindlegs are joined. Disjoint the small hams on the nearest joint to the body and begin at this point to bone them, leaving the hams on the whole pig. Only the feet remain with the bones in.

Sprinkle salt mixed with spices over the boned part, fold the carcass and set it aside until the filling is prepared.

Some additional meat is needed for the filling of one suckling pig such as lean pork, back fat, ham, ox tongue, pork liver, and a little heavy cream and white wine. The ingredients for the filling are as follows:

Ingredients:

8 lbs. lean loin of pork	½ glass white wine
2 lbs. back fat	2 ozs. Cognac or Madeira
2 lbs. pork liver	1 cup peeled pistachio nuts
½ pint, heavy cream	Liquid from 1 can of truffles

Cut 6-inch long square strips of lean ham one-half inch thick and the same of salted ox tongue. Also cut back fat (larding bacon) in the same size strips. About eight strips of the ham, ox tongue, and back fat are needed.

If a center garnish in the filling is desired, skin a large pork tenderloin and sauté with butter before using. Cut the filling meat—not the strips—into squares and run through the grinder. Transfer into the chopper and as the meat gets finer and finer, little by little add cream and white wine. Also, for better binding, add four egg whites.

The seasoning is added while the bowl is still rotating. To season a filling of this sort demands a feeling in the fingertips and tongue. Keep in mind that any filling gains in salty flavor during cooking so hold back with the salt and give rather a delicate flavoring with spices—galantine spices, finely crushed mixed herbs, or special Paris pâté condiments. A wise mixture of marjoram, basil, cloves, and sage may be used. Do not run the filling too long in the chopper as the fat will separate from the meat and result in an uneven product.

Lay the boned pigling out flat. Plaster a two-inch layer of filling over the whole inside. Next set the insert strips lengthwise on the filling beginning with the truffles in the middle and follow with back fat, ham, and tongue. Follow with more strips until all are used. If a tenderloin is used, place it on top of these strips after a thin layer of filling has been placed over the strips. Sprinkle a generous amount of pistachio nuts into the filling.

The balance of the filling goes on top creating a small mound shape to fill in the piglet's belly. Clean the outer edges of the skin free of any filling before closing the skin by sewing.

Use needle and twine to sew the body together to resemble its former shape. Be sure that the cavity of the whole pig is not over-stuffed to avoid the danger of the skin breaking open during roasting. The filling will expand a little as it roasts.

With a moist towel, clean the whole outside of the pig. Cut a wood plank the same length and cover it with aluminum foil. Place the pig on the aluminum foil and tie the front and hind legs to the board. Be sure they are securely tied so the form of the animal remains in its natural shape throughout and after the roasting process.

Set the oven thermostat at 220° and place the pig on the board on a baking sheet. Baste the surface of the pig with bacon rind and roast for three and one-half hours, basting from time to time with bacon rind. This keeps the skin from cracking and colors it a beautiful brown. Protect the ears and tail with foil during most of the roasting time; otherwise they will crack. When the roast has cooled, set in the refrigerator over night.

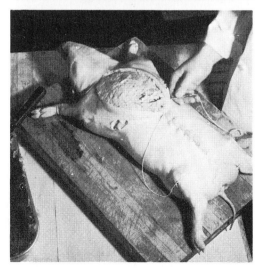

In the early days a mosaic of tender bits was put into the pâté and the slices were a beautiful sight. Today some modernistic attempts are made, using whole pieces of very tender parts of meat such as tenderloins and goose liver.

When the garde manger has completed his contribution to the pâté, he passes it on to the pastry chef who finishes with an artistically decorated pastry cover.

Preparation of a Pâté

The basic recipe is more or less always the same whether meat, game, poultry, or other meat is used. The main effect is achieved through a flavorful "farce" or fine meat filling. This filling, once cooked, must be tender, homogeneous, of a fine texture, and must have the characteristic taste and aroma of the particular kind of meat used.

To make a Polynesian-style decoration, prepare grapefruit baskets filled with raw cranberry jelly and apple slices, cocoanut shells with scalloped edges filled with Waldorf salad decorated with peeled grape halves, bananas decorated with pimientos, and a pineapple filled with marinated pieces of fresh pineapple and maraschino or mint cherries.

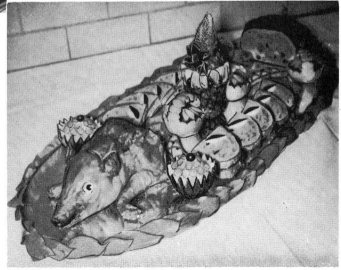

Cut half-inch thick slices from the center of the pig. Each slice will yield two large portions or several smaller ones. Glaze the surface of the slices with aspic and present on a large platter with the garnishings.

Do not cut a freshly baked pâté. It should be allowed to age in a cool place for several days. This will improve the taste and aroma tremendously because a certain fermentation and development occurs among all the spicy ingredients after two or three days' rest.

Four separate procedures are necessary in making a pâté:

1. Preparation of the special dough
2. Preparation of the filling (farce)
3. Baking
4. Preparation of jelly

Dough for a Pâté

3 lbs flour	1 to 2 pints of lukewarm water
¾ lb. lard	2 egg yolks
1½ ozs. salt	

Form a well with the flour, salt, lard, and water. Begin to make a dough from the middle by adding flour a little at a time. Work the dough until homogenous. Form in the shape of a loaf and cover with a damp cloth. Let it rest for four or five hours.

Preparation of Filling

Basically the ingredients are the same for all fillings except for the addition of the particular meat that is needed to give the pâté its characteristic flavor. Usually a combination of fresh lean pork, veal, back fat, and liver are used. Veal liver may be omitted if plenty of goose liver or canned foie gras is available. But pork or veal is needed to give the filling a good homogenous structure. Recipes for fillings are given later under each separate type.

Be sure the meat for the pâté is entirely free of sinews and tough parts before grinding. Cut the meat in large cubes, mix with the correct amount of lard, then run through the meat grinder twice or three times until fine. After that, place it in the chopper. Finally, strain it through a wire sieve that will remove the last of the remaining sinews and the result will be a filling of very fine texture.

After the meat filling is ready, add for each pound of it, three-fourths of an ounce of salt mixed with one-half teaspoon of fine ground mixed spice. Special spices for the pâté which are imported from France are preferable but it is permissible to use a mixture of spices and herbs mixed in the kitchen. White pepper, black pepper, paprika, ginger, cloves, bay leaves, mace, nutmeg, basil, thyme, and marjoram give good results.

The filling is used like plaster, as a covering of all the larger pieces of meat such as strips of tenderloins and livers. The taste must be delicate and never over-salted.

Baking the Pâté

After the pâté dough has rested for five hours, shape it to a square block and roll it out to fit the mold. In France they have specially-designed pâté molds which are rippled on the sides and are either oval, round or rectangular in shape similar to bread molds. These special molds come in two pieces which are hinged together during the baking. When the pâté is cold, the hinges are opened on one side. This makes it easier to remove the pâté without breaking the dough which occurs when the dough is rolled too thin or baked until it is too crisp.

Roll the dough one-half inch thick, fold it over lengthwise, and place it in a well-buttered mold. Press the dough against the sides, being careful not to make any thin places in it. The dough must be evenly spread on the bottom and sides of the mold with two inches hanging over the edges. The whole surface of the dough in the mold is then spread with thin slices of fat bacon.

The dough is now ready for the filling. One layer the thickness of a finger is then spread on the bottom and the sides. Then comes the inserts in the form of strips which may be imbedded into the rest of the filling so the slices, after the pâté is baked and aged, resemble a neatly assembled mosaic. Each recipe has its own inside decoration.

From the left-over dough, roll out the cover slightly thinner than for the bottom and sides. With a dough cutter, make round cutouts in the cover for a chimney to be inserted later. Baste the sides of the dough to make the cover adhere and put it in place. Do not stretch it too tightly but give it a little leeway for baking. Pinch the surfaces together where the dough cover meets the sides and cut the remaining dough away. Brush the surface with egg white and add a thin ring of dough around the cutouts.

From thick paper, roll a short chimney and place it in the cutouts so no juice will run out during the baking. Half moon decorations made from dough may be placed on the cover.

Baking a pâté demands close attention. An excessively hot oven may break the crust. Also, if baked too fast the filling will expand forcing the cover to break loose on the edges. This allows the juice to run out and the pâté is a failure.

Be sure that the cover of dough is firmly fixed to the sidewalls and that no thin places are present. Roll the dough to a thickness of one-half inch. The cover may be a little thinner.

Set the oven temperature at 350° to 400°. If the crust takes too much color, the oven is too hot. Sometimes a damp wrapping paper placed over the pâté protects it from taking on too much color. The baking may be tested with a thick larding needle. Push it into the pâté and when the needle point feels very warm, the pâté is ready to take out of the oven. Now, after the pâté is cool, pour in the cool aspic as directed below.

Preparation of Aspic for the Pâté

Aspic used to fill the space between the crust and the shrinking filling should be slightly stiffer than usual because the pâté will be cut into slices. Also, the aspic has to follow the knife. For various pâtés different types of aspic must be used. A family-style pâté may be filled with a regular meat aspic. Pâté made from fowl must have a poultry aspic and for game, a game aspic.

It should be poured into the pâté after it has cooled almost to ice box temperature. Do not pour it while the pâté is still warm. Cool the aspic until it appears like syrup. Use a goose-neck pitcher and a funnel and fill the aspic in through the chimney which is the round opening on top of the pâté, left open during the baking process for steam to escape. Fill aspic right up to the top. Do not soak the outside of the pâté or the crust will soften.

Pâté de Foie Gras Strasbourgeoise

For a large pâté of 25 large portions or 50 to 75 small portions use the following ingredients:

12 ozs. tenderloin of veal	4 ozs. salt mixed with pâté spices
12 ozs. tenderloin of pork	
36 ozs. fresh back fat	2 eggs
12 ozs. fresh or canned foie gras (goose liver)	3 ozs. Madeira wine with liquid from truffles
	2 ozs. Cognac

6 large fresh gooselivers stuffed with truffles

Carefully remove all sinews from the veal and pork, cut into cubes, mix well with the spicy salt, and grind several times until a fine mass is obtained.

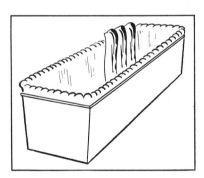

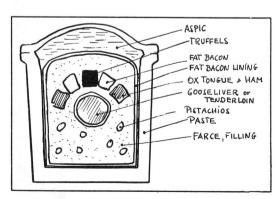

ASPIC
TRUFFELS
FAT BACON
FAT BACON LINING
OX TONGUE & HAM
GOOSELIVER or TENDERLOIN
PISTACHIOS
PASTE
FARCE, FILLING

Representation of pâté in preparation. The dough is in the sides and bottom and one thin slice of bacon has been inserted. These thin slices extend around the mold inside the dough, covering the sides and bottom.

Representation of a slice of pâté showing how the mosaic effect is achieved. Starting with thin slices of fat bacon, the bottom and walls are plastered with a finger-thick layer of filling. Pistachios are sprinkled over this layer and a second layer of filling added. Then the center decoration is imbedded in the filling —a tenderloin of veal, pork, game, or poultry, wrapped in bacon. Around this center another layer of filling is built to a dome shape. On this is placed the inserts in strips—truffles, fat bacon, ox tongue, and ham. Finish the top with another layer of filling built to a slight dome shape and place the overlapping bacon slices from the sides over the meat. Place the cover directly on the bacon slices.

After baking, the meat will recede leaving some empty space between the meat and the dough. This space is then filled with aspic.

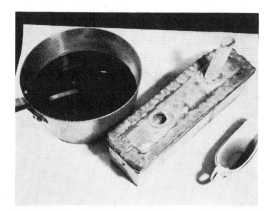

After the pâté is baked and cooled, aspic is poured into it through the small "chimneys" with the help of a sauce bowl until the space between the filling and cover is completely filled. Do not cut the pâté until the aspic is cooled to sufficient stiffness. Note the paper tube placed in the "chimney". This prevents the juice from getting on the outside of the crust during baking. These holes are placed in the crust to permit steam to escape.

Presentation of a Pâté for the Buffet

The slices of the pâté cannot be cut too thin because the flakey crust will break. For this reason they are cut into slices of about one-half inch thickness and then, if desired, cut into two or three equal pieces. In this illustration the tray is garnished with orange sections filled with jelly; and artichoke bottoms with Waldorf salad. However, a pâté may be presented entirely free of garnishes in which case Waldorf salad and Cumberland sauce is served on the side.

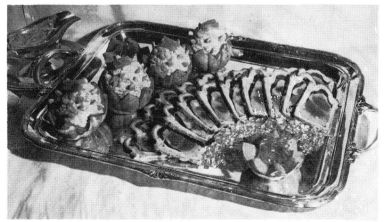

Pâté of Deer or Other Game

The pâté is cut in slices and presented in fan shape. The salad is made from rice and fruit with mayonnaise dressing filled into halves of cantaloups and served with Cumberland sauce.

143

Add Madeira and Cognac in small quantities. If a fine wire sieve is available, press the filling through this fine mesh so a grainless mass results. Set aside for further use.

Dough:

2 lbs. and 4 ozs. flour	1½ ozs. salt
6 ozs. lard	2 eggs
12 ozs. water	

Preparation:

The bottom and sides of the mold must be covered with fat bacon slices from fresh, unsalted bacon with the ends hanging over the edge. Plaster the meat three-fourths inch thick over the bottom and sides in an even layer. The size of the mold will determine how much of the fresh or canned goose liver can be placed in it. These raw goose livers have first to be stripped of skins and sinews, then stuffed with truffles and marinated for hours in a covered tureen, sprinkled with Madeira and Cognac. When the livers are tightly pressed into the meat, a layer of meat must cover them until the filling is built into a mound. The overhanging bacon ends then close over the top.

From the remaining dough a cover must be rolled out and two steam holes cut out with the aid of a small round cutter. Around these openings place a ring of paste. Otherwise, during the baking juice will rise inside the pâté and run over. It is wise to make a chimney from heavy paper which closes tightly around these steam holes.

The edges of the dough should be pasted with egg so cover and side wall will adhere to each other during the baking. For decoration the edges may be pinched together with a special dough pincer. This pâté will take about one and three quarters hours to bake.

In case fat runs out of the pâté during baking, be sure it is replaced. The same fat may be used if it has not darkened too much and acquired a bitter taste.

Goose liver pâté is not filled with aspic as most others are.

As soon as the pâté is cold, remove from mold and cut into slices of one-third to one-half inch in thickness.

Family Style Pâté

Filling:

10 ozs. lean pork	8 ozs. lean veal
8 ozs. pork liver	14 ozs. back fat

Garnish for inside of pâté:

Sliced ham, sautéed tenderloin of pork, chopped parsley and shallots, and pistachio nuts.

Preparation:

Same as previously explained.

Pheasant Pâté

Filling:

14 ozs. chicken liver purée	8 ozs. lean pork
8 ozs. lean veal	1½ lbs. back fat

Garnish for inside of pâté:

Larded breast of the pheasant, tiny lardings with truffles, and ox tongue marinated in brandy.

Inserts:

Truffles, tongue, back fat, and pistachios

Preparation:

The same with a port wine-flavored aspic used for filling.

Any type of game bird may be used for a pâté.

Popular Ham and Veal Pie (English Style)

Filling:

Strips of cooked ham, blanched bacon slices, marinated filets of veal or pork, truffles, and pistachios.

Prepare some fine ground meat as for Family Style Pâté. On the bottom, place the ground meat, then a layer of veal, followed by a layer of ham, etc., until mold is full. The tenderloins have to be pan-fried quickly in butter so the meat flavor is retained and so that they do not shrink too much in the pâté or become brown outside and raw inside. Add a spoon of chopped shallots before the filets are removed from the pan. After a moment of sautéing, add a glass of dry white wine or Madeira. Proceed in the usual way.

Rabbit or Hare Pâté

In Switzerland the Pâté de Lievre is most popular as the taste of the game pâté is outstanding.

First, bone the rabbit and free the meat completely from all sinews. Use the meat of the loins for inserts. Grind the legs and forelegs together with the same amount and kind of meat mentioned in the Family Style Pâté. Fry the loins quickly in butter, add a spoonful of chopped shallots and four ounces of Cognac. Bring to a boil and remove from the stove. Cool and proceed in the usual way in making the pâté.

Liver Pâté (Terrine)—Prepared in mold, not in paste.

Filling:

4 lbs. fresh calves' pork or chicken livers	2 glasses of red wine
2 lbs. back fat	Salt, pepper, mixed spices to taste
1 cup finely chopped shallots	Add 1 lb. small diced back fat for garnish if desirable
1 garlic clove	

Preparation:

Remove sinews and skin from the liver and place the liver in hot water for a few minutes. Take off any remaining skin and grind finely. Cut the fat bacon in small pieces and boil it with chicken stock until tender. Chop fine. Mix with sautéed shallots, ground liver, bacon, and stock. Place in a casserole and heat. Add the spices and salt necessary to make a tasty paste which, with increasing heat, will thicken. As soon as the mass gains consistency, take from the stove and fill it into a cake mold which has been completely lined with thin fat bacon strips. Place on a baking sheet and bake in a medium hot oven at about 220° to 275° temperature for one to one and one-half hours.

After baking, let cool and then place a weight on top of the liver pâté. This keeps the pâté level and it cuts nicely when ready to serve.

When unmolding, hold the cake mold an instant in hot water and unmold on a cutting board. Remove bacon slices and cut pâté with a hot knife into adequate slices. Serve with aspic croutons.

Salmon Pâté

Fish pâtés are prepared similarly to the foregoing. Carp, pike, and fresh snapper are excellent to use. They work up easily into a pâté, imparting their characteristic flavor necessary to this dish. Inserts for the filling are delicate filets of fresh salmon.

Fish Filling:
For a medium-size pâté about 20 inches in length:

2 lbs. pike or carp meat	1 lb. butter
15 ozs. dough (see recipe)	6 egg whites

Use salt, pepper, tabasco, or cayenne, and Accent for seasoning.

The dough is used to make the filling smoother and to give it proper consistency.

Dough or Panade:

1 cup milk	Salt
1 cup flour	Butter the size of an egg

Stir with a wooden spatula while heating the mixture until it forms a paste. Remove from the stove and add three egg yolks, one at a time. Cool.

Preparation:
The bone-free fish meat and dough (see filling) are ground or chopped until fine. The mass must be strained through a fine wire mesh sieve. Put into a bowl and place on crushed ice for a while. Add the six egg whites in mixing into the mass with a wire whip. Season to taste.

Make boneless filets from fresh salmon or lake trout. Cut these into strips one inch thick and the length of the pâté. Marinate these strips for one-half hour with salt, pepper, lemon juice, chopped parsley, and shallots.

Prepare the mold with the pâté dough. Put one layer of filling on the bottom of the mold. On the filling arrange the pre-cut strips of salmon. Fill the empty space between the strips with more filling, add more strips and more filling until the pâté mold is nearly filled to the top. Cover with the dough cover in which one or two chimney holes are made. Bake in a moderate oven for about one hour. Make a needle test before removing from the oven.

After the pâté has entirely cooled off, some empty space will be left between the filling and the top of the crust. This space must be filled with fish aspic. Serve a mayonnaise sauce with the salmon pâté. Potato or cucumber salad and deviled eggs is an adequate accompaniment.

The Terrine

Terrines, like pâtés, consist of fine stuffings but instead of being baked with a crust they are steamed in fire-proof earthenware dishes. They are made from poultry, foie gras, and especially from game, liver, and game birds.

Presenting terrines on a buffet demands a carver with a sharp-edged spoon to serve portion by portion. It is possible to present a terrine without the earthenware. Unmold the meat carefully after dipping the mold into hot water. Free the edges of grease with a sharp knife.

Take a mold slightly larger than that in which the terrine was steamed and place in it a one-half inch layer of aspic. Decorate it with egg whites from hard-boiled eggs made into flowers. When the aspic is stiff, place the terrine on top of this decoration and fill the remaining space between meat and mold with jelly. Be sure that this jelly will become stiff enough to hold around the terrine. Then cool the entire dish in the refrigerator overnight but never freeze.

Terrine de Canard (Terrine from Duck)

This is considered the best terrine. It is made from duck meat and goose liver and is worthy of the painstaking decoration—a mosaic of truffles, egg whites, and tongue. Here it is accompanied by poached apple halves filled with sour wild cherries.

When ready to serve, unmold it like an aspic in the center of a platter. Place slices of a second terrine around it and garnish with suitable garnishes. Serve salad separately.

Except for the terrine of foie gras, all others of duck, pheasant, snipe, grouse, partridge, woodcock, quail, wild duck, plover, etc., have the same preparation.

Basic Preparation of a Terrine

The feathered game must be boned completely and skinned. The breasts of smaller birds remain whole or parted in the center. Larger birds must be cut into smaller pieces. The remaining bones, sinews, and meat are made into an aromatic concentrate. This concentrate is made by sautéing these remainders over a swift fire and thinning them out with Cognac. If a mortar is available, stamp all to a mass and work through a wire sieve. Because of the wonderful aroma this concentrate gives to the terrine, it is a *must*, either in liquid form or as a purée.

The pieces of breast which are to be used as filling, must be marinated in Cognac, chopped shallots, and spicy salt and placed in a cool place for several hours.

Filling:

The earthen tureen must be made ready with a thin layer of fresh fat bacon. Place a layer of stuffing on the bottom and on the sides. Next, place one layer of the delicate breast pieces, one layer of stuffing, and another layer of breasts. A layer of stuffing should close the top of the mold. If foie gras can be placed in between these layers the terrine gains in flavor. Do not fill the terrine to the very top as a thin cover of melted butter or gooseliver fat should be poured on during poaching. Also the meat will expand a little. Sometimes a bay leaf on top will give a good spicy aroma.

A tureen filled in this way is to be set in a flat casserole or bain marie and placed in an oven of moderate temperature. The cooking time is about the same as that for baking a pâté. A needle is used to determine when it is thoroughly cooked.

Pain de Foie

This is a curiosity in gastronomic wording but a delicacy of first grade if prepared properly. The ingredients must be assembled into a tasty but not too firm paste.

There is not much difference between a *pain* filling and the pâté except that most of the meat in this dish is pre-cooked and then driven through a sieve and mixed with a few egg yolks and flavored delicately with Madeira wine, truffle juice, and spicy salt.

The *pain* is baked slowly in a cake mold. It can also be poached in a water bath in the oven. Bake until the whole mass is thoroughly heated.

Ingredients:
4 lbs. of fresh chicken or turkey livers (mixed with foie gras if the pain should be fine).

2 lbs. back fat
2 soup spoons of fine chopped shallots
2 egg yolks
2 glasses Madeira wine
Salt, mixed spices, or galantine spice (French Import)
Truffles

Preparation:
Cut up all ingredients into cubes, season, and place back fat cubes first in a large sauté pan and melt some of the fat. Add the livers and heat further. Cool. Run through a chopper and add wine and egg yolks, spices, and salt to taste. Strain all through a fine sieve. Again mix thoroughly.

Prepare the mold with thin slices of back fat. Fill in mold to a height of three inches. Fold over bacon ends so that whole *pain* is completely surrounded by a thin layer of back fat. Put a bay leaf on top. Set the mold in a shallow pan with a little water. Place in a moderate oven and poach rather than bake the mold until the mass is thoroughly heated. This takes from 40 to 60 minutes.

Cool the *pain* overnight in the refrigerator. When ready for service, unmold the *pain* and cut into exact slices about one-half inch in thickness. Arrange these slices on a pastry rack and glaze the top of each slice with a thin coating of aspic. Place on a glass platter and set on ice if desired.

This type of *pain* may be served also as an appetizer before any full course meal. A dill pickle or a small mushroom salad or Waldorf salad may also be an adequate garnish. Sometimes Cumberland sauce is served with it.

To make the *pain* more appealing, sprinkle small cubes of truffles, ham, and bacon into the filling. Pistachio nuts may also be used.

One may also use different kinds of raw material to make a *pain* such as ham, tongue, or pheasant if these can be made into a fine purée.

Mousse

The varieties of mousse are used not only in connection with the meats from which they are made but are also used as decorative items on their own. A proper mousse is not only a tasty and popular buffet food; it is also economical and simple in preparation. Left-over ham, tongue, and seafoods are a few of the many sources of mousse material.

Since it is really a heavy purée, the garde manger should keep in mind that only small amounts of it should be distributed on the various items. Mousse is rich in content and flavor and for that reason should not be served in large portions.

The raw material must be made into a fine purée. This is done with the grinder followed by the chopper. After that, mix it well, strain it through

Decorated Ham with Mousse Cubes

Pour mousse three-fourth inch thick into a stainless steel pan. Be sure the surface is smooth. Place in the refrigerator for complete cooling. For decoration, they may be cut into any shape with a cutter. If a decoration is required it should be put in place and then a thin layer of aspic added. When the aspic has stiffened, the appropriate form may be cut out of the mousse. In this illustration cubes were cut out with a knife.

Virginia Ham Cornets

Above, Right: A ham mousse, partly of Virginia ham, is prepared. From raw Virginia ham, thin slices are cut and formed into cornets. These are filled with mousse from a piping bag and then cooled. They may be decorated with a point of truffle and a few drops of aspic on the mousse—not on the ham roll.

Below, Right: The cornets may be arranged on any decorated ham platter or served as appetizers with pickled vegetables or salad. In the illustration a wheel barrow, made from raw potato strips, is used as a decorative container and some of the cornets arranged to resemble a flower bed.

a fine wire mesh and perfect it with cream and aspic. If a so-called "mousse-line" is needed, straining through a fine sieve is a *must* because any granular material would show up in the fluffy appearance of a mousseline which is handled with a mold and cannot be treated the same as the mousse.

The mixing of the mousse is accomplished with the correct amount of aspic and slightly whipped cream in an adequate container with or without ice cooling, depending upon the end use.

The amount of softening agents such as cream sauce, cold liquid aspic, or whipped cream should be determined by an accurate recipe. This depends upon the end use—just how stiff the mousse should be.

Ham Mousse

This recipe may be increased or decreased by multiplying or dividing the ingredients accordingly. As it is, it will decorate two large ham platters, or will make about 60 squares, or fill 60 to 80 ham rolls.

Recipe:
>   2 lbs. of ham (no rind but fat left on if desired. Also, a small portion
>   of lean Virginia ham may be used for a tasty mousse)
>   2 cups of cream sauce
>   4 cups liquid aspic
>   ½ cup of partly whipped cream (one cup when used in piping bag).
>   ½ cup Madeira wine
>   Salt to taste (according to saltiness of ham)
>   Pinch of cayenne
>   A little red coloring

Procedure:
1. Cut ham in cubes and grind, then chop fine in chopper.
2. When fine enough and the chopper is still rotating, add the cream sauce.
3. Next place in an earthen bowl and incorporate the liquid aspic.
4. Add Madeira wine.
5. Cool the mousse on ice to the degree desired, fold in the partly whipped cream, season, and add the coloring matter.

Note: If a molded mousse, do not place on the ice but mix the ingredients in the above manner and then pour into a mold. If it is to be used in a piping bag for filling ham rolls, half eggs, bouchées, etc., wait only long enough for the mousse to have the necessary stiffness.

Mousse may be used in many ways—almost an unlimited number of applications are known. Following are a few of these.

Bouchée Charcutiere

Tiny puff paste patty shells may be filled with mousse, decorated with a truffle slice, and a thin cover of aspic on top. Do not wet the crust with aspic.

Profiterolles of Ham

Small profiterolles from eclair dough are filled when cooled.

Eclairs with Salmon Mousse
Small eclairs are baked, cooled, and filled with a mousse of salmon.

Artichoke Ecarlate
Cut eight even sections from each artichoke after removing the stem and one-third of the tops. Remove the seeds and plunge the artichoke quarters into lemon juice, water, and salt. Pour a little oil into this and cook until the artichokes are done. After cooling, arrange on a china platter and fill with a mousse prepared from salted cooked ox tongue. Place a small decoration on top.

Barquette a la Bouchere
A small boat-shaped shell of puff paste or other plain dough is filled with ham mousse and decorated.

Tiny Tomatoes Filled with Mousse
Cut the top from tiny tomatoes and take out centers. Place them upside down on a rack until all the juice runs out. Fill with any mousse and replace the top so a little mousse is visible. Give an aspic glaze and decorate.

Cucumber Boats or Barrels Filled with Mousse
Peel cucumbers and cut in sections two and one-half inches in length. Cut each lengthwise and take out center to form a boat shape. Small cucumbers must be used. Plunge them into boiling salt water slightly sour with vinegar. Bring to a boil, cook for about two minutes and cool quickly under cold water. Remove and let dry on a towel. Place them in a row on a rack, fill with mousse, decorate and glaze with aspic. Cucumbers may be cut into barrel shapes and filled in the same way.

Celestine with Mousse
Make 12-inch thin pancakes with crêpe batter. When cool, spread with a layer of mousse one-fourth inch thick. Roll tightly and place in refrigerator for a few hours. Cut into one-half inch slices and glaze before using.

Tomato Quarters Filled with Mousse
Peel medium-size tomatoes, cut in quarters, cut out centers and seeds and place quarters on a rack in a row. Use a piping bag in filling these tomato half-moons with mousse. Decorate with a small piece of truffle or pistachio, and glaze.

Artichoke Bottoms with Mousse
Tiny canned or fresh artichoke bottoms may be filled with mousse. Decorate on top. Any kind of mousse may be used.

Avacado Quarters Filled with Mousse
Cut small avocados into quarters, dip in lemon juice. Fill with mcusse.

CHAPTER XII

Cold Ham

Ham is the most popular item on the cold buffet. An imaginative chef can create a magic of cuisine with ham that will delight the connoisseur as well as the person who merely delights in good and colorful food. It is the presentation that makes the difference between "just a slice of ham" or a portion of delicious food unsurpassed by anything else available.

High grade ham is generally available throughout this country whether packed by the great meat packing houses or by smaller companies specializing in home-cured hams. When poor ones are encountered it is usually the fault of poor salting and curing procedures. Hams containing too much liquid are just as bad as those that are too dry. It is true that the country-cured ham has that special taste which the speedily-cured commercial type cannot have. The whole treatment, from slaughtering through the curing and smoking processes, is responsible for that extra flavor.

Although the Virginia hams and similar products in this country are first in taste, we still find in most states a home-cured and smoked ham par excellence and always dependable. Slow-curing in a brine containing sugar, pickling spices, and garlic in addition to saltpeter and salt usually give the best results. The fast salting process is modern and is probably used today in all pork-packing plants. In this fast procedure, a solution is injected into the meat and it spreads through the veins to most parts of the ham effectively and rapidly. Such a ham will not shrink during the curing process and therefore is more economical than country-cured and smoked ham. In some brands such as Virginia ham, Prosciutto, and air-dried ham, the loss through shrinkage is sometimes as much as 75 per cent greater than when cured the other way.

Westphalian ham, like Italian Prosciutto, is often served uncooked, sliced in paper-thin slices.

153

The preparation of the cuff must be careful and exact. The smaller of the two shank bones is removed with a saw. The skin is cut either in the shape of scallops or an even line, and the superfluous fat trimmed off. If the ham is only for presentation, all uneven spots may be molded and flattened out with shortening which is spread smoothly with a spatula.

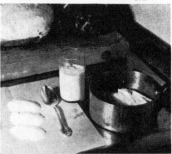

For the preparation of a small amount of covering sauce (chaudfroid ordinaire), take two ladles of thick cream sauce, a half glass of thick cream, and three teaspoons of granulated gelatin. Mix the gelatin with the cold cream and dissolve over hot water. Then add smooth cream sauce slowly and mix with the gelatin mixture. Strain the sauce through a cheese cloth and put on ice to cool. Stir during the cooling process until the sauce reaches the right consistency for coating as explained.

As soon as the sauce coats the spoon, it is ready for use.

In decorating the ham, the decoration should suit the occasion. For instance, a car motif should be used on a buffet for car dealers; a jockey, horse shoe, or spurs and a whip for a racing event; a putting green with a flag for golfers. The illustration shows a floral motif with butterflies which will suit any occasion. It is well to draw a sketch of the planned design first.

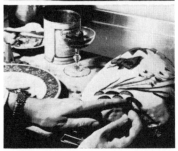

154

For buffet display purposes, choose the best shaped golden brown smoked ham with the bone in. The illustrations herewith show how easily a regular, bone-in ham may be prepared for a beautiful buffet piece. The ham need not be cooked if it is to be used only for the purpose of decoration. Also a decorated ham may last a week if put back into the cooler and clear aspic glazed over the surface after each presentation.

It is not practical to present the ham without a coating of demonstration chaudfroid. This chaudfroid is not made the classical way as it is too costly to use just for display. Recipe No. 2 in Chapter VII is recommended for this purpose. In the illustrations another recipe for fast work is explained.

After the coating with chaudfroid sauce, the ham is set in the cooler so the covering stiffens enough for the decoration to be added. After decoration, the ham is placed on the back of the platter and sliced ham or ham rolls or both arranged around it. A Madeira aspic, cut in cubes, will brighten up the platter. Asparagus tips go well with ham as does Russian salad in tomato baskets. Any type of green salad or regular vegetable or potato salad is appropriate also and may be presented on the side in glass bowls.

For the butterfly, pour a thin coat of jelly on a plate or glass platter and make the wings of the butterfly with red pimientos. The outlines and body are made with truffles or thin, black olive strands. Apply jelly carefully with a jelly brush until the decor is evenly coated. Allow this to set and then cut along the outlines. By using a glass platter this procedure may be used for difficult designs by placing a sketch under the platter and following the outlines. Of course, it is better to apply the decoration directly on the ham.

The finished show piece, with asparagus tips, melons filled with pickled or spiced melon rind, gelatin cubes and sliced ham or ham rolls used here as garnish. This may be served with the chef's favorite salad.

Below, top: This illustrates another use of truffle lettering. Cutters for these letters are available. The border for the heraldic design is made from round-cut truffles, boiled egg white, and leek, interlocked. The squares on the platter in front of the ham are made of ham mousse.

Below, bottom: This is a ham decoration of fast execution. Ripe olives are used to simulate a huge bunch of grapes. The ribbon is made from pimientos and two twigs from a green bush with the leaves intact. The whole arrangement is placed on the ham without the use of chaudfroid.

Decorated Ham for Mother's Day

Cut the rind off the ham leaving the well cleaned bone in. The bone is not visible in this illustration. Brush the ham with concentrated aspic (Glacé de Viande) and pour a white chaudfroid sauce over the ham. Surround the edges with sliced Canadian bacon held in place by invisible toothpicks. The decorations on the ham are explained in the chapter on decorating material. Green onion tops, truffles, and radishes were used and cutters used to cut the letters out from truffles. Ham rolls stuffed with ham mousse were arranged around the platter decorated with a slice of gherkin and two half wheels of truffle. Clear aspic cubes lighten up this platter effectively. The truffle lettering here is used to great advantage.

This ensemble resulted very brilliantly despite the massive dark areas cut from truffle aspic. The ham rolls with truffle garnish make an effective foreground and lend themselves well for speedy service.

Ham rolls with tangerine sections. The decorations were placed on the ham, free hand, with truffle strings. The motif, being a seascape, would go equally well on fish.

A ham decoration for the Easter buffet since the lily is used. After the lily is outlined with truffle strings, the outer edges of the petals are linted with very thin slivers of pimiento. The stuffed ham rolls are decorated with cut-out rounds of truffles and the whites of boiled eggs, then glazed with aspic.

Another type of ham decoration surrounded with ham slices and rolls and eggs stuffed with Waldorf salad.

Ham for an Easter Sunday Buffet

The shank meat has been cut from the bones of this ham so the modeling may be done with the bone as a base. Wire it first before starting to model. The ham should first be covered on the front with chaudfroid sauce which is the base for the truffle and pimiento decoration. With Westphalian Ham the rococo style of decoration is achieved by dipping the slices into cooling aspic. For modeling the rabbit, check with the chapter on decoration where modeling in margarine is discussed. Stuffed egg halves are given the shape of little chickens and the ham rolls are filled with ham mousse.

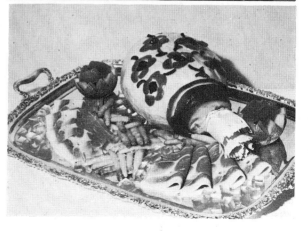

This type of decoration will be particularly suited for the busy chef. Thin slices from the tomato skin are used to form the corn flowers with five petals each, a truffle slice in the center.

CHAPTER XIII

Poultry on the Cold Buffet

The correct presentation of poultry demands more time than any other item. For this reason it is reserved for the higher-priced menu items. It also demands great skill; otherwise the result is not successful.

Throughout the years of culinary artistry, quite a number of different cold poultry dishes have been developed. Here we have attempted to present a few of the most beautiful in a more modern way.

Capon

Of all the poultry buffet pieces, the Chaudfroid of Capon is the most classical. The chaudfroid treatment has often been criticised during the past few decades because of a preference for food more naturally presented. People in general do not like food items completely covered by a sauce and if they have a choice, the food shown in its natural state is more popular. One cause for this probably is that the sauces are not properly made. Covering up a boiled capon with a stiff sauce containing too much gelatin is not the chaudfroid of capon of which the culinary artists are so proud.

Despite this controversy, no one can deny the beautiful effect of a buffet which has a selection of chaudfroids. In addition to the capon or other whole poultry, small chaudfroids may be made from bit-size pieces of breast meat. These breast slices must be cut into finger-long medallions. The shape should be identical for all pieces, either oval or oblong or round on one end of the slice and pointed on the other. It is advisable to make them with a cutter. With a table knife, a spoon-size quantity of goose or chicken liver purée is placed on top of the meat so a mound-shaped medallion results.

These medallions are then placed on a rack and cooled to ice box temperature. Place each medallion on a table fork, cover with the chaudfroid sauce, return them to the rack and cool again.

Chaudfroid of Capon

Poach the capon slowly in its broth until done. Allow it to cool overnight in the liquid. Then remove skin and extract breast meat. Care must be taken that the legs stay in place. Cut out the breast bone, leaving the wings tied to the back. Return to the cooler. Prepare chaudfroid sauce and cool it until it reaches the proper thickness. Pour it over all parts of the emptied carcass and the legs. Avoid drippings on the surface and smooth out any drippings on the underside of the feet and legs. If a second layer of sauce is needed apply it only after the first layer is stiff.

After the chaudfroid has cooled and stiffened, fill in the empty space where the breast was removed with a mousse of ham. Dip a table knife frequently in hot water and even off the surface of the mousse. It is very important to model the mousse to the shape of the breast. Return to the cooler.

The breast meat must be cut in very thin slices. Cut off the excess meat on the edges of slices. Place the slices, sized from smallest to largest, side by side on a rack or wax paper. Prepare a chaudfroid sauce. When it reaches the proper temperature and begins to cover the upheld ladle evenly, pour the sauce carefully over the slices and place them aside to cool.

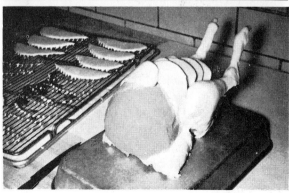

The difficult part comes in placing the slices on top of the mousse. Use the smallest slices first and finish off with the largest ones, each time two of the same size to a row—one for the left, one for the right side of the breast slightly overlapping. Toothpicks will help in setting the slices in place until the whole arrangement is finished and glaze with aspic which will hold the slices without the picks. It is well to use a little mousse underneath each slice where it will not be seen to hold the slices in place. Also, use a little pressure, to make sure each slice remains in its proper place.

160

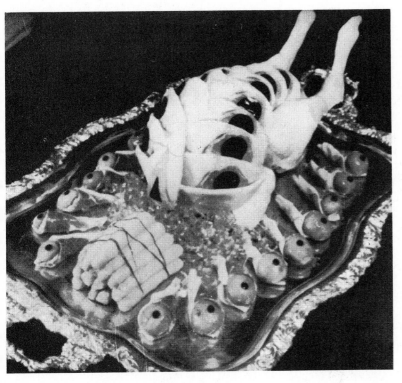

The finished capon shows how each slice is decorated with a thin slice of ham or Canadian bacon. These are slipped in between each capon slice and a round truffle slice finishes the decoration. The whole is glazed with clear aspic. Form cornets with thin slices of Virginia ham. Fill them with ham mousse and close with a mushroom and truffle point. Add white asparagus spears in a bundle tied with green strings of leek or green onion tops. Arrange on a silver platter which has been spread thinly with clear aspic. Tiny cubes of fine Madeira aspic finish the platter with sparkling effect.

Decorate each medallion with truffles, pimientos, mushrooms, etc., or cut out, with the aid of fancy cutter, the desired shape of a decoration. Then glaze the medallions with aspic in the usual way. They may be presented with the whole capon or with any bird treated in the following way:

Chaudfroid of Capon

After the breast of the capon has been carefully removed from the bone, fill in the empty space with a chicken liver purée, ham mousse, goose liver mousse or with a finely diced jellied vegetable mayonnaise or Waldorf salad.

The filling depends largely upon the character of the bird. There are still existing a few classical recipes of this kind such as Jeannette, Bristol, Lambertye, Neva, Rose de Mai, and York. These buffet pieces demand top performance from a good garde manger. Much experience and practice is necessary before such dishes as the one illustrated of the *Poularde à la Virginia* can be executed.

The tediousness and time necessary for preparing this piece of culinary art is somewhat lessened by using turkey and, instead of the petite medallions, use slices of the breast to cover the whole front of the bird. A few pictures show the preparation for this kind of presentation. However, one has to learn to handle the knife for this type of food layout. Only good tools and exact workmanship will bring satisfaction.

This illustration is a "Chaudfroid of Capon Printaniere." It is prepared in much the same way as
Chaudfroid of Capon but here the breast is filled
with mousse and the sauce poured over the whole
bird at the same time. The breast meat must be
sliced very thin and cut out with a cutter or knife
and covered with a mound of chicken liver, goose
liver, or any adequate mousse. The small medallions must also be covered with the sauce and decorated the same as the capon. The breast part is
decorated with a springtime motif made from leek,
onion tops, chive strings, radishes, and truffles.

In addition to whole poultry arrangements, the boned breast of chicken, either boiled or roasted, may be used. After cooking the breasts they should be put under some pressure so they will have a more even form and are more easily decorated. Such breasts, portion size, may be combined with aspic rings in the center of the platter. White or brown chaudfroid may be applied as desired.

Among cold poultry, duckling is very popular with connoisseurs. Roast the correctly tied duckling and set it aside to cool. The breast is extracted from the bone and cut into portion-size pieces which are served naturally or covered with a brown chaudfroid sauce to which the gravy from the duckling is added. The breast may be filled with Waldorf salad and presented with the breast pieces around it. Young goose may be prepared the same way.

Of the game birds, the pheasant is tops. Woodcock also belongs in this category. Most of these birds are presented with foie gras and truffles.

In this picture series, two types of *Chaudfroid of Capon* are shown. The one with chaudfroid slices is the most complicated one to make but after a few practice sessions it will be a rewarding buffet piece.

The second one is easier to prepare. The remodeled capon gets a coat of chaudfroid on which a decoration is placed.

Turkey

Turkey, quite often now, holds the place of honor formerly occupied only by the more expensive capon and poularde. By applying the same treatment as for capon, turkey becomes a popular item on the buffet. Therefore, step-by-step pictures show the different approaches for cold turkey preparation.

Capon Neva

Take out the breast bone without damaging the breast. Fill with fine uncooked chicken meat. Close with needle and string and cook in chicken stock. After cooling, remove the skin and cover the whole bird with white Chaudfroid sauce. Decorate with truffle. Place extra chicken medallions stuffed with goose liver purée and covered with chaudfroid sauce around the capon, surrounded with chopped aspic and truffle points.

Top Left: The capon or turkey must first be roasted to perfection. After cooling, the breasts are cut out from the carcass and a chicken or liver purée is prepared. The breast is cut into slices from which the medallions for the small turkey chaudfroids are made.

Top Right: The liver purée is placed in the breast cavity so a full-breasted bird is presented.

Lower Left: With a spatula, the surface is smoothed out. Brush the roasted legs and wings with concentrated natural gravy of the turkey or with heated *Glacé de Viande*. The medallions are covered with the same liver purée, cooled and covered with white chaudfroid sauce. Decorate each medallion with a pimiento star and truffle.

Lower Right: First, cover the turkey's legs with wax paper. Next, put one to three layers of chaudfroid sauce on the breast to get a smooth even surface. After cooling, apply the decoration. Here the small bowls at the left contain truffle, pimientos, etc., ready for use. In foreground, pickled fresh cucumber shells filled with a miniature Russian salad, topped with pimiento, are ready for aspic glazing. In the bowls back of the cucumbers are other garnishes: orange halves filled with raspberry gelatin; artichoke hearts decorated with truffle slice; pears and prunes stuffed with cream cheese; grapefruit baskets filled with fruits in lime jelly; banana shells filled with Waldorf salad and decorated. Cranberry sauce, raw cranberry molds, spiced fruits, and many other items may also be used as a garnish for turkey with equal decorative effect.

With a set of cutters this type of decoration may be made in a short time and it is effective.

It is not always necessary to make a chaudfroid sauce for a decorative setting. Fruits of various kinds may be used to advantage. In these two illustrations turkey is shown decorated with fruit.

The breast of the turkey may also be of a different filling. Instead of a liver purée or a mousse, a Waldorf salad thickened slightly with gelatin may be the base for the pineapple slices cut one-fourth inch thick. A few thin slices of turkey have been cut off with the help of an oval-shaped cutter and placed in front of the bird. These slices are decorated with truffles and edged with thin truffle strings. Truffle points are placed in the centers of the pineapple slices which serve to break up the flat color of the pineapple.

In the lower illustration, a large platter is used and breast slices are arranged attractively and with precision around the turkey.

Left: Bananas are used in this illustration to cover a celery salad. Use a toothpick to make each banana slice remain in place. The bananas are edged with truffle strings, the entire breast is glazed, and the toothpicks removed.

Below: Sliced turkey presented with a jellied Waldorf salad. Here sliced turkey is glamorized with the help of stuffed pineapple and a jellied salad which bears a truffle decoration. For this salad a terrine has been made as explained in Chapter XI.

This Indian face with a head dress is a very impressive piece, frequently seen and relatively easy to make. Modeled from cooked sweet potatoes, the face is built on the breast of the roasted turkey. Slices from an additional turkey breast are used to construct the head dress which is decorated also with pimientos and truffles. The platter is garnished with tomatoes stuffed with Waldorf salad topped with sweet potato and truffles built up to represent an Indian tepee. Small foie gras aspics are placed between each tepee to fill in the vacant places.

Cold Cornish Game Hen with Mandarins and Waldorf Salad

This same arrangement may also be applied to leftover poultry of any kind. Cut the bird up and remove the meat from the bones. Place the meat on a platter as shown, the leg pieces underneath, the breast pieces on top. Each group should have a decoration of two mandarin sections and a grape. The platter is presented with an empty pineapple shell filled with a cream celery and apple julienne (à la Waldorf), the celery cut from celery roots. Slices of pineapple are topped with the same salad and decoration. Two large bunches of grapes placed on crinkled aluminum foil finish off the platter.

Chaudfroid of Duckling

First, the breast meat of the duckling is extracted from the bones. To form the border, these are covered with a mound of goose liver paste over which brown chaudfroid sauce is poured. When cooled completely, they are decorated with thin lines of butter. The white from boiled eggs may also be applied. The empty breast is then filled with mousse. The top decoration is made with banana slices and glazed. The small balls in the border are made with goose liver, truffles, and surrounded with aspic cubes.

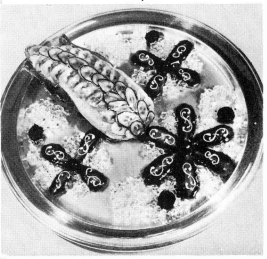

Cold Roast Duckling

Here leftover duckling makes a good cold poultry platter. One duckling is used as a center piece by extracting the breast meat which is sliced and placed back on the carcass and decorated with pineapple wedges. The meat from the remaining birds is cut into small pieces and placed around the center. The whole is surrounded by small liver paste aspics, making a fine buffet platter.

167

Pheasant

Pheasant is the most important among the feathered game birds for the cold buffet display. In early days, no royal buffet was complete without the royal bird. Today, the pheasant still has its great value on any distinguished cold buffet.

In this country, this bird is available throughout the hunting season. Still others are raised on farms and it has become not too luxurious an item. If we follow the French cuisine, most cold pheasant dishes are presented with the classic and delicate *Parfait de Foie Gras* (goose liver or goose liver paste). This flavor combination is unsurpassed. But the garde manger will find other possibilities in dressing up cold pheasant that are just as flavorful.

Still another presentation is *Faisan en Voliere*. In this dish the beautiful feathers are preserved. With the help of wooden or wire sticks, the head, wings, and tail are used. The single parts with the sticks protruding about three inches, are stuck into a bread crouton or a heavy turnip. All visible parts of the sticks must be covered by the feathers which remain on the neck, the wings, and tail. In this way an amazingly true copy of a pheasant in flight may be achieved. This presentation, despite criticism by the juries of culinary shows will bring atmosphere to any buffet.

If such a decoration is chosen for a buffet, make sure that the feathers of the bird do not come in contact with the food but place it on a separate standard which can be entirely covered on the sides and place the platter containing the food in front of it.

Pheasant à la Bacchus

Two pheasant cocks are needed for this display although only the carcass of a single one is used for the build-up. Both birds are roasted but not until they are too dry. One of them should have the feet correctly dressed for presentation. This is done by tying both feet together after the claws and first joints are removed. An aluminum foil wrapping will protect them from breaking or burning.

When the pheasants have cooled, cut out the breast meat and slice it into thin slices, lengthwise.

The carcass is then built up to its original shape with a mousse of chicken and goose liver. Then arrange slices on it beginning with the smaller ones and ending with the larger ones, leaving a triangular front part open for the front decoration. This may be made with small oval goose liver medallions decorated with truffles and pistachio nuts. Glaze with clear aspic.

The slices of the second breast are set in correct rows on a rack and garnished with an artificial truffle made from a ball of foie gras purée, rolled in chopped truffles and wild cherries, sour-sweet, then glazed with aspic.

For further garnishes, 12 small apples are peeled half way, cored, scalloped with a knife, dipped in lemon juice, and baked in the oven with white wine and sugar until done. Cover the apples while baking with a buttered wax paper so they will not take on color. Cool the apples and decorate with

Pheasant with Cailles in Nest

See text for preparation of pheasant and quail.

Illustration of nests.

The finished dish with the Faisan en Voliere as described in the text.

169

peeled grape halves, wild cherries, and truffles in imitation of a wild fall flower. Two bunches of large hot house grapes are further garnishes and underline the Bacchus motif.

Pheasant with Pineapple and Cailles in Nest

Still another superb pheasant platter is prepared the same way as *Chaud-froid of Capon Virginia,* but the slices are left without decoration. The pheasant is roasted as in the preceding recipe. When cold, the breast meat is cut off the bones and sliced very thin. The legs are brushed with a thin layer of reduced hot natural juice from the roasting pan. The breast bones are cut down with a heavy sizor. Make a Waldorf salad with celery knobs finely julienned mixed with the same amount of diced pineapple and added to a creamy mayonnaise stiffened with a small amount of gelatin. Place the salad on ice and when it begins to thicken, place it in the empty breast and dress it up to the original shape. Then place the slices on the salad, overlapping each slice with a half-moon shaped slice of pineapple between each. Give the whole pheasant a glaze.

The *cailles* (quail) are roasted for approximately eight minutes, set to cool on a rack, then coated with a thin layer of brown chaudfroid sauce. From foie gras make a paste, roll into small balls slightly flattened on two sides and place on the border of a plate. These balls are to represent the heads of the quail. Coat them also with a layer of chaudfroid sauce.

From boiled egg white, truffles, and almond stick, make eyes and beak. Glaze the heads with aspic and when completely cooled, place the heads on the breast of each little bird.

This very attractive cold dish may be made somewhat finer if the breasts are boned and the legs removed from the carcass. With an egg-size foie gras or game mousse the body is formed, the legs placed on the sides, the boneless breast coated with brown chaudfroid sauce and the heads are added.

CHAPTER XIV

Roasts on the Cold Buffet

Who does not get a glow of anticipation when he views a nicely turned roast, be it rib or round, being removed from the oven and glistening in its brown tasty crust of fat and juices? And the cold roast loses none of its splendor when it rests in royal glory on the buffet table surrounded by its loyal subjects, the colorful salads, shining gelatins, and hors d'oeuvre.

The cold roast has a most respectable lineage. The Puritans of New England knew it well because their religious beliefs permitted no cooking on their day of worship. In old London, the standby breakfast was cold beef, a loaf of bread, and a tankard of ale.

Hence we see that the cold roast, in the hands of a chef with imagination, has unlimited possibilities.

All first class roasts may be used on cold buffets as well as some second class pieces such as corned beef, pot roasts, etc.

These meats should be shown with some vegetables in display form. There are some salads that go particularly well with these meats such as tomato, potato, and cole slaw. Several ways that garnishes may be used effectively are shown in the illustrations. These add not only nutritional value but their brilliant color makes a dull colored roast much more appetizing to view.

All large buffet pieces of such roasts should be prepared as follows:

Preparation of Roasts for Display

Cut the finished roast in half, racking the best end for display. Make sure the cut is clean and the roast trimmed. The remaining piece should be sliced in medium portions.

Since buffet pieces must be prepared hours before they are to be served, pour a very thin layer of clear aspic on the bottom of the platter, place the portion of the roast for display in position and allow it to cool in the refrigerator. This not only keeps the roast in place but insures against any metallic taste.

When the jelly has stiffened, the sliced portions may be arranged as desired. The choices of arrangements are numerous. The main rules to follow are:

1. The meat must be sliced carefully and arranged in an exact pattern beside the presentation piece.
2. Once they are placed on the platter, do not move them as rearranging will mar the clear reflection of the aspic base.

It is wise to draw a quick plan either in the mind or on paper before setting to work. Sketch variations of the same piece with the slices between appropriate garnishes.

With the roasts or large pieces many small cold pieces may be prepared such as stuffed chops, medallions, scallopini, sliced and rolled meat, cornets, noisettes, supremes of poultry, chaudfroids, etc.

Leftovers of this type may easily become best sellers on a buffet if correctly prepared and presented.

Cold Beef Tenderloin, Belle Jardiniere

This is made from a select roast beef tenderloin trimmed and roasted to perfection and garnished with a classical "jardiniere." As roast beef has a tendency to lose some of its juice when sliced, it is advisable to roast it almost medium well done. Prepare a base of bread, flat and square, for the presentation piece. This will absorb any overflow of juices so they will not mar the appearance of the platter.

Cut the tenderloin in one-fourth inch slices and arrange around the main piece. All the corners and bare places on the platter should then be garnished with the vegetables or "jardinere." Such vegetables should be cooked especially for this purpose and flavored with lemon juice. They may also be prepared as in Greek salads by steaming with vinegar, white wine, oil, and mixed spices. However, with this presentation, although the salads may be tastier the vegetables have a tendency to lose their lovely color.

Suggestions for the vegetables to use are:

Flowerets of cauliflower, cooked and marinated and pressed in a towel to form small round balls of equal size, placed on a rack and topped with mayonnaise.

Green beans put together in small bundles and held with an onion ring.

Small spring carrots of equal size.

Brussels sprouts.

Stuffed miniature tomatoes.

Asparagus made into bundles—about five to each bundle—held together with strips of pimiento.

Arrange all vegetables on a rack, cool in the refrigerator and then paint over the surface of the vegetables, using a pastry brush, with a layer of syrupy jelly.

Tenderloin of Beef Wellington

This is one of the more impressive buffet pieces. Roast the tenderloin, which has been larded, until it is brown—about 15 minutes. Cool off and cover it with a thin layer of Duxelle. This is a foie gras and mushroom filling. The recipe is given below. Place the filet on a paste which is similar to puff paste or a fluffy pie dough and envelop it completely to resemble a loaf. Decorate with strips or cut-outs of paste and brush with egg yolk. Bake another 25 minutes until golden brown. Cool and slice in portions about three-fourths of an inch thick. Chefs tossed salad goes very well with the Wellington.

Duxelle Farce for one Filet Wellington

Chop three-fourths pound of fresh mushrooms and sauté in butter with shallots. Add a small amount of white wine, lemon juice, salt and pepper and simmer slowly until thickened. Next, add an equal quantity of purée of foie gras or, for economy, chopped chicken livers puréed. Mix well with a wooden spatula until very hot, then add two egg yolks and a little chopped parsley. Take from the fire, cool, and use on the filet.

Tenderloin of Beef Wellington

Preparation of a Cold Prime Rib of Beef

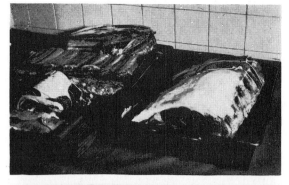

Remove excess fat and cut off the short ribs at the correct place. Saw off the bony part of the ribs and back bones to give an even appearance—as shown in the first illustration. Take out one or two slices of meat beneath the fat on the front part of the ribs—that part nearest the neck of the animal. Replace the fat cover and you have a fairly flat appearing roast rather than a rounded one.

For a cold buffet, roast the meat until it is fairly well done. If it is too rare it not only looks unappetizing but the juices will flow out on the platter and mar the appearance. After roasting and thorough cooking, some trimming is necessary. Do not cut off the natural roasting cover but only the small pieces which protrude. The slices should be fairly thin for a buffet and may be served either alone or with garnishes.

If the roast is to be served with garnishes, these are prepared ahead of time. It is important to anticipate an adequate supply of vegetables. It is impossible, of course, to place 30 servings of vegetables on a platter holding 30 servings of beef. Separate platters of vegetables are recommended—also bowls of Chef's Salad, Potato or Beet Salad.

This is the finished platter. A base of bread has been placed beneath the roast to catch any juices that may escape.

174

Pork Loin

Here are slices of a pork loin being decorated with softened butter, slices of hard boiled eggs, radishes, capers, and tomato aspic.

After decorations are completed, place the slices in a pan which is filled with cooled aspic. After the aspic is stiff from thorough cooling, cut out the slices with a sharp knife.

Here is a very attractive dish prepared from roast pork loin in aspic and a fruit jelly mold.

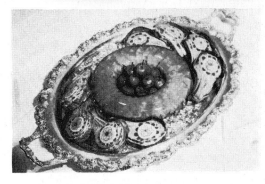

Cold Prime Rib of Beef

A cold prime rib of beef also makes a beautiful buffet platter. It may be arranged in the same way as Beef Tenderloin Jardiniere.

Filet Mignon Rossini

Grill or broil a filet mignon over a hot fire until medium well done. Cool on a rack allowing all the fat to drip down. When cold, cut into equal parts and cover the bottom part with a layer of purée of foie gras. Press the top part into it and then spread the purée around the filet. Decorate the top, finishing with a truffle slice. Cool well and finish with a thin layer of jelly.

Make a suitable salad from knob celery, Waldorf style. Be careful to keep the salad a little dry so no juice will run onto the platter. Make a center piece of a salad bowl surrounding it with nicely arranged filet mignon slices and mushroom heads.

Ox Tongue with Tongue Aspic

The point of the tongue is left whole and its top decorated with a
design made from carrot slices and truffle.

Tournados Richelieu

Use the recipe for Filet Rossini above except the top of each slice is
decorated with small strips of carrots and truffles. Each slice should weigh
from six to nine ounces.

Corned Beef

A corned beef buffet platter may be made very appealing by placing the
presentation piece at one end of a platter and arranging slices in front.
Decorate with thick slices of tomatoes covered with a delicate cole slaw
or sauerkraut. Finish with thin slices of dill pickles.

Corned Brisquet of Beef may be prepared the same way as ham, glazed
with brown sugar and dry mustard and studded with cloves.

Beef à la Mode

In France this is used with great success on the buffet. It tastes much like
cold pot roast and differs little in the presentation. Cold pot roast that is a
leftover may be used.

To prepare beef à la mode, use a large square mold. Pour in about one-half
inch of clear aspic, cool, and then place a garnish of carrots, pickles, white

turnips, or asparagus tips in the aspic. Pour in more aspic to hold the garnishes in place. If the sides of the beef are to be garnished, place the mold in a container of ice and give the sides a thin layer of jelly, turning so the stiffening aspic stays on the sides of the mold. Add jelly while turning until it is about one-half inch thick. Now the sides may be decorated with vegetables, sticking them to the sides in the jelly.

Around the sides of the mold alternate small slices of pot roast on top of the garnish with pot roast sauce which has been thickened with gelatin, until the mold is filled. Be sure the sauce is thick enough to hold when the whole dish is finally taken from the mold.

Cured Ox Tongue

Tongue is a good buffet item. In the classical kitchen, tongue, after cooking, is pressed into the shape of a shoe and covered with either a white or brown chaudfroid sauce. Mark the shoe laces in with strips of truffles and place in the center of the platter. Place slices of tongue around the center piece and garnish with various fruits—pineapple, peaches, pears, and cherries.

For repeat buffet business, a dummy may be prepared from bread. Shape the bread and cover with chaudfroid sauce. Decorate the same as for the real tongue.

Ox Tongue with Piquante Salad

Slice the center of the tongue in slices one-third inch thick. Place the slices in a straight or circular arrangement and garnish the top of each with a mound of vegetable salad. Decorate the tops with a radish rose.

Ox Tongue Waldorf

Follow the recipe for Ox Tongue with Piquante Salad but use Waldorf Salad instead. Spicy mustard or sweet mixed pickles may also be used on each slice of tongue instead of the salad.

CHAPTER XV

Game

Because local game laws limit the use of game for buffet presentation, it cannot be used too frequently. Nevertheless, it is always a special treat, highly rewarding to the connoisseur, and must be set up properly with a festive platter representative of the particular game—a saddle of deer, a pâté of hare or venison, or a stuffed boar's head.

The preparation of game is, with one exception, the same as for other meats to be roasted or cooked by other methods. The exception is that game *must* be aged. It should be hung long enough to become tender and develop the "haut gout"—the fine flavor admired by gourmets. For animals with an especially strong game flavor, a marinading process is required before cooking. Young animals are preferred for their tenderness.

For buffet work only the best parts of the animal are chosen—usually the saddle or legs. If delivered with the hide on, care must be taken when skinning to prevent hair from remaining on the flesh. Also, the inside of the carcass should be cleaned with a towel wet with vinegar.

Though game has little fat, the skin is tough and care must be taken in skinning not to lose any of the meat. To offset the lack of natural fat, the saddle and legs are usually larded before marinading.

There are three outstanding methods of marinading game: (1) the skimmed milk marinade, (2) the wine marinade, and (3) the dry marinade.

Skimmed Milk Marinade
Marinading in skimmed milk for a few days helps to tenderize the meat. Put the meat in an earthenware pot and cover with milk. Place the container in a cool place.

Saddle of Venison Orientale

Wine Marinade

The following proportions are given for a wine marinade for tender pieces of deer, hare, and young wild boar:

1 quart red or white wine	1 juice glass of oil
2 teaspoons peppercorns	½ teaspoon sugar
1 bay leaf	1 pinch of thyme
1 small bunch parsley stems	1 onion
1 juice glass of vinegar	1 carrot

Chop the carrots and onions very fine and sauté slightly in oil. Add the condiments and liquids. Cook slowly and when cooked, the marinade is ready for use. For game such as moose, bear, elk, and older deer, the amount of vinegar is increased to one part vinegar to two parts wine.

Dry Marinade

This is a short process. Rub the oven-ready meat first with plenty of oil. Sprinkle broken pieces of spices over it and cover the surface completely with peeled lemon slices. Cover with wax paper and allow to set for 24 hours in a cool place. The following ingredients are used for the dry marinade:

Lemons, peeled and sliced	Sliced shallots or onions
Oil	Parsley stems
Peppercorns, crushed	Thyme and marjoram leaves

Saddle of Venison Orientale

This is among the most classical of buffet presentations of venison and is certainly the most colorful and delicious of buffet items. Deer is used in most instances but other game may be used such as elk, wild boar, or bear.

Prepare the short loin of the animal in perfect shape and tie with string. The meat has to be larded and roasted with perfection which means until it is slightly pink close to the bones. A deer loin may require about 40 to 50 minutes slow roasting.

Cool thoroughly and cut out the filets in even, unsevered pieces. These filets must then be cut into small slices of about finger thickness.

If they are cut on an angle they give a better effect when arranged on the platter. (See illustration). On the rib bones place a thin layer of liver paste on which the meat is placed in the same order as cut. In the illustration a slice of ox tongue has been placed between each deer slice. When the saddle is completely together again allow it to cool and pour aspic over the saddle. Garnish with pineapple sections and mushroom heads finished with white chaudfroid sauce and a truffle star. Place the saddle on a platter which is covered with a thin layer of aspic. Decorate with orange baskets filled with Waldorf salad, orange gelatin sections and pineapple rosettes.

Leg of Deer

The legs of deer may be prepared in the same manner as the saddle. After removing the skin and hip bone, prepare the same as for a leg of lamb. Lard the surface. Use a dry marinade for young deer; a wine marinade for older deer.

The leg should be roasted for approximately one hour and 15 minutes. This should leave the meat pink around the bones. Cool the roast thoroughly before time for the buffet. For presentation, bone the meat into two sections and slice into one-fourth inch slices on the machine. Handle the slices carefully and keep them in order as they must be placed back on the bone exactly as they were removed to give the natural appearance of the leg before boning.

Serve with Waldorf salad and Cumberland sauce. Decorate the platter with the same fruits seen in the illustration of the *Saddle of Venison Orientale*.

Wild Rabbit or Hare

The best parts of the rabbit are the back and hind legs. Rabbit makes a fine game platter for hot as well as cold service. However, for the buffet, the rabbit is best presented as a pâté. The recipe for this is found in Chapter X.

Stuffed Head of Wild Boar

Variations in the size of heads makes it difficult to give a precise recipe. Therefore, refer to the treatment of the stuffed suckling pig in Chapter XI. The stuffing is the same and meat from the boar may be used for this.

General Instructions:

Cut off plenty of neck rind because the back of the head must be closed by

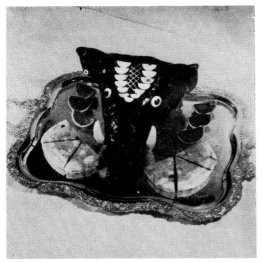

Stuffed Boar's Head

After the head has been prepared in accordance with the instructions in the text, cut slices from the rear as directed. This leaves the front intact for display purposes in case two heads are not available.

sewing over the opening a round piece of bacon rind. Wash the head thoroughly and singe completely with a red-hot iron or open flame. Wash again and bone from the back of the head. Sew up the openings of the eyes and mouth. The ears are poached within a towel.

The inside of the head is filled in the same manner as demonstrated for the suckling pig, Chapter XI. With a piece of bacon rind laid across the neck, the head is closed by sewing the rind to the neck skin. Place the head on a board of the same size cut from wood and tie it firmly with a cloth so it will retain its natural shape. With the bones, vegetables, and spices, a flavorful stock is prepared and the head and ears are poached in the stock for three and one-half to four hours. Cook it very slowly and remove the ears after one hour.

Cool the head in the same stock, then remove the cloths and tie it up again in clean cloths so the head still retains its natural shape. Replace it in the stock and stand it aside for the next two days. Remove it from the stock after this time, drain well, remove cloths, and fasten the ears to the head with toothpicks.

Place on a rack and with a table knife fill in all the uneven spots on the surface of the head with goose liver paste. Glaze with a mixture of *glace de viande* and thick aspic to an even golden brown. Decorate with the whites of boiled eggs as illustrated and glaze the entire head with aspic.

The head is carved from the back or neck side. The larger slices will require dividing into smaller portions. Place the slices on a rack for glazing.

Waldorf-type salad and Cumberland sauce go well with this outstanding buffet piece.

181

CHAPTER XVI

Various Buffet Styles

The Smorgasbord

The smorgasbord is a daily affair in Sweden and in most other part of Scandinavia. The modern smorgasbord is a descendant of the festive boards laid out in the great halls of the Viking chiefs to celebrate the return of the northern warriors from successful raids upon their enemies.

On long wooden tables, piled high with food from the land and the sea, were placed large vessels of beverages from which the Vikings would fill the skulls of their slain enemies and drink to their victory. From this practice came the phrase "Skol."

Today the Scandinavian toasts his guest with "Skol" with the same hearty good wish for merriment and pleasure at the smorgasbord but without the skull (skol in Swedish) of his enemy. The Scandinavians have few enemies and many friends to whom they play host at the festive board for which they have become famous in this 20th Century.

The proper smorgasbord may be all cold food or it may display a choice of hot items along with the cold. Almost the same food—mackerel, stroeming, herring, eel, and smoked salmon (roekt or gravel lax) along with delicacies from the land, is found on their smorgasbord today as it was centuries ago.

Among the seafoods are shrimps, tiny and of medium size. Large shrimps of outstanding flavor are brought to the table with their shells on; only the smallest ones are peeled. Lobsters are abundant and are mostly prepared as a salad mixed with mayonnaise. No smorgasbord is complete without shrimps or lobster. Denmark, contrary to the practice in Sweden, Norway, and Finland, serves most items on bread which is buttered. One of the greatest specialties in the restaurants of Copenhagen is a base of bread with a towering structure of 100 shrimps. In Norway's capital you may wander along the harbor and buy a paper bag full of fresh cooked shrimps right from the hand of the fisherman and eat them as you stroll. In a fine restaurant in Stockholm, the Belmansro, a salad is served with the biblical name of "Jonas." This salad consists of most everything in the line of seafood with caviar sprinkled over the top.

The most fantastic canape assortments are those one can see prepared by the pantry women with great speed. The Rainbow Restaurant in Oslo serves lunch largely from these canape trays and is famous, known to all globe-trotting gourmets.

Food on a smorgasbord must be prepared very colorfully. This means that flowers may be used in decorating the various food platters. In Sweden the sweet pea is used all summer long. Cheese platters, fruit trays, and baskets colorfully decorated with dahlias are not unusual. Many of these blossoms are used during the short summer months.

Nowhere is the food so glamorized as when the crayfish season opens. A dozen crayfish is the usual portion when you eat them in a restaurant but your friends in Scandinavia will place before you an immense platter towering with fiery red "Kraeftor" (crayfish) and decorated with dill crowns. With this, aquavit or brandwin is served, cold as ice. Beer is also an appropriate beverage with smorgasbord. Aquavit is served before the meal and beer with the meal. Sherry is also a preferred beverage with the hot foods.

Herewith is a sketch showing a suggested arrangement for a smorgasbord. If a great many people are to be fed, two tables with the same arrangement may be used. If a very long table is available, each side of the table may have the same arrangement.

Following are a few typical hot dishes for the smorgasbord:

Boiled Lamb with Dill Sauce (Kokt lamm med dillsas)
Boil the breast or shoulder of lamb in salt water seasoned with bay leaf, dill, and a few peppercorns. Simmer one and one-half hours until the lamb is tender. Cut in pieces and serve in a chafing dish with dill sauce and boiled potatoes.

Dill Sauce: Use the stock from the meat to make the sauce. To this, add a few tablespoons of vinegar, sugar, and dill. Season to taste. Add beaten egg yolk at last but do not cook after egg yolk is added.

Braised Beef Rouladen (Oxrulader)
From a top round of beef cut thin slices and pound until all are of the same thickness. Stuff each slice with a strip of fat bacon, roll, and fasten with a toothpick. Brown in a skillet. Braise in the usual way until tender, turning occasionally. Remove the meat and mix cream and flour and add to pan liquid. Simmer and then pour over the rolls. Serve with loganberries on the side.

Cabbage Rolls (Käldolmar)
These are very popular with Smorgasbord.

Creamed Sweetbreads (Stuvad Kalvbraess)
Five pounds of sweetbreads will serve about 16 to 20 people. After soaking the sweetbreads in cold water for several hours, place them in a casserole

Cheese Platter

Crayfish with Dill

Fruit Platter

Fish Platter

Platter of Wild Fowl

and bring to a good boil. Rinse in cold water and remove the skin. Cook in salt water for 10 minutes and allow to cool in the same water and cut in cubes. Make a white sauce with the sweetbread stock. Season. Add the cubed sweetbreads and heat. Serve in a chafing dish with either toast triangles or in patty shells or on Holland rusks or as filling for an omelette.

Kidney Sauté (Njursaute)

Cut slices or cubes from calf's kidney and sauté in butter. Add the same amount of mushrooms, thinly sliced. Sprinkle with flour and blend. Add a little brandy or sauterne and cream, stirring constantly. Cook slowly for 10 minutes and season with salt and pepper.

Loin of Pork with Prunes (Plommonspaeckad Flaeskkarre)

    10 pounds loin of pork
    50 prunes, pitted
    Salt, white pepper, and ginger

Bone the roast loin of pork while it is uncooked and over the entire length of the loin cut three deep parallel incisions. After rinsing the prunes in

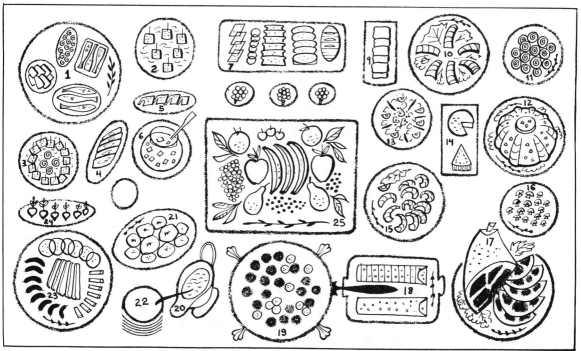

Explanation of Sketch

1. Various kinds of marinated herring, sardines, and anchovies in their original cans, cover neatly removed (Sill Brika)
2. Herring filets in sour cream
3. Herring filets in vinegar (Inlagda Sill)
4. Smoked salmon (Rökt Lax)
5. Smoked eel (Rökt ål)
6. Herring Tidbits in Marinade (Inlagda Sill)
7. Rye crisp and other breads such as pumpernickel and rye
8. Butter rolled to tiny balls by using two wooden spatulas
9. Liver paste (Leverpastej)
10. Lobster salad (Hummersallad)
11. Pickled sliced beets (Inlagda Rödbator)
12. Fish and shrimps in aspic (Fisk i Gele)
13. Potato salad (Potatissallad)
14. Cheese (Ost)
15. Fresh cooked shrimp in shells (Räkor)
16. Mushrooms (Svampstuvning)
17. Boiled ham (Kokt Skinka)
18. Jellied pork and veal (Flaesk-och Kalvsylta)
19. Small meat balls (Sma köttbullar)
20. Lingonberries
21. Boiled potatoes, garnished with dill sprigs
22. Stack of plates
23. Salami and other sausages and corned beef
24. Radishes
25. Fruit basket or platter (Fruit Brika)

A corner of the Smorgasbord at the Grand Hotel Royal in Stockholm. The photograph, made by Ake Lange, was submitted by Chef Emil Ackermann. The Smorgasbord contains nearly 40 different dishes.

In the left lower corner, sill Bricka, different herrings presented in their original containers placed in silver inserts. The next row above, from left to right: stroemings, a marinated local fish—fish roe—sour cream dressing. Third row: Individual cocottes of fish mayonnaise—beefsteak tartare—stuffed eggs. Fourth row: Platter containing smoked salmon and eel—cold meat platter with breast of wild birds and cold pot roast—cheese platter.

In the raised center portion are salads of different kinds: lobster, shrimp, herring, meat, greens, and vegetables. Notice the use of the starched and neatly broken napkins. Nowhere is food touching the metal. The eggs and marinated items are presented in earthenware.

The platters and containers are not of uniform size but those are chosen which best suit the food items they contain. This gives variety and interest to the Smorgasbord.

warm water, cut them in halves and insert in these incisions. Tie the meat with a string and roast in the usual way. Cut the loin into thick slices and serve on the Smorgasbord in a chafing dish with a country gravy.

Roasted Spareribs (Ugnstekt Revbenaspjaell)

This is very similar to the usual type of pork sparerib preparation. Season with salt, white pepper, and powdered mustard or ginger. After rubbing the broken spare ribs with the seasonings, roast slowly in a braise pan until the meat is tender. Stock or water is added during the roasting but only after the ribs have browned.

Swedish Hash (Pytt i panna)

This dish is very popular but it must be made correctly. All the ingredients must be cut in exact cubes and the meat freed from all skin and tissue.

3 pounds leftover meat, diced into one-third inch cubes
3 pounds cubed boiled potatoes, diced same size
6 medium-sized onions, chopped
Butter, salt, and white pepper

Sauté the onions to a golden brown and remove from the skillet. Brown the potatoes and meat in butter and mix with the onions. Season to taste. Sometimes the pytt i panna is made into an omelette shape and the pan reversed on the serving platter. Fried eggs may be placed over the top of the dish and the edge of the platter garnished with sliced dill pickles.

Swedish Meat Balls (Köttbullar)

1 pound beef, ground	2 eggs
1 pound fat pork, ground	1 medium-size onion, chopped
1 cup bread crumbs	3 tablespoons butter
2 cups of cream, half and half	3 tablespoons salt
	½ teaspoon white pepper

Soak the bread crumbs in cream. Sauté chopped onions in butter until golden brown. Place the meat in a mixing bowl and add all ingredients. Mix until smooth. With the help of two tablespoons, dipped in water, shape into balls. Fry in butter until brown, shaking the pan so they retain their round shape. Do not broil them. Often a gravy is made from the pan drippings by adding a little flour and cream or milk. This gravy, similar to country gravy, may be poured over the meat balls or served separately in a sauce bowl.

Buffet on the Terrace

Depending upon the location of the terrace, a buffet may be an attractive addition to a restaurant or hotel. If food is served on the terrace, a buffet may be a drawing card and at the same time take care of an overflow of business without over-burdening the hot cuisine department. Local specialties may be the main dishes on the buffet. On the coast such dishes might be lobster, crabs, clams, and fish salads; in inland locations, perhaps chicken, turkey or pork; in the tropics, tropical fruits.

The purchase price of such items must be lower than the average food costs. Only in this way is the necessary generosity possible on a buffet as the guest should be allowed to help himself as often as he likes. This will create repeat business.

A terrace buffet should be glamorized by its surroundings, decorated with local flowers, green plants, and perhaps some additional decorative objects. Such objects may be placed on a separate table which can be set aside after its use without disturbing the overall arrangements so it may be used again. Around this center table, a large round table may be placed on which the buffet is arranged—or U-shaped tables may be used with the fourth side against the wall. If possible, place the buffet out of the way of the waiters or waitresses going to and from the kitchen so that the guests do not interfere with the flow of service.

The control system of such a buffet, where hot food is served from the kitchen is somewhat more difficult but should be overcome by spot checks and by counting plates that are put on the buffet tables. This will give a fairly good estimate of sales.

To keep the cold food in good condition, ice pans should be constructed. The tables with the food on them should not be exposed to direct sunlight but should be placed in a shaded area.

The Beach Buffet

There is nothing more pleasant than to eat, picnic style, in the open air. Such occasions are rare because of the many problems involved in setting up the buffet far away from the kitchen. Also the weather is uncertain and a cloudy sky or a very windy day makes the meal something other than pleasant. Otherwise, a buffet on the beach or in the garden differs little from the terrace buffet, but they require thought in the preparation.

The Breakfast Buffet

The breakfast buffet has gained popularity, particularly on Sunday morning when it extends right through the luncheon period and is called a "Brunch." A great many dances and other special functions in hotels go into the wee small hours of the morning. In too many instances, no arrangements are made for feeding the guests. At such an hour a good buffet breakfast is both appetizing and nourishing, may be served quickly, and at a profit. Labor may be a problem but since much of the food may be prepared in advance, proper planning can reduce the labor cost.

Food should be served buffet style in hot chafing dishes with a waiter behind each hot item to serve. This keeps the line moving well. The following menu is easy to prepare and serve:

Scrambled Eggs	Special Link Sausages
Broiled Canadian Bacon	Potato Patties
Home-Baked Sweet Rolls	Strawberry Preserve or Marma-
Butter	lade

Coffee

For the above menu, one cook is able to take care of 150 orders. With a coffee maker in the pantry, the whole operation should go smoothly.

Normally, fruit juices or fruits will be eaten first. The management should decide whether this type of food will be a part of the buffet presentation. It can more easily be brought by the waiter from the kitchen as such a set-up on the buffet makes an ice pan necessary. However, a beautiful fruit stand is a must.

Here, as in all catering, price is determined by the variety of dishes. From the simple breakfast mentioned above to one of rich display and great variety, there are many possibilities. In this chapter there are two suggestions for breakfast buffets. The one above is simple as we have explained and as the sketch will show. The Hunt Breakfast which follows is more complicated and involves much more labor and food cost. It depends upon the occasion and the people who attend whether the buffet breakfast should be extended to include fancy foods such as smoked salmon, caviar, cold smoked ham, and other delicacies.

The Hunt Breakfast originated in England. After fox hunts it was served out of doors or in a veranda-style setting. Many hotels in Scandinavian coun-

Suggested Arrangement for a Large Buffet Breakfast
The variety of foods displayed here is listed in the text.

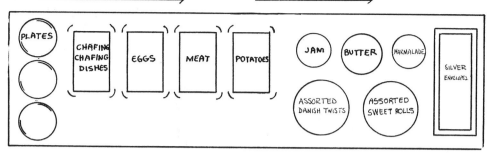

An Easy-to-Serve Breakfast Buffet

This sketch shows the menu organization. The guests approach from the left. There the plate is picked up. Next the hot food in chafing dishes followed by jam, butter and sweet rolls. The silverware, wrapped in a napkin is at the end of the table. When the guests are seated, waiters serve coffee at the tables.

tries serve a breakfast buffet style in which several ham and sausage items, cheeses, and smoked fish play a large part. The guests select the buffet items and beverages are brought from the kitchen to the guests at the table.

The Hunt Breakfast

To set up a hunt breakfast or a "brunch," it is wise to make a list of the main items in their proper groups and then select from each group a number of dishes which seem appropriate to the occasion. The different groups are:

1. Beverages
2. Fresh Fruits
3. Stewed Fruits
4. Juices
5. Breakfast Meat from Pork
6. Other Breakfast Meats
7. Hot Smoked Fish
8. Hot Fresh Fish
9. Eggs
10. Cheeses
11. Different Breads and Crackers
12. Smoked or Marinated or Salted Fish (cold)

Beverages

The usual breakfast beverages—coffee, tea, hot chocolate, and milk are offered. On some special occasions alcoholic beverages in a punch bowl or champagne are acceptable.

Fresh Fruit

Grapefruit, either pre-cut in halves or sections in an iced glass cup.

Oranges, sliced and sprinkled with a little granulated sugar.

Papaya, in portion slices with a wedge of lime, on ice.

Pineapple, either in quarters freed from the rind, or thick wheels, or chunks. If the occasion demands these wheels or chunks may be placed back in the rind to dress up the dish. A little sugar and a few drops of Kirsch may be added for flavor.

191

Grapes, arranged either in small or large bunches. If the latter, place fruit scissors beside them so the guests may help themselves to a serving.

Bananas, served with the skin on because of discoloration. The guests may order them sliced and served with cream.

Melons, must have reached the peak of ripeness before being presented to guests. They should be served on crushed ice, the smaller ones in equal halves, the larger ones in sections with the seeds removed, of course. Mint leaves are correct decorations for melons—also fresh raspberries and strawberries when in season. Melon balls mixed with berries and served in a glass bowl are also possible.

Figs, may be presented fresh in the cases in which they are shipped by merely removing the lid. If peeled, they discolor after a short time so that only a few orders of ready-to-eat figs may be placed on the buffet table. Stewed figs may also be a part of the buffet.

Mangos, a tropical fruit from which the hard skin must be removed. The golden meat is cut in as large chunks as the close-fitting seed permits and served in a glass cup or dish—eaten plain or with whipped cream.

Pears, Apples, Persimmons, as well as citrus fruits may be arranged on a three-tiered fruit stand or in baskets.

Peaches, when in season, are presented sliced in a crystal bowl on ice. To prevent discoloration, a plain syrup with a small amount of Sauterne and lemon juice should be poured over them. Champagne may also be used. They may also be presented in a fruit basket for decoration or, if they are of the large selected type, in the original package.

Berries, in season are a must on such a buffet. The largest strawberries are presented with their green stems still in place on a bed of ice or on a large leaf of some kind lining a silver tray stand. Raspberries, boysenberries, blackberries, and blueberries are presented in glass bowls on ice. Plain cream or whipped cream should be placed nearby for easy use.

Stewed Fruit

All types of fresh fruit may be stewed in a heavy syrup and allowed to cool in the juice. Pears, peaches, pineapples, or figs, make fine breakfast items. They should be presented in glass bowls.

Juices

Usually a selection of from two to four different juices, among them tomato juice is possible. They should be in clear glass pitchers for easy recognition, standing in ice and water for constant cooling with juice glasses near by.

Breakfast Meat from Pork

This consists of ham, bacon, pork links, or sausage cakes. Canadian bacon is well suited for the buffet breakfast because of its size and mild flavor. A small amount of these items are cooked ahead of time and placed in a chafing dish in orderly lines. Hash brown potatoes are served in a nearby chafing dish.

Other Breakfast Meats

Loin lamb chops, lamb kidney on a skewer, calves' liver, calves' sweetbreads, chicken legs, small club or sirloin steaks, small filet mignons or thin slices of beef tenderloin (Filet Paillard), beef Stroganoff, chicken á la King, kidneys and mushrooms are a few selections from which to choose. These meats must be presented in clean chafing dishes. Clean those dishes containing sauce often so they will have an appetizing appearance at all times.

Smoked Fish, Hot

These usually consist of kippered herring and smoked finnan haddie.

Fresh Fish, Hot

Except for small trout and flat fish, these are usually prepared in filet form. Well suited for breakfast are salted mackerel, fresh filets of sole, redsnapper, pompano, pike, Lake Superior whitefish, soft shell crabs (meuniere or a l'amandine) except for the salted mackerel which is poached and served with melted butter. Sometimes fresh oysters on the halfshell, placed on crushed ice are suitable for a Hunt Breakfast.

Eggs

In any basic method of preparation, these are suited for buffets. Easiest to serve from the buffet are scrambled eggs as fried or poached eggs pose a problem.

A chafing dish containing Canadian bacon and sausage links

A sweet roll display for the buffet breakfast

Cheeses

An assortment of various cheeses on a wooden cheese tray with radishes or celery is a must. Such cheeses as Swiss, American cheddar, and similar ones may be cut into slices. However, only a small amount of pre-cuts should be made, the others placed neatly in their original wrappings with the labels visible. A knife for cutting the cheese by the guest is placed on the cheese board.

Breads

In addition to the usual breads, rolls, and toast, a specialty such as Parisian croissants or Brioches may be added. Pumpernickel, rye crisp, Melba toast, and sweet rolls are other possibilities. Those frequently served with cheese should be placed near the cheese board.

Smoked, Salted, or Marinated Fish

Herring, salmon, eel, oysters, and caviar may be the choice of many gourmets who enjoy this type of Hunt Breakfast.

There is no doubt that a hotel or restaurant can gain wonderful publicity by offering, at least on Sunday, this type of breakfast. If the price is right, a wonderful business can be built up that will last right through the day and other departments will benefit as well.

CHAPTER XVII

Salads

America's greatest contribution to the culinary art is the salad. This country has created more combinations of salads and salad dressings than any other in the world. There are now so many famous salads that it would take a much larger book than this to name and describe them all but an attempt will be made to mention a few of the most famous ones.

General Information on Salads

Salads, whether for the buffet or for other service, are divided into two classes:

1. Simple salads (vitamin rich).
   Those made entirely from greens or from other vegetables, the latter fresh, frozen, or canned.
2. Combined salads (protein rich).
   Fish salads, fresh, frozen, canned, pickled, or smoked.
   Gelatin and molded salads.
   Fruit salads, fresh, canned, frozen, or dried.
   Combined salads, with several types of ingredients.
   National salad specialties.

Salad is served as an appetizer, an accompaniment to the entree, or as the main course of a meal. For this reason, the size of the portion is varied, although the combination remains the same.

In this chapter single portions of salad are illustrated. The names of the salads are those selected by various hotels. They are sometimes garnished in different ways but the ingredients remain the same.

Adapted to buffets, many of these salads may be used to advantage. Gelatin salads are of particular interest as they may be arranged attractively on platters and are very bright and colorful.

195

Salad greens are used for building up a refreshing and eye-appealing salad and are the source of natural vitamins. The treatment of salad greens is, therefore, very important. The green leaves must be clean, crisp, and chilled. It is possible to core, wash, and strip lettuce leaves a day before they are to be used if they are placed in a covered container under refrigeration. A few pointers may be advantageous.

1. Buy fresh supplies daily if possible.
2. The greens must be crisp and fresh.
3. Wash thoroughly under running water to remove all sand, dirt, and insects.
4. Do not allow to remain in water as soaking removes both flavor and vitamin content.

In addition to the favorite Iceberg lettuce, many other salad greens may be used and are a welcome change in the daily salad menu. Such greens are romaine, Boston lettuce, chicory, curly chicory, bibb or limestone lettuce, Belgian endive, young fresh spinach, Brussels sprouts, Chinese cabbage, green cabbage, escarole, watercress, dandelion greens, and many more.

Any one of the above greens, either alone or in combination, may be used for the large salad bowl on the buffet. The salad should be tossed with an adequate dressing. Bear in mind that green salads, once mixed with a dressing, are difficult to keep crisp for any length of time. The heavier the dressing the sooner the salad wilts. Light plain dressing (oil, vinegar, salt, pepper, and herbs) will keep the salad on a lengthy buffet attractive until the last.

To give distinctive character to a dressing for green salads, add flavored vinegar, herbs, mustard, spices, horse radish, garlic, shallots, chives, green or ripe olives in slices or chopped, freshly ground pepper, Maggi seasoning, Worcestershire sauce, chutney, chili sauce, ketchup, cheese, and bacon. There is an old proverb to the effect that "it takes four persons to make a salad dressing: a spendthrift for the oil, a miser for the vinegar, counselor for the salt, and a madman to stir them up."

An additional garnish over the top of the green salad creates interest. Such garnishes may be radishes, hard boiled eggs in slices or chopped, anchovy filets, tomato wedges or slices, diced or shoestring beets, avocados sliced or cubed, cucumbers, and ham, tongue, turkey, chicken, cheese, or green peppers julienned.

As salads are the least expensive food item on the buffet, they should be combined in lovely color combinations and selected from foods of different character. It is wise to distribute two simple and four to ten combined salads throughout the buffet.

The decoration of the combined salads also play an important role as they glamorize the buffet. So, with good decoration one may give even an economical salad counter or buffet table a rich look.

Choice of containers for the salads also play their part. They may be placed on glass or wood. Because of destructive acids in certain metals, great care must be taken in the selection of dishes for salads. Badly plated silver dishes may result in food poisoning due to the fact that salads often stay on the buffet over a long period. Make sure, therefore that the dishes are in perfect condition.

One or several different dressings may be placed beside the salad bowl which is lined with plain salad leaves and preferably standing on cracked ice, so that guests may help themselves.

Below we mention a few desirable dressings, the recipes for which are given in Chapter VII.

French Dressing	Lorenzo Dressing
Thousand Island Dressing	Roquefort Dressing
Russian Dressing	Blue Cheese Dressing
Maurice Dressing	Vinaigrette Dressing
Green Goddess Dressing	Remoulade Dressing
Caesar Dressing	Orange Cream Dressing
Lemon Cream Dressing	

Simple Green Salad Combinations

For these salads any of the following five dressings may be used. Their recipes are found in Chapter VII.

Plain French Dressing
French Dressing
Vinaigrette
Roquefort Dressing
Thousand Island Dressing

For buffet use, the oil-vinegar dressings are better suited because of the necessity to keep the salad crisp and firm over a period of time.

Belgian Endive and Watercress Salad: Arrange endive and watercress attractively on a plate and serve with French dressing.

Cole Slaw: A very fine shredded cabbage marinated with salt, pepper, vinegar, onions, garlic, and oil. Add a little sugar if desired.

Cole Slaw Hawaiian: Add shredded pineapple to cole slaw, marinate with creamy mayonnaise and chopped nuts.

Cole Slaw Mexican: Add shredded carrots and green peppers to cole slaw and serve with a slice of Spanish onion.

Cole Slaw Nordic: Very fine shredded red cabbage marinated in French dressing.

Mimosa Salad: Mixed greens topped with sprigs of watercress and hard boiled, chopped egg yolks.

Mixed Green Salad: Contains all green leafy vegetables.

Panache Salad: Tossed green salad topped with julienne of beets.

Spring Salad: A combination of all leafy greens of the spring season.

197

Preparation for a Salad Bowl

In preparing an individual salad bowl as for Chef's Salad, mixed green with shrimp, crab, lobster, etc., form a lettuce bowl within the salad bowl. Take a crisp head of lettuce and cut the stem about one inch above the outer leaves. It depends on the size of the head whether it should be cut in half as shown at the top of the picture or whether the cup-shape unbroken leaves should be extracted from the smaller head. It is essential that the leaves, grouped together, make a bowl within the salad bowl. Uneven leaves should be cut into strips as seen at the left and a handful of these placed in the center of of the lettuce bowl to make a bedding for the salad which is placed on them.

Tossed Green Salad: A combination of romaine, iceberg, chicory, endive, escarole, Chinese cabbage, celery, cucumbers, green peppers, watercress, chives, etc.; varied also with tomatoes, radishes, hard boiled eggs, onions, spinach, grated carrots, etc.

Vegetable Salads

Most left-over vegetables in good condition may be used for many of these salads. However, if the vegetables are cooked for salad purposes, they should be cooled quickly by placing under running cold water. Drain immediately and place in a pan of sufficient size to accommodate one layer only. Never pile the cooked vegetables in heaps. Marinate these with either a plain French dressing or vinaigrette sauce.

Alligator Pear Salad: Two types—1. Half of the fruit set on ice, filled with any tangy dressing. 2. Avocado cut parisienne on romaine or lettuce and garnished with green peppers. Serve with French dressing.

Argenteuil Salad: Lettuce, asparagus tips, and red peppers. Serve with vinaigrette dressing.

198

Asparagus Tip Salad: Two types—1. Three asparagus tips on bed of shredded lettuce. Chopped red peppers. Serve with French dressing. 2. Add julienne of ham over asparagus. Dash vinaigrette dressing over salad just before serving.

Asparagus Vinaigrette Salad: A bouquet of asparagus tips on lettuce leaves, garnished with a pimento strip. Dash vinaigrette dressing over the asparagus at the last moment.

Avocado Salad: Slice skinned halves of avocado and place, hollow side down, on lettuce or any green. Use any of the preceding dressings.

Beatrice Salad: String beans and strips of pickled beets on bed of shredded lettuce. Serve with French dressing.

Bon Ton Salad: Three asparagus tips placed on a slice of tomato and arranged on lettuce or romaine. Serve with any dressing.

Bretonne Salad: After cooking and cooling dry white beans, marinate with vinaigrette and arrange in a bowl. Garnish center of dish with small cubes from peeled and seeded tomatoes, chopped parsley, and chives.

Brazilian Salad: Lima beans, with celery and green peppers cut in strips. Proportion: one half beans, one fourth celery, one fourth green peppers. French dressing.

California Tossed Salad: Prepare the following ingredients for this marvelous green salad combination. Chopped onions or shallots, finely sliced green onions, chives, chopped parsley, chopped crisp bacon, grated parmesan cheese, a little garlic, chopped ripe olives, fine cut radishes, olive oil, wine vinegar, pinch of Accent, salt, pepper from the hand mill, and lemon juice.

Mix in a large wooden bowl: oil, vinegar, lemon juice, onions, shallots, green onions, garlic, radishes, salt, pepper, Accent.

Mix in the salad only at the last moment: chives, bacon, parmesan cheese, and olives.

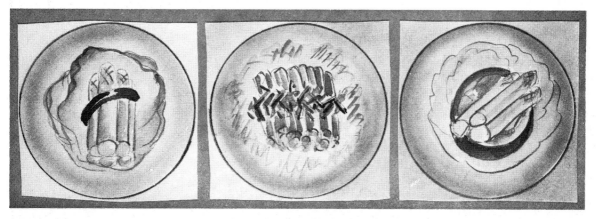

Argenteuil Salad   Beatrice Salad   Bon Ton Salad

Cendrillon Salad: Knob of celery covered with small quarters of chopped apples and potatoes. Cross with asparagus tips and serve with vinaigrette dressing.

Carmelite Salad: Diced potatoes, beets and onions. Two slices of hard boiled egg. Top with anchovy filet. Serve with French dressing.

Cauliflower Salad: Boiled cauliflower broken or cut in buds. Use either vinaigrette, mayonnaise, or ravigote dressing.

Caesar Salad: Four heads of romaine, washed and chilled, one cup crisp croutons, eight tablespoons garlic-flavored salad oil or a little crushed garlic, four tablespoons oil, three tablespoons of grated Parmesan cheese, one tablespoon Worcestershire Sauce, two raw or slightly boiled eggs, juice of three lemons, four anchovy filets, pepper from the peppermill, coarsely ground, and salt to taste. Break romaine into a big salad bowl, add other ingredients, the eggs last with the lemon juice, toss all very lightly from the bottom and serve immediately. Above quantities are for 6 to 8 portions.

Preparation of Caesar Salad

Cendrillon Salad   Carmelite Salad   Chatelaine Salad

Celery Mayonnaise Salad: Three types: 1. Pour a generous amount of lemon juice over celery root finely julienned to keep white. Mix with heavy cream and mayonnaise. Salt and cayenne pepper to taste. 2. Cook celery roots. After cooking, cut in cubes and mix with heavy cream and mayonnaise. Salt and cayenne pepper to taste. 3. Fine shredded Pascal celery mixed with lemon juice, finish with mayonnaise.

Celery Victor: Cut celery stalks in three inch sections, place them in rows in a square steam pan, pour following marinade over and steam or cook until celery is tender. Marinade: four parts water, one part vinegar, one part oil, lemon juice, and spice bag. After celery is cooked in this liquid, cool in same liquid. Serve on salad cup of greens with a little marinade poured over it. Celery Victor is often served with either shrimp, eggs, anchovies, or crab meat around it and it makes an excellent appetizer or a cold entrée.

Chatelaine Salad: Romaine, watercress, asparagus tips, and beets. Serve with French dressing.

Chef's Salad: 1. Same as tossed salad with the addition of julienned ham, turkey, cheese, etc., to give more richness. Also special attention is given to the dressing which is often prepared before the guests.

Chef's Salad: 2. Take an abundance of small leaves of lettuce, romaine, cut chicory, and escarole. In a large wooden bowl build the leaves up to a dome shape and place a ring of tomato slices around them. Garnish the top with sections of julienne ham, tongue, turkey, and Swiss or American cheese. Place a bouquet of watercress in the middle. Chill in refrigerator and on serving, pour a little French dressing or a plain oil and vinegar dressing in which a little garlic and chopped shallots has been mixed. Sprinkle with finely cut chives or green onions.

Chiffonade Salad: Equal parts of romaine, lettuce, chicory, escarole, cucumbers, and quartered tomatoes mixed with French dressing. Chopped beets, eggs, and parsley are sprinkled over the salad.

201

Cosmopolitane Salad: Line the bowl with leaves of lettuce. In the center place a cooked cauliflower rose. Take four different colorful vegetables and arrange in mounds around the cauliflower, each mound to be separated by shrimps or slices of lobster. Serve with French or Lorenzo dressing.

Cubaine Salad: Place diced tomatoes and small squares of red and green peppers on lettuce leaves. Decorate top with slice of Bermuda onion, stuffed olive slices, and anchovies. Serve with French dressing.

Cucumber Salad: Three types: 1. Remove skin and if cucumber is too mature, remove seeds also, slice very thin, sprinkle with salt and let salt remain for several minutes to draw liquid. Press and pour liquid off. Mix cucumbers with oil, vinegar and pepper from the mill, to taste. Cucumbers usually take more vinegar than other vegetables. 2. *Hungarian style*—Marinade with salt, pepper, vinegar and a small amount of crushed garlic. Pour off almost all liquid, mix with thin sour cream. Sprinkle top with paprika. 3. *Swedish style*—The skin is left on. Use only small cucumbers. Cut in thin slices and marinade with salt, pepper, sugar, chopped dill, parsley, and vinegar. Serve with wine vinegar.

Dandelion Salad: The word "dandelion" is derived from the French word Dent de Lion and means lion's teeth. These are small leaves, bitter in taste, and purchased in early spring for spring salads. Plain dressing or vinaigrette is used, sometimes with crumbled Roquefort.

Cubane Salad   Dolly Salad   Geneva Salad

George Salad

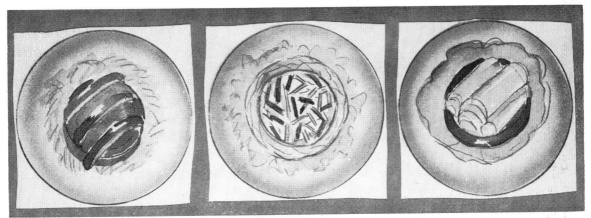

Grand Union Salad   Jockey Club Salad   Jordan Salad

Dolly Salad: On a bed of endive and romaine, place slices of alligator pear. Between slices dress with julienne of celery and Roquefort cheese. Serve with French dressing.

Doucette Salad: A field salad. Preparation is the same as that for dandelion salad.

Espagnole Salad: Shredded outer leaves of lettuce. String beans, quartered tomato, and slices of red and green pepper. Serve with oily vinaigrette, a slice of Spanish onion, and one ripe olive.

Gauloise Salad: Julienne of heart of romaine, asparagus tips with celery and mushrooms. Decorate with truffles. Serve with French dressing.

Geneva Salad: Slices of beets and hard boiled eggs alternately dressed on hearts of romaine. Serve with French dressing.

George Salad: Sliced avocado on shredded escarole. Serve with tart mayonnaise.

Grand Union Salad: Cole slaw, green peppers, and tomatoes. Serve with French dressing.

Imperial Salad: Cut the bottoms of artichokes in slices and serve with alternate layers of peeled slices of tomatoes and green peas on lettuce leaves. Cover with thin mayonnaise and decorate with truffles.

Jockey Club Salad: Place an artichoke bottom on shredded escarole. Cover with julienned celery knobs, and truffles. Serve with dressing of choice.

Jordan Salad: Hearts of palm on a slice of tomato. Serve with mayonnaise.

Lentil Salad: Cook lentils, drain and cool. Add finely chopped onions, salt, pepper, vinegar, oil, and a few drops of Worcestershire sauce or Maggi seasoning.

Lorette Salad: Place beets and cooked celery roots alternately on leaves of lettuce, placing field salad around it. Serve with French dressing.

203

Monte Carlo Salad: Lettuce, sliced tomatoes, watercress, and sliced eggs. Serve with vinaigrette dressing.

Mother Hubbard Salad: Mixed green salad with fine grated carrots. Garnish top of salad with asparagus tips which are crossed by red pimentos. Serve with French dressing.

Pickled Beet Salad: Slice and cube beets or baby beets pickled for a few days in a marinade. Prepare marinade with boiling water, vinegar, sugar, salt, onion, and a spice bag. When cool pour over beets, which are in turn placed on lettuce leaves. Oil may be added.

Plantation Salad: Cut iceberg lettuce into large cubes and separate leaflets. Add diced tomatoes, finely sliced celery, and green peppers. Mix this salad with French dressing. The top is garnished with rippled cucumber slices and sliced stuffed olives.

Potato Salad: Three types: 1. Use small potatoes and boil with the jackets on. Skin while still hot. Cool and cut in thin slices. Add salt, pepper, chopped onions, beef stock, vinegar, and oil. Mix carefully because the thinly sliced potatoes break easily. 2. Cook potatoes the same as above, but cut into cubes. Add small diced eggs, mayonnaise thinned with beef stock, small cut green onions, salt, and pepper. 3. Hot potato salad. Prepared the same as No. 1, but do not cool potatoes too much. Mix with hot beef stock and keep salad warm.

Princess Salad: Stuffed tomato, asparagus, and pimentos. Serve with French dressing.

Printemps Salad: Mixed, broken escarole and romaine, topped with quartered tomatoes and asparagus tips. Serve with French dressing.

Rachel Salad: On a lettuce leaf set dainty bouquets of julienned artichoke, celery roots (cooked), tomato, and asparagus tips. Use truffles to decorate the bright colored vegetables. Serve with French dressing.

Rejane Salad: Cubed celery roots, artichokes, and tomatoes. Place separately on salad leaf and garnish with red pimento. Serve with French dressing.

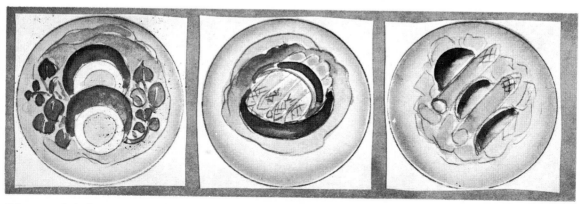

Printemps Salad   Princess Salad   Monte Carlo Salad

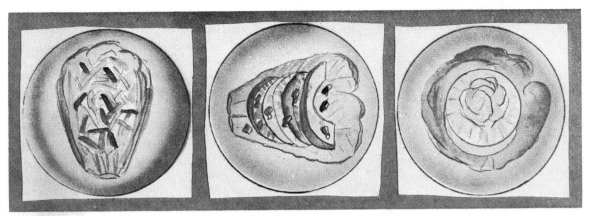

Tosca Salad   Alma Salad   Antoinette Salad

Robin Hood Salad: On a lining of romaine, place a whole medium-size cooked artichoke bottom. Decorate the center with egg slice and truffle and small diced pimentos. Use oil and vinegar dressing.

Tomato and Asparagus Salad: Place tomatoes and asparagus on lettuce leaves. Serve with dressing of choice.

Tomato and Cucumber Salad: Skinned tomato halves, filled with cucumber salad in marinade, placed on lettuce leaves, and decorated with chopped parsley.

Tosca Salad: Romaine, celery, string beans and tomatoes. Serve with any dressing.

Fruit Salads

Alberta Salad: Slice of pineapple with mound of cream cheese in center. Sprinkle with chopped green and red peppers and dust with paprika. Serve with dressing of choice.

Alexandra Salad: Hearts of romaine, julienne of celery, and a slice of grapefruit. Sprinkle with chopped walnuts. Serve with mayonnaise.

Algerienne Salad: Sliced pineapple, orange, grapefruit, and banana on lettuce. Serve with mayonnaise with lemon juice.

Alice Salad: Apples and celery diced and mixed with mayonnaise (leave skin on apples), dressed into a mound on lettuce and garnished with thinly sliced red apples which have been soaked in grapefruit juice. Serve with mayonnaise.

Alma Salad: On romaine, arrange sections of grapefruit, avocado, and orange. Garnish top with red and green peppers and pickled walnuts. Serve with French dressing.

Antoinette Salad: On lettuce leaves, place pineapple slice which in turn is topped with a small heart of lettuce. Serve with mayonnaise mixed with tarragon vinegar and chopped chives.

205

A Group of Fruit Salads

206

Banana Salad

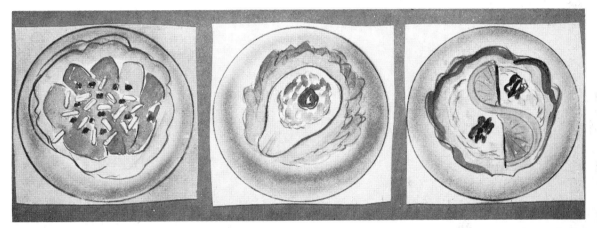

Bombay or Caribi Salad   Diana Salad   Diplomat Salad

Banana Salad: A split banana filled with cream cheese and topped with fresh strawberries. Serve with creamed mayonnaise.

Blackstone Salad: A very famous salad from the Blackstone Hotel in Chicago. Fine cut celery, apples, and grapefruit dressed on half a head of romaine (or a third if a half is too large), covered with mayonnaise. The top of the salad is decorated with orange sections and small strips of green peppers and pimentos.

Bombay or Caribe Salad: Sliced mangoes topped with chopped red peppers mixed with boiled rice. French dressing with curry is used.

Diana Salad: Stuff a hollowed Bartlett pear with pineapple, oranges, and strawberries. Serve with pink mayonnaise.

Diplomat Salad: Half slice of pineapple beside a mound of chopped apples, celery, and walnuts. Serve with mayonnaise.

207

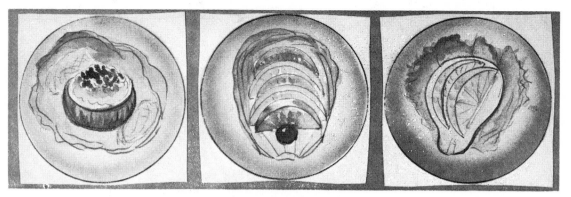

Excelsior Salad   Floridienne Salad   Frontenac Salad

Excelsior Salad: A scooped out apple filled with mixture of chopped apple, celery, and nuts. Serve with shreds of pineapple in mayonnaise.

Florida Salad: Banana shell filled with creamy fruit filling of grapefruit, orange, banana, celery. Creamed mayonnaise, sprinkled with paprika is served on the side.

Floridienne Salad: Romaine, grapefruit, orange, and maraschino cherries. Serve with dressing of choice.

Frontenac Salad: Heart of endive with halved pears and grapefruit. Serve with creamy mayonnaise.

Frozen Peach and Pecan Salad: Place peach halves in tray. Mix cream cheese, pecans, and whipped cream and place over peaches. Freeze for three quarters of an hour. Proportion: 1 cup cream cheese, 1 cup mayonnaise, 1 cup chopped pecans, 1 cup heavy cream, whipped.

Hawaiian Salad: Center slice of pineapple with cream cheese. Surround with Malaga or Tokay grapes and garnish with watercress. Serve with French dressing.

Japonaise Salad: Sliced oranges with chopped red peppers on romaine. Serve with light creamy mayonnaise and dust with paprika.

Jockey Club Salad: On bed of romaine, arrange orange sections in semblance of a saddle. Garnish with watercress and put a strawberry or ripe olive in the middle topped with a cream cheese ball. Serve with French dressing.

Ladies' Delight Salad: Pineapple and orange sections on shredded romaine, with dots of cream cheese. Garnish with red and green cherries, or strawberries. Serve with sweet mayonnaise or French dressing.

My Lady's Choice: Line a bowl with romaine and place in it alternate slices of pineapple and avocado. Garnish with cubes of cream cheese and sprinkle the whole with chopped pecans. Serve with dressing of choice.

Pineapple and Cottage Cheese Salad: On lettuce cup, arrange one spoon of cottage cheese. Garnish with pineapple slice, strawberry or cherry. Serve with fruit dressing.

208

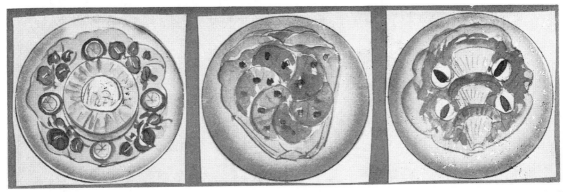

Hawaiian Salad   Japonaise Salad   Ladies' Delight Salad

Saratoga Salad: On heart of romaine, arrange sections of grapefruit, orange, banana, diced green peppers, and strawberries. Serve with French dressing.

Sunburst Salad: On heart of romaine, arrange sections of grapefruit, oranges, banana, diced green peppers, and strawberries. Serve with French dressing.

Sunburst Salad: On chicory, place pineapple, strawberries, grapefruit, orange, and green pepper in an arrangement to resemble the sun with its bright rays. Sprinkle chopped fruit jello and whipped cream in between. Use any dressing in the mayonnaise line.

Tehachapi Salad: On rosette of watercress, arrange sliced oranges, seeded grape halves and sprinkle chopped nuts over all. Serve with French dressing.

Tropical Salad: Line a salad bowl with romaine. Cut out a large pineapple. To the meat of the pineapple add pear and avocado for filling. Place the empty pineapple shell, topped with pineapple sections on the romaine. Serve with lemon cream dressing.

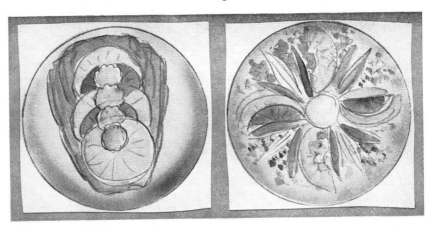

Saratoga Salad   Sunburst Salad

Veronique Salad   Waldorf Salad   American Beauty Salad

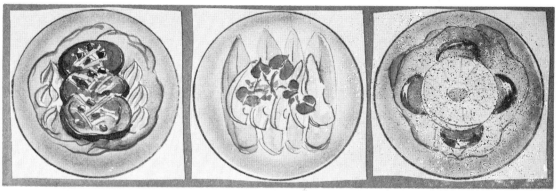

Anna Salad   Belge Salad   Caprice Salad

Veronique Salad: Romaine hearts or lettuce slices are spread out on a glass tray. Garnish the green with slices of large strawberries and seeded hothouse grapes. The grapes may be filled with cream cheese. Decorate with pimentos. Serve with French dressing and grated nuts.

Waldorf Salad: Chopped apples and celery mixed with mayonnaise, shaped into a mound and topped with half apple slices and chopped nuts.

Combined Salads

American Beauty Salad: Lettuce, cottage cheese, beets, and green peppers. Serve with French dressing.

Anna Salad: Sliced tomato on heart of lettuce sprinkled with julienne of celery, apples, and chopped nuts. Serve with mayonnaise or French dressing.

Assez Salad: Inch-long cut cooked macaroni, mixed with diced peeled tomatoes, finely shredded lettuce, and boiled ham. Dress on bed of lettuce, garnish with watercress. Serve with Thousand Island dressing

Astoria Salad: Prepare a Waldorf salad and garnish with sections of avocado. Serve with mayonnaise.

Augustine Salad: Lettuce, alligator pear, and grapes. Serve with mayonnaise.

210

Belge Salad: Endive, sliced spiced pears, and watercress. Serve with French or Roquefort dressing.

Caprice Salad: Lettuce, sliced pineapple, and tomatoes. Serve with French dressing.

Chicken Salad: Cut breast of chicken into strips or small cubes. Add to it about one third the amount of cut celery. Use mayonnaise to mix the salad. Line the bowl with green salad leaves. Place the salad on this and decorate with egg, tomato, and pickle.

Cocette Salad: On lettuce leaves set small artichoke hearts which are marinated in vinaigrette. On top, sprinkle small strips of ham, turkey, and celery. Serve with vinaigrette dressing.

Chicken Salad Bowl

Use a greater percentage of the white meat of chicken either julienned or diced. Mix this with celery diced very fine, green peppers, onions, or, as a matter of taste and economy, onion tops. Prepare this mixture with mayonnaise being careful not to get the salad too sour or too salty. The illustration shows the finished product—the lettuce lining topped with a portion of chicken salad. A few strips of julienned chicken breast is sprinkled over the surface and the garnishes are slices of tomato, egg slices, asparagus tips, radish, dill pickles and an olive. Mayonnaise or French dressing may be served on the side.

Doctor's Salad: Lettuce, tomatoes, cottage cheese, chives, and watercress. Serve with dressing of choice.

Dumas Salad: Diced beets, tomatoes, and cucumbers. Garnish with anchovies, hardboiled eggs, and fine herbs. Serve only with mayonnaise.

Fantasie Salad: On romaine, alternate slices of celery, apples, and pineapple. Garnish with mint leaves. Serve with vinaigrette dressing.

Health Salad: With apples and celery, prepare a Waldorf salad and garnish the top with shredded carrots and raisins.

Herriot Salad: Prepare a mixed green salad with julienne of chicken, rice, and green peppers. Circle with sliced tomatoes. Garnish with asparagus tips. Serve with French dressing.

Hawley Salad: Heart of endive, watercress, and sliced mushrooms. Serve with dressing of choice.

Hortense Salad: Julienne of celery, apples, and carrots on romaine. Serve with French or Thousand Island dressing.

Iron Salad: Endive, cottage cheese, dates, and raisins. Serve with French dressing or mayonnaise.

Jeunesse Salad: Prepare a mixed green salad and border the dish with spoons of cottage cheese, each topped with a peach slice. Serve with dressing of choice.

Louise Salad: Two types: 1. Mound of chopped celery and apple surrounded by four sections of orange, alternating with grapes. Top mound with grape. Use cream dressing. 2. Heart of lettuce, julienne of chicken and ham. Use cream dressing.

Palm Beach Salad: Lettuce, alligator pears, tangerines. Serve with French dressing.

Poinsetta Salad: Large tomato, asparagus tips, cottage cheese, chopped egg, and watercress put together to resemble the poinsettia flower. Serve with French dressing.

Progress Salad: Top a bowl of mixed green salad with julienne of celery and tomatoes. Circle with egg slices. Serve with Roquefort dressing.

Molded and Frozen Salads

Ring forms are very useful for buffet work for these salads. Any packaged flavored gelatine may be used and the instructions on the package should be followed.

In order to decorate these molded salads attractively, pour some gelatin into the bottom of the molds and arrange the ingredients of the salad in this gelatin in an orderly manner. When these ingredients hold firmly to the bottom layer of gelatin, fill the mold to the top with the balance of the gelatin. Many different effects may be achieved with various ingredients. These salads must be prepared well ahead of the time for serving as the gelatin must have time to stiffen.

Doctors' Salad

Dumas Salad

Hawley Salad

Hortense Salad

Iron Salad

Louise Salad

Palm Beach Salad

Poinsettia Salad

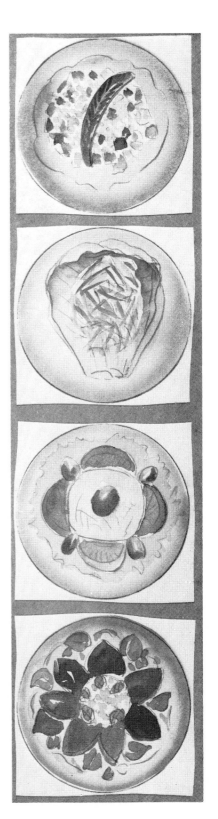

Avocado Molded Salad: Use half grapefruit juice and half water and place in this the packaged lime gelatin. Heat this liquid and when gelatin has thoroughly dissolved pour into the mold after the fruit has been added as described above. Grapefruit sections and avocado sections cut to the same size may be placed in the bottom of the mold. Chill, unmold on lettuce leaves and serve with mayonnaise dressing.

Avocado Mousse Salad: Mash avocados. Heat half grapefruit juice and half water and dissolve gelatin. Add salt and lemon juice and mashed avocados. Serve with mayonnaise and whipped cream.

Frozen Fruit Salad:

6 eggs, yolks and whites separated	Juice of 2 lemons
6 tablespoons, flour	3 cups, heavy cream, whipped
6 tablespoons, sugar	½ gallon fruit cocktail, drained
1 teaspoon, salt	6 bananas
	Sections of 2 oranges
2 cups apricot nectar, papaya juice, or juice from the fruit cocktail	

Combine all ingredients except fruit and beat in a pastry basin over a steaming hot pot until mixture thickens. Cool. Fold in whipped cream and the stiffly beaten egg whites. Fold in fruits.

Pour into cake molds which have been lined with wax paper. Place in deep freezer for about three or four hours. Unmold, slice into portions and place on lettuce leaves. Serve with any desirable dressing.

Ginger Ale-Melon Mold: Dissolve package orange, lemon, or lime flavored gelatin in a small quantity of boiling water. Add to this the amount of gingerale which the recipe on the gelatin package calls for in liquid. Add a little salt and lemon juice, and set aside to cool and thicken.

When the gelatin mixture begins to thicken, add melon balls (preferably of different colors) and pour into molds. Chill until firm. Unmold on crisp lettuce and garnish with a sprig of fresh mint. Serve with a fruit salad dressing.

Tomato Aspic:

½ gallon, tomato juice	Juice of 4 lemons
3 teaspoons, gelatin	Salt to taste (preferably celery salt)

Take one dipper of tomato juice and heat it with the granulated gelatin until smooth. Add to the balance of the juice.
Fill into square pans or loaf molds and cool until jellied.

Salad Specialties of Other Countries

Despite the fact that America can be truly given credit for the perfection of salads generally, there are European countries that claim a few original salads among their other great dishes. In combining salads for buffet dining, any salad specialties from other countries will be an asset. There are dozens of local salad specialties throughout America which apply to this section as well.

Gaspacho Salad: This Andalusian salad specialty is a splendid buffet item. Make layers of the following ingredients which are seasoned to taste: Small pieces of dried bread crusts, thin slices of Spanish onion, cucumbers and tomatoes. Garnish with bread crumbs. Have the bowl in which this is served lined with either romaine or lettuce leaves. Serve with plain or French dressing.

Italian Salad: Cooked carrots, celery knobs, cooked white turnips and potatoes finely diced, mixed with green peas, a few diced anchovies and ham. Use thick mayonnaise to make a tasty salad which is dressed up in a bowl to a dome shape. The edge is filled in with hearts of lettuce or romaine and the top of the salad nicely garnished with cornets of salami, egg quarters, capers, olives, and anchovy rounds. Sometimes small beets or tiny shrimps are added.

Russian Salad: Cubed cooked vegetables such as carrots, celery knobs, turnips, green peas, and potatoes mixed with mayonnaise. Dress salad into dome shape on a platter or tray and cover with mayonnaise which should be smoothed out with a spatula. Decorate the top with sliced hardboiled eggs, each garnished with a center of caviar.

Guacamole Purée:

4 avocados	6 canned green chili peppers
2 tomatoes	2 cloves of garlic

Mash avocados, add salt, lemon juice and grated onions to taste. Add tomatoes, chili peppers or tabasco sauce. Heap in a bowl, which is rubbed with garlic cloves, chill, serve on lettuce, garnish with tomato or corn chips if desired. This Mexican-style avocado purée may be served by filling it into the empty half shells of avocados.

Fish Salads

Tunafish Salad: Flakes of tunafish mixed with a small amount of diced celery, mayonnaise, lemon juice, salt, and pepper. Sometimes tunafish salad is filled into different vegetables such as emptied tomatoes, artichokes, etc. Decorate with sliced egg.

Crabmeat Salad: Preparation similar to tunafish salad. Often a Louis dressing is called for. Decorate with egg slices, ripe olives, tomatoes, or asparagus tips.

Cosmopolitane Fish Salad: Arrange four different kinds of vegetables on a salad dish. The middle is decorated with shrimps or crabs. French dressing is served.

Herring Salad: This may be prepared from either marinated or salted herring. However, the salted and slightly watered herring filets make the best salad. Cut herring into small bits and mix it carefully with an equal amount of potato salad. Add sour cream if desired. Add finely chopped onions, a little garlic, and chives for flavor. Decorate the top with sliced onions and sour pickles.

← Shrimp Salad Bowl

This salad may be prepared with tiny Alaskan shrimps or larger ones. The lettuce lining is topped with shrimp salad to which celery may be added. The decorations consist of shrimps in the center, hard boiled egg quarters, tomato wedges, ripe olives and lemon sections. Thousand Island dressing is usually served with this salad, although this is a matter of individual taste.

Calavo (or Avocado) Stuffed with Shrimp

Avocados are delicate in texture. They must be sun-ripened on the tree in order to have flavor. Although they are harvested while still hard, they must be thoroughly softened for eating. Keeping them in a warm room hastens the softening process. To test them, press the whole fruit gently in the hand. Heavy pressure bruises them.

If the fruit must be peeled some time in advance of service, a lemon bath will help them retain their original color. Some people use salt water. If they are cut in half before peeling, the process is much easier.

The illustration shows a salad bowl with half an avocado stuffed with shrimp, and decorated with egg slices, tomato wedges, asparagus tips, and ripe olives. Lemon and any desired dressing may be served with this salad, Roquefort, Thousand Island, and French being the dressings most commonly used. Avocados may also be stuffed with crab meat or chicken salad.

← Crab or Seafood Salad ˙

Top the usual lettuce lining with a portion of crab salad prepared with one quarter finely diced celery, chopped onions, and mayonnaise. For decorations use egg quarters, tomato slices, olives, asparagus spears, radishes, green onions, lemon wedges and crab legs placed in the center.

A Salad for the New Year Buffet

The aspic, filled with a shrimp salad is placed in the center of a glass platter. Soft boiled eggs (six minutes) are laid around the border of the plate, the figures representing the hours, cut from truffle. Aspic cubes fill the spaces between. The mosaic made from truffle, egg white and ox tongue is very effective when used in aspic.

Lobster Salad: Cut lobster meat into half-inch pieces. Season with salt, pepper and lemon juice. Drain, mix with mayonnaise and lemon juice. Make a dome on lettuce leaves and garnish with hardboiled eggs, tomato wedges, claws of lobster, capers, and pickle slices. Celery may be added.

Pasadena Salad: Line bowl with romaine. Circle bowl with wedges of avocado treated with lemon juice. In center of bowl place a mound of shrimps covered with cocktail sauce.

Louie Salad: Line bowl with lettuce leaves and use shredded lettuce to cover bottom of bowl. Mix crabmeat with diced celery, lemon juice, and pepper to taste. Shape into a mound on the lettuce, and cover with Louie dressing. Garnish with slices of tomato, eggs, chives, green onions, and wedges of lemon.

Crab Louis

Top the usual lettuce lining with a portion of crab meat. Pour Louis dressing over this sprinkled with chopped eggs. Decorate with crab legs and tomato slices, and chopped chives. Follow recipe for Louis dressing in Chapter VII.

CHAPTER XVIII

Suggestions for Hot Buffet Dishes

There are many things to be considered when the problem of hot food on the cold buffet arises; the type of establishment, the guest and the price he is willing to pay, the location, and the season. It is true that the "Continental Buffet," a combination of both hot and cold dishes, is quite popular at many hotels and restaurants throughout the country.

The hot food may be adequately served from chafing dishes, silver Escoffier dishes, and the like. From the point of view of correct dining, however, it is questionable whether it is wise to permit the guest to put hot and cold food both on the same plate at the same time. However, the usual customer seems to be happy with a plate of chicken à la King combined with cold food such as herring in sour cream, cole slaw, etc. Most stomachs will accept mixed food but the damage to the digestive system may be easily imagined. In addition, various delicacies such as hors d'oeuvre and desserts, should be eaten with more discrimination.

Actually, there are few cold foods that go well with a hot food display with the exception of appetizers, salads, a few cold meat items, fruits and cheeses. And despite the fact that a mingling of hot and cold foods on the same plate is not ideal service, there seems to be no satisfactory solution in the average dining place where the food cost must be watched. Since most of the clientele prefer a low price and do not mind mixing hot and cold foods, the business possibilities cannot be ignored. The price of the complete buffet dinner or luncheon must be determined by the catering management—the chef and the maitre d'hotel. After a check of the clientele's wishes as to price, it is possible to find the necessary food cost for either a cold buffet or one that has both hot and cold dishes.

Enough margin for food cost should be allowed so the chef can put out first class food and usually one or more hot dishes. If the cold meat and pantry section can work off some of the better left overs, the result should not be included in calculating the final food cost. A 33 per cent food cost may be the average.

Too many selections in the hot food line kills any reasonable profit and the finesse of the buffet will suffer. Attention must be concentrated on one well-prepared meat dish, the vegetable, and the potato or garnish that goes with it. Two hot meat dishes will demand good judgment to include left overs which must be sold to avoid a loss. Keep in mind that any type of meat, poultry, fish, or seafood may be served on the hot buffet. Roast beef holds the first place in popularity followed by roast poultry, broiled chicken, cacciatore, scallopini, and any type of Newburg.

Roasts

Roast Sirloin of Beef

Completely boned, medium rare roasted is the best way to serve this meat on the buffet. The sirloin is acceptable because the cooking time is slightly over an hour and can be roasted and the buffet replenished as the dinner is progressing. It is also one of the easiest roasts to carve in front of guests but the cost is high.

Roast Rib of Beef

This needs the proper aging so it will be tender. Have the rib roast correctly prepared for carving.

Roast Round of Beef

This should be a well-aged, medium size leg of beef with the rump and shank off, properly square cut for better carving in front of the guests. This is a very popular roast. The cooking time is around six to seven hours at 225°. One round is sufficient for 70 to 90 buffet-size portions.

Roast Beef Tenderloin, Larded

This should be a larded tenderloin of seven to eight pounds each. This is an expensive roast but very practical and well liked. One tenderloin should yield from 10 to 12 portions. Carve two small slices for each portion instead of one thick slice. As the cooking time is not more than 35 to 40 minutes, it can be well controlled and cooked while the buffet is proceeding.

Luncheon Beef Roast

This may be taken from the cheaper cuts such as top sirloin, shoulder cloth, rib eye, and top round. With these cuts long aging is a must. Otherwise the meat will be tough.

Roast Leg of Lamb

Leave the leg bone in so the roast may be more easily held for carving.

Roast Turkey

Prepare with a special stuffing.

Fish

Baked Salmon on Plank

This fish should be presented with the head on.

Snapper Filets Fried in Butter

Fresh or fresh-frozen fish should be chosen.

Colorado or Idaho Natural Water Trout Amandine

Fish weighing from 9 to 12 ounces should be used. Pan fry them to a golden brown. Marinate the fish first in lemon juice and Worcestershire sauce seasoned with salt and pepper. Then add, half and half, cream and flour and pan fry with half butter and half oil. Place in even rows in the chafing dish and cover generously with sliced almonds browned with fresh butter.

Broiled Salmon Steaks

From a 12 to 15 pound salmon, cut steaks of six to nine ounces each. Marinate and season as for trout. Dip in oil and charcoal broil directly on the broiler or on a rack. Crisscross for nice appearance and place in a chafing dish in exact rows. Pour over warm maitre d'hotel butter.

Pompano

A very desirable buffet fish that comes from the coast of Florida. The portion-size fish is treated the same as trout, either amandine or with meuniere butter. Also delicious if broiled.

Halibut Steak

Only fresh fish should be used. Frozen halibut becomes tough and dry. Prepare it broiled with anchovy butter.

Seafood

Maine Lobster, Broiled

Live lobsters cooked especially for the buffet are preferred but if they are not available, pre-cooked lobster may be used. A small whole chicken lobster may be used and split in two. Take out the stomach but not the green liver. Separate the claws from the two points. Divide them lengthwise later and simply crack them with a wooden mallet. With a small size lobster, serve two halves, two claws, and four joints—the live weight about one and one-quarter pounds. If it is desirable to serve a half lobster, buy the jumbo size.

When ready-cooked lobsters are used, stuff the front part of the lobster halves with a dry, New England-style bread stuffing. This is made from very small diced dry rolls with plenty of butter to moisten them and flavored with salt, pepper, chopped parsley, a little crushed garlic and a generous amount of Worcestershire sauce. This stuffing may also be made with white bread crumbs. While the lobster halves are being broiled, care must be taken that the bread stuffing does not burn. Drip butter over the flesh of the lobster, then brown under the broiler and bake until thoroughly hot.

Place the halves side by side in a chafing dish, the claws and points in front of each lobster half. Place small chunks of butter on top before putting on the buffet. Have only a small supply on the buffet and make up fresh as the orders come in. Drawn butter must be kept in a sauce warmer beside the dish containing the lobsters.

Lobster Newburg

Follow the usual method of preparation and present in a hot chafing dish with rice in another dish.

Lobster Creole

Usual preparation.

Lobster Thermidor

One and three-quarter pound lobsters are most desirable for this type of lobster dish. If baked with a little Hollandaise sauce over the top of the lobster thermidor mix, a better more regular appearance for buffet service may be obtained.

Lobster in Whiskey Sauce

Instead of sherry such as in Lobster Newburg, whiskey is used. No paprika whatever should be used so that the dish remains white. Puff paste crescents around the edge of the dish give a better appearance and taste.

Shrimps

Shrimps may be prepared in exactly the same way as lobster. A count of 21 to 25 shrimp to the pound is best for buffet service.

Curried Shrimps

Prepare a tangy curry sauce. Sauté the shrimps first with finely chopped onions before mixing with the sauce. Flakes of mango chutney, dry raisins, red pimiento bits, and walnut or pecan pieces put irregularly over the shrimp in the chafing dish makes them more appetizing.

Jumbo Shrimps on the Skewer

Wooden skewers as well as stainless steel or silver ones may be used to hold portions of butter-fried jumbo shrimps. Heat a butter-oil mix in a sauté pan. Place the skewered shrimps in the pan and place the whole under the broiler for a little color. Finish the shrimp by baking in the oven until done. Six jumbo shrimp make an order of good size. Different effects may be obtained by adding mushrooms, onions, peppers, zucchini, etc., to the skewer. A hot sauce may be served on the side.

CHAPTER XIX

Ice Carving for the Buffet

Ice carvings are among the most decorative additions to the buffet. The ice is carved and not molded as the layman might think. Out of a more or less large piece of ice, a figure is carved with the help of various chisels. The hard ice presents difficulties as it breaks easily and once broken all that can be done is to freeze the parts together again into one piece. Therefore, the technique of carving ice must be acquired by experience and practice.

A requirement for carving real art pieces is the talent of a sculptor, but many subjects may be carved without great talent and they will give an artistic touch to the buffet table.

The purpose of ice carvings may be to present them as decorative center pieces or as practical containers for food that must be kept on the ice during the serving period. From small ice bases or standards (socles) to gigantic buffet pieces weighing 2,000 pounds, almost anything may be achieved with the chisel. Fine art pieces are made from one solid piece of ice. It is also possible to piece together a few blocks of ice in the deep freezer and then carve whatever one wishes. But it is never as artistic a piece as a talented artist can carve from one single block.

In most major cities throughout the country, ice carvers have set up a place with an ice plant where the hotel or restaurant may buy a ready-carved ice piece. But outstanding work is done in the kitchens of hotels, restaurants and clubs by some of the better trained cooks. Ice plants are capable of freezing crystal clear ice and making delivery in a very short time to the hotel or restaurant kitchen. The average blocks weigh from 250 to 300 pounds and have approximate measurements of 45 x 20 x 10 inches. With

224

1

2   3

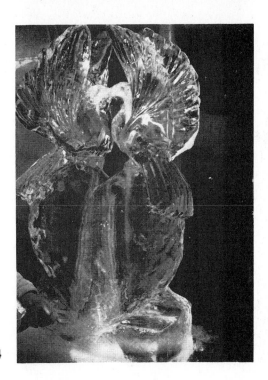

1. The outlines of the figure are transferred with roughly chiseled scratches. The paper sketch should always have exactly the same proportions as the finished carving. By watching the sketch carefully a well-proportioned carving is sure to result.

2. It is wiser to cut out flat surfaces and straight lines with the saw or steam knife to prevent the finer parts of the carving from splitting. Here a line is cut between the wings and the body.

3. This shows details of the cutting more clearly. Much work with the saw has been done in cutting out the ice between the wing tips and the beak—also from the heads down to the feet.

4. Finished ice carving for a wedding reception.

4

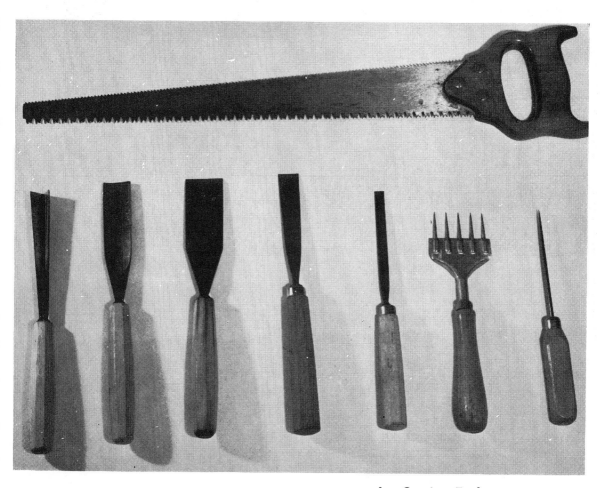

Ice Carving Tools

From right to left: (1) ice pick, not much used and difficult to control; (2) ice shaver, very handy for preliminary smoothing work; (3) small chisel for boring holes in the ice one-fourth inch wide; (4) small straight chisel, three-fourths inch wide; (5) straight chisel, one and one-half inches wide for general carving; (6) half-moon shaped chisel for rounded figures; (7) three-cornered chisel for marking and carving; Top: carpenter's hand saw, preferably with very rough teeth.

these blocks an almost unlimited choice of forms may be carved. For larger ice sculptures or awkward shaped figures, additional pieces of ice may be frozen to the main piece. This can be done with snow which is wet and used like plaster. The additional piece must be supported until both pieces are frozen solidly together. However, to repeat for emphasis, a pieced ice carving lacks the beauty of a piece carved from one block and is only recommended as a last resort.

The ice need not necessarily be carved under refrigeration. A fast artist finishes any type of carving in a time short enough so that it will not melt too greatly even under room temperature up to 70°. Choose a place for carving where there is good floor drainage and not much traffic or many on-lookers. With the help of ice tongs, the blocks of ice may be moved by sliding or by the use of a dolly.

The best results are achieved when the ice is carved at a convenient height— about 18 to 20 inches. A barrel rack made of wood is ideal as the ice stands quite solidly on it and may be turned easily as the work proceeds. A small piece of burlap placed under the ice holds it in place and prevents sliding. A partly carved block demands strong hands and much care as the slightest bump will cause cracks or breaks in the thin places.

In the picture series is a demonstration of what can be done in ice carving. It is an art which can come to its greatest development by practice—mastering the use of the tools and understanding the material.

Tools Used in Ice Carving

It is not absolutely necessary to own a full set of ice carving tools. For the beginners, two or three chisels and a carpenter's hand saw are sufficient. The advanced carver may wish to use gadgets such as the steam knife or melting iron and various chisels with different faces. All of the demonstrated ice pieces shown here are made with the set of tools shown in the illustrations. The steam knife can be made by any plumber. It is a steam hose that has an attachment for the steam pipe and a flattened copper pipe about two and one-half feet in length attached and welded to a fitting in order to insure that no steam escapes.

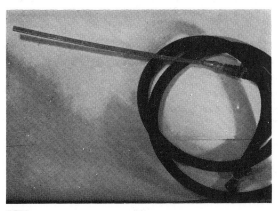

Steam hose with copper pipe flattened like a knife, handy for removing rough spots before the actual carving begins.

The Technique of Ice Carving

Since it takes much practice to make a master ice carver, in the limited space available here there is no room for more explanation than a good start. From that point on it is up to the beginner to try more complicated models.

The easiest type of ice carving is that which will be used as a container or base (socle) to keep food cool. Caviar, foie gras, and fruits such as melon or pineapple are kept on such bases which may have any desirable shape. With the steam knife they may be cut with ease and placed back in the deep freeze until needed. A few sketches may be helpful.

In carving larger models, planning is required. The drawing must be made first and in the same proportions as the large model. For example, an inch on the drawing may represent a foot on the actual ice carving. This scale work on paper must be correct or the parts will come out short or long. Some carvers, in order to be sure their proportions are correct, draw on sheets of kitchen paper the same size as the finished piece to avoid possible errors.

Once the drawing is made, the ice is placed either flat or erect on the scaffold or roller. Next, take the three-cornered chisel and mark on the surface of the block the correct size of the pattern by drawing a cross—the vertical line marking the height and the horizontal line the width. Then, with the same chisel, make an outline drawing of the model from the paper. The paper drawing of the motif is important for one can easily correct the lines on paper but the actual ice work is difficult to correct once an error has been made.

Small ice bases (socles) for various purposes (to hold dishes containing fruits, caviar, mousse, etc.). The designs show readily how a base may be obtained with the help of a saw and a three-cornered chisel.

Bird on a Branch

1. Start drawing the outlines of the bird on the ice with the three-cornered chisel.

2. Take the saw or steam knife and cut out odd ends and corners. This saves time and eliminates breakage.

3. Go over the entire figure with the shaver and give the preliminary shaping.

4. Use the straight and hollow chisels to finish the carving. Any type of bird may be carved in this way. The distinguishing features are the head and beak.

Top: The lighted figure is placed on the buffet.

229

Ice Carving of Donkey

This animal is carved from a 200-pound cake of ice. The middle saddle-section is carved so that the two baskets may be placed and frozen to the body with the help of wet snow. Keep in the freezer for a few hours and drop a little water at a time in the snowy cracks so it freezes solidly. The basket later may be filled with flowers.

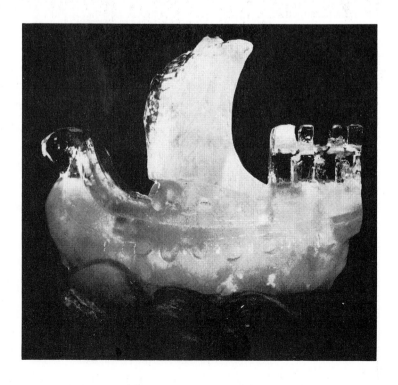

As soon as the lines on the ice appear satisfactory one must decide how to do the actual sculpturing without unnecessarily weakening part of the ice. It is not wise to finish one part ahead of the others because that part will melt faster and be out of proportion. It is best to have the whole picture in mind and rough it in and do the finer chisel work later.

The first tools used are usually the hand saw and the steam knife. The general outline of the model will decide the erect or prone position of the ice block. If the steam knife is used for taking off surplus ice, the block should remain in the same position from start to finish. The steam knife will do a faster job but it should not replace the chisel entirely for it fails to give the piece an artistic or authentic appearance. It will not look *carved*.

After odd ends and corners are sawed or steamed away, and a fairly good outline of the figure is obtained, the roughing down begins. For this purpose, the ice shaver is best. Always keep a picture of what is desired in the mind while working with the shaver and from time to time take the three-cornered chisel and re-emphasize the outlines that have disappeared under the chisel and shaver.

← Ice Carving of a Ship

1. Start as usual with saw or steam knife.

2. Watch the upper line of the whole ship, especially the bow. Work the line from the bow to the castle into an elegant curve. This curve determines the entire shape of the ship's body. Carve the front of the bow into a spiral using the shaver to get the general shape.

3. With a hollow chisel work out the inside of the boat. Leave the edge on the side of the boat two to two and one-half inches thick, allowing greater thickness toward the bow. Work with the same chisel upward to the bow.

4. Carve the waves around the bottom of the boat before taking more ice off. As soon as the waves have enough contour to be recognized work in the lower part of the ship's body. With the saw, finish the castle.

Ice Carving of a Fish

1. Start as usual with saw or steam knife.

2. Cut the top fin squarely to a thickness of four inches.

3. Shave the body round leaving the breast fins solid.

4. Work in the head and mouth with chisels. This part should be overdone slightly so that in melting it will not lose all the details.

5. Use the steam knife in making the top fins; work fast and avoid melting.

6. Cut in deeply with a three-cornered chisel the scales, tail fins and eyes. Shape the bottom to resemble rocks.

The proper technique is not to cut away all possible ice to reach a desired sculpture but to leave as much excess ice as one can and still have a work of art in the finished piece. By close study of the drawing and a clear mental picture of what is desired, this is possible.

As most blocks are rather thin, deep reliefs present a problem and in choosing a model the carver must reject unsuitable patterns.

As the sculpture begins to take form more care should be taken in the choice of tools. After the shaver, the different chisels are taken up. Large flat areas are handled with the large flat chisel. Smaller areas of work call for the smaller chisels. Curves and rounds are done with the round-faced chisel. With thoughtful work the carver can present a work of beauty.

Last comes the smallest chisel, the three-cornered one. This tool is for the highlights, and the claws of a bird, the eye, and the feathers. Also the scales of a fish are accentuated and help give a natural impression. When lighted up with a back light, these marks will sparkle like diamonds.

By this time the ice will have begun to melt and the marks and impressions will have need of deeper grooving to insure that the features are retained. This work is done with the three-cornered chisel. The saw may be used to advantage in marking thin delicate flats such as the tail feathers of a bird or the fins of a fish. If the marks are handled correctly, later melting will only emphasize the features and the sculpture will last for hours.

Valentine Heart

This double heart is made from one cake of ice in one piece. The flowers are placed in a cutout in the center.

Flower with Leaves

This is carved from one single ice cake. It is a beautiful carving when displayed with lights.

Boot and Spurs

Carved from one cake of ice and very appropriate for a cattleman's convention.

As soon as the carving is finished, put it into the deep freeze. Care must be taken in removing the piece from the freezer for presentation. The sudden change of temperature from intense cold to warm or hot air will sometimes cause the carving to splinter. The change in temperature should be made gradually. Naturally, the same applies to the block of uncarved ice in the beginning.

Quite often a customer may demand a colored ice piece. This is not practical for the ice will not take coloring and retain its crystal clearness. It will look like colored snow and the details of the carving are lost in this flat colored ice.

Instead, the colors may be obtained by the use of colored lighting. With small batteries and light placed inside the ice, one may obtain the desired effect. But it is much more practical and effective to have portable lights placed from three to six feet behind the piece where photo floodlamps may be used and cause the piece to appear to the best advantage. A colored rotating spotlight may also be used. Sometimes green foliage properly arranged will give a more pleasing effect and at the same time protect the eyes of the guests from the glare of lights.

An ice pan should be constructed to hold the drippings from the carving and to protect the floor. It should be somewhat larger than the carving it is to accommodate. Usually a pan 24" x 36" should be practical for most carvings.

233

Special Menus

Special Menus

Special Menus

Special Menus

Special Menus

Special Menus

Special Menus

Special Menus

Plans for Table Arrangements

Plans for Table Arrangements

Plans for Table Arrangements

Plans for Table Arrangements

Buffet Set-Ups

Buffet Set-Ups

Buffet Set-Ups

Buffet Set-Ups

Index

A

Abalone shell, 114
Alaska shrimp, 110
Alberta salad, 205
Alexander salad, 205
Algerienne salad, 205
Alice salad, 205
Alma salad, 205
Alligator pear salad, 198
Aluminum foil, 21
American beauty salad, 210
Anchovies, 45; for decoration, 32
Anchovy filet, 32
Andalouse sauce, 80
Anna salad, 210
Antipasto, 64, 74; Italian, 56
Antoinette salad, 205
Apples, 32, 58
Aquavit, 183
Argenteuil salad, 198, 199
Artichoke, bottoms with mousse, 152; Ecarlate, 152; for decoration, 40
Asparagus, 33; salad, 172; and tomato, 205; spears, 64; spears for decoration, 32; tip salad, 199; vinaigrette salad, 199
Aspic, 124; artificial, 131; of crab legs San Francisco style, 115; cubes, 124; of ecrevissse, 117; of filet of Dover sole, 129; fish, 128; for foie gras, 129; ingredients for clarification, 127; ingredients for reduction, 127; ingredients for stock, 127; of langouste, 106; of lobster, 101, 130; of lobster with caviar, 105; of lobster with truffles, 104; mold, 124, 126, 132; tongue with ox tongue, 176; preparation of, 125; recipes, 127; regular, 128; salmon, 95; shrimp, 130; of shrimp and Maine lobster, 102, 105; tomato, 214; truffle, 157; use of, 131
Assez salad, 210
Astoria salad, 210
Au bleu, fish, 85
Augustine salad, 210
Avocado molded salad, 214; mousse salad, 214; quarters with mousse, 152; salad, 199; sections, 64; stuffed with shrimp, 217

B

Bacon, Canadian, 193; bacon-wrapped hot hors d'oeuvre, 48
Baked salmon on plank, 221
Baking the pâté, 140, 141
Bananas for decoration, 166, salad, 207
Barquette à la bouchere, 152
Barquettes, 48
Bases, ice, 228
Batons, 49
Beans, green, 33, 172
Beatrice salad, 199
Beach Buffet, 189
Beef, 47; à la mode, 176; cold prime rib of, 175; corned, 176; prime ribs of, 174; roast, 221; roast, luncheon, 221; rolls, 65; rouladen, braised, 183; round of roast, 221; sirloin of, 212; tenderloin, cold, Belle Jardiniere, 172; tenderloin, roast, larded, 221
Beer, 183
Beet salad, pickled, 204
Beets, 33
Belge salad, 210, 211
Belmansro, 183
Berries, 58
Beurecks, 49
Beverages, 190
Bismarck herring, 44
Blackstone salad, 207
Bleu cheese dressing, 81
Blinis, 44, 50
Boar's head, stuffed, 181
Boiled lamb with dill sauce, 183
Boiling fish, 85
Bombay salad, 207
Bon Ton salad, 199
Bouchées, 49; charcutiere, 151
Boysenberries, 60
Braised beef rouladen, 183
Braising fish, 86
Brandwin, 183
Brazilian salad, 199
Bread base, 109; for canapés, 71
Breads, 194
Breakfast buffet, 189, 190, 191, menu for, 189; fruit, 190; meats, 192
Breast of chicken in aspic, 126
Bretonne salad, 199
Broccoli, 33
Broiled Maine Lobster, 222
Broiled salmon steaks, 222
Brunch, 189; menu for, 190
Brussels sprouts, 33, 172
Buffet arrangement, 16; beach, 189; breakfast, 189, 190, 191; continental, 22; ham for Easter Sunday, 158; large functional, 20; lay-

out of, 15, 24; length of, 25; low-price, 19; on
the terrace, 188; pâté for, 143; piece, Easter,
157; salad for New Year, 218; scaffolds for,
25; seafood, 100; selections, 26
Buffets, cocktail, 48
Buissen d'ecrevisse, 98, 117
Butter modeling, 41, 42
Butterfly decoration, 155

C

Cabbage rolls, 183
Cacciatore, 221
Caesar salad, preparation of, 200
Cailles, 170
Cakes, 18, 27
Calvo stuffed with shrimp, 217
California dressing, 79, tossed salad, 199
Canadian bacon, 193
Canapé, Alsacienne, 69; anchovy, 67, 68; Antoine,
70; bacon and cheese, 68, 70; Bismarck herring, 66; Bohemienne, 69; Bouchere, 69; caviar,
66, 67; caviar and shrimp, 67; Charlie, 70;
cheese, 68; Clermont, 70; crab leg, 67; cream
cheese, 68; ecrevisse, 66; egg spread, 67; foie
gras, 69; Gauloise, 69; ham, 68, 69; ham
mousse, 68; herring, 66; liverwurst, 69; lobster, 66; Lorenzo, 50; Massena, 70; meat ball,
70; Midinette, 68; roast beef, 69; roquefort, 68;
roquefort and anchovies, 68; Rose Marie, 70;
salami, 69; salmon caviar, 66; sardine, 66, 67;
sardine or bristling, 66; sausage, 70; shrimp,
67; smoked salmon, 66, 67; tongue, 70; tongue
spread, 70; tuna fish purée, 66
Canapé tray, contents of, 72
Canapé trays, 183
Canapés, 65; arranged for service, 72; bread for,
71; decoration of, 73; preparation of, 65, 71;
with center piece, 73
Cantaloupe, 64
Capers, 33
Capon, 132, 159; and foie gras, galantine of, 135;
Argenteuil, galantine of, 135; chaudfroid of,
159, 160; galantine of, 133, 134, 135; galan-
tine, preparation of, 132; Neva, 163; prin-
taniere, chaudfroid of, 162
Caprice salad, 210
Caramel coloring, 130
Carmelite salad, 200, 201
Carp, 46
Carpenter's work, 15, 24
Carrots, 34, 172
Cauliflower, 33, 172; salad, 200
Caviar, 33, 43; eggs with, 119
Celery, leaves, 33; mayonnaise salad, 201; Victor
salad, 201
Celestine with mousse, 152
Cendrillon salad, 200, 201
Center-square layout for buffet, 25
Centerpiece, 15, 24; grapefruit, 73; melon, 73;
pineapple, 73; salmon Oregon, 92; canapés
arranged with, 73
Ceramics, 21
Chafing dishes, 220
Chantilly sauce, 78
Chatelaine salad, 201
Chaudfroid of capon, 160; capon printaniere, 162;
duckling, 167; sauce, brown, 82; sauce, green,
82; sauce, pink, 82; sauce, white, 81

Cheese balls, 50; cream, 60; platter, 184
Cheeses, 194
Chef's salad, 201
Chemisér, 131
Cherries, sour, 33
Cherrystone clams, 118
Chicken, broiled, 221; salad, 211; salad bowl, 211
Chiffonade salad, 201
"Chimneys" in pâté, 143
Chinaware, 21
Chives, 34; for decoration, 35
Chops, stuffed, 172
Chutney, mango, 64
Citrus fruit cocktails, 58; sections, 60
Clam fritters, 51
Clams, 117; cherrystone, 118; Little Neck, 118
Classes of fish, 84
Cleanliness, 30
Cocette salad, 211
Cocktail buffets, 48; glasses, 57; melon ball, 58;
melon supreme, 59; oyster, 62; oyster Olympia,
62; shrimp, 62; supreme, fruit, 58
Cocktails, 57; fruit, 58; seafood, .58; supreme, 58
Coffee service, 189
Cold food, 26
Cold hors d'oeuvre, 16, 56
Cold meat section, 29
Cold roast duckling, 167
Cold sauces and dressing, 75
Cold section of kitchen, 28
Cold whole salmon, 88
Cold whole salmon, preparation of, 86
Cole slaw, 197; Hawaiian, 197; Mexican, 197;
Nordic, 197
Collee, mayonnaise, 80
Coloring, caramel, 130
Combined salads, 210
Containers, cocktail, 57; salad, 196
Continental buffet, 220
Cooking fish, rules, for, 85
Cooking time, lobsters, 101; shrimp, 111
Corn, 34
Corned beef, 176
Cornets, 172; Virginia Ham, 150
Cornish Game Hen, 167
Cosmopolitan salad, 202; fish salad, 215
Cottage cheese salad, pineapple and, 208
Court bouillon, 111; for fresh water fish, 85;
with white wine, 85
Crab, 98; crab delight, Monterey, 114; Dungeness,
112, 113, 114; Irlandaise, dressed, 115; Louis,
114; salad, 216, 219
Crab legs, aspic of, 115
Crabmeat salad, 215
Crabs, 99, 111; cracked, 112, 113; cracked,
hardshell, 116; hardshell, 111; softshell, 111
Cracked crab, 98, 111, 112, 113; hardshell, 116;
softshell, 111
Crayfish, 116, 183; and dill, 184
Creamed sweetbreads, 183
Creole, lobster, 223
Croissants, 51
Cromesquis, 51
Croquettes, 51
Croûtes, 51
Crown of ecrevisses, 117
Crustaceans, fish and, 26; preparation of, 84
Cubane salad, 202
Cubes, aspic, 126
Cucumber barrels filled with mousse, 152

251

Cucumber boats filled with mousse, 152
Cucumber decorations, 36; salad, 202; salad, Hungarian style, 202; Swedish style, 202; salad, tomato and, 205; skin, 34; slices for decoration, 40
Cucumbers, 34; pickled, 34
Cumberland sauce, 83
Curried shrimp, 223
Cutters, 31

D

Dandelion salad, 202
Dartoise, 52
Decorated Ham for Mother's Day, 158; with mousse cubes, 150
Decorating material, 30; materials recommended, 32
Decoration, butterfly, 155; of canapés, 73; cucumber, 36; fruits used for, 165; ham, 156, 158; Indian head, 166; truffles for large scale, 40; Polynesian style, 139; tools for, 30
Decorations, 15, 22, 27; holiday, 22; miscellaneous, 40; olive, 36, 39; radish, 38, 39
Deer, leg of, 180; pâté of, 143
Delicacies, 43
Desserts, 18, 27
Deviled eggs, 119
Diana salad, 207
Dill, 34; crayfish and, 184; sauce with boiled lamb, 183
Diplomat salad, 207
Doctors' salad, 213
Dolly salad, 203
Doucette salad, 203
Dough for pâté, 140; for pâté de foie gras, 144; for salmon pâté, 146
Dover sole aspic, filet of, 129
Dressed crab Irlandaise, 115
Dressing, bleu cheese, 81; California, 79; garde manger, 78; green, 78; green goddess, 79; lemon cream, 80; lime cream, 80; Lorenzo, 78; needles, 31; orange cream, 80; Plaza, 78; roquefort, 81; Russian, 79; Thousand Island, 77
Dressings, salad, 197
Dressings and cold sauces, 75
Drip pans, 25
Dry marinade, 179
Duck, terrine from, 147
Duckling, 163; chaudfroid of, 167; cold roast, 167
Dumas salad, 212, 213
Dummy items, 22
Dungeness crab, 112, 113, 114
Duxelle farce, 173

E

Easter buffet piece, 157
Easter Sunday buffet, 158
Eclairs with salmon mousse, 152
Ecrevisse, 98, 116; à la Nage, 116; aspic of, 117; crown of, 117; Swedish style, 117
Edible items, 22
Eel, 182
Egg plant skin, 34
Eggwhite for decoration, 35
Egg yolk purée, 119
Eggs, 119, 120, 121, 122, 193; Benedict, 52; Cardinal, 119; caviar-stuffed, 64; Danish style,

123; for decoration, 32; deviled, 119; Foo Yong, 52, Gourmet, 123; Italian style, 123; Jardiniere, 123; lobster, 34; soft boiled, Bristol, 123; soft boiled San Francisco, 123; Russian style, 123; with caviar, 119; with shrimp, 119
Electric slicer, 31
Endive and watercress salad, 197
Entrées, 17
Escoffier dishes, 220
Espagnole salad, 203
Excelsior salad, 208

F

Faisan en volière, 22, 108
Family-style pâté, 144
Fantasie salad, 212
Farce, 140; Duxelle, 173
Figs, 60
Filet of Dover sole, aspic, 129
Filet Mignon, Rossini, 175
Filets, anchovy, 32; salmon, 94; salmon Italienne, 92, 94; salmon, portion size, 93; salmon, preparation of, 93
Filling, family-style pâté, 144; galantine of pheasant, 136; galantine of veal, 136; pâté, 140; preparation of, for pâté, 140; suckling pig, 138
Fish, 17, 21, 221; aspic, 128; au bleu, 85; balls, 53; classes of, 84; and crustaceans, 26; filling for salmon pâté, 146; fresh, 46; fresh hot, 193; and Game Commission, 101; jelly, 88; marinated, 62; pickled, 62; platter, 185; preparation of, 84; rules for cooking, 85; salad, Cosmopolitan, 215; salads, 215; smoked, hot, 193; smoked, salted, or marinated, 194
Flood lamps, 22
Florida salad, 208
Floridienne salad, 208
Foie gras, 35; capon and, galantine of, 135
Foil, aluminum, 21
Food, cold, 26; cost, 220; presentation of, 15, 18; relationship of, 15
Formula for truffles, 40
Fowl, platter of wild, 185
Frills, 22
Frontenac salad, 208
Fruit, breakfast, 190; cocktail supreme, 58, 59; a meal from, 61; platter, 61, 184; salad, frozen, 214; salads, 205; salads, frozen and molded, 212; salads, group of, 206; stewed, 192
Fruits, 18, 27, 60; used for decoration, 165; and fruit juices, 189

G

Galantine, 132; of capon, 133; of capon Argenteuil, 135; of capon and foie gras, 135; capon, preparation of, 132; of pheasant, 136; stuffing for, 133; of suckling pig, 136; of turkey, 133, 134, 135; of veal, 136
Game, 47, 178
Garde manger dressing, 78
Garnishes, 30; for langouste, 108; for salmon, 87, 91
Gaspacho salad, 215
Gauloise salad, 203
Gelatin, 124
Geneva salad, 202

George salad, 202, 203
Glasses, cocktail, styles of, 57
Glassware, 21
Ginger ale melon mold, 214
Goose, 163
Gooseliver pâté, 139, 144
Grand Union salad, 203
Grapefruit, 58, 60; centerpiece, 73
Grapes, peeled, 60
Gravel Lax, 46
Green dressing, 78
Green goddess dressing, 79
Greens for decoration, 35
Gribiche sauce, 80
Grosse pieces, 17
Guacamole purée, 215

H

Halibut, 95; moderne, 95; steak, 222
Ham, 22, 65, 153; air dried, 153; cold, 153;
    cornets, Virginia, 150; decorated for Mothers'
    Day, 156; decorated with mousse cubes, 150;
    decoration, 156, 158; Easter Sunday buffet,
    158; finished show piece, 155; mousse, 151;
    preparation of cuff, 154; profiterolles, 151;
    Prosciutto, 64, 153; rolls, 157; slices, 65; and
    veal pie, 145; Virginia, 153; Westphalian, 153
Hard-shell crabs, 111; cracked, 116
Hare, or rabbit, wild, 180; pâté, 145
Hash, Swedish, 188
Hawaiian salad, 208, 209
Hawley salad, 212, 213
Head of wild boar, stuffed, 180
Health salad, 212
Herring, 44, 62, 182; Bismarck, 44, Matjes, 44;
    salad, 215
Herriot salad, 212
Holiday decorations, 22
Hors d'oeuvres, bacon-wrapped, 48; cold, 16, 56;
    hot, 48; meat, 65; mixed, 64; Riche, 57
Hortense salad, 213
Hose, steam, 227
Hungarian style cucumber salad, 202
Hunt breakfast, 191

I

Ice bases, 228; blocks, 227
Ice carving, 16, 224; of bird, 229; of boot and
    spurs, 233; of donkey, 230; of fish, 231; of
    flower with leaves, 232; of heart, 232; of ship,
    230; technique of, 228; tools, 226; for a
    wedding, 225
Ice carvings, 22
Ice socles, 228
Imperial salad, 203
Indian head decoration, 166
Inedible items, 15
Iron salad, 212, 213
Italian antipasto, 56, 74; salad, 215

J

Japonaise salad, 208, 209
Jelly, 30
Jelly fish, 88; mold, 124

Jeunesse salad, 212
Jockey Club salad, 203, 208
Jordan salad, 203
Juices, 190

K

Kidney Sauté, 184; stew, 53
King crab, 94
Kitchen, cold setion of, 28
Knives, 31

L

L-shape layout, 25
Ladies' Delight salad, 208, 209
Lamb, boiled with dill sauce, 183; roast leg of, 221
Langouste, 98, 99, 106; à la Parisienne, 98, 106,
    108, 111; aspic of, 106
Larding needles, 31
Layout of buffet, 15, 24; center square, 25; L-
    shape, 25; long renaissance, 25; u-shape, 25
Leeks, 34
Leftovers, 62, 172, 221
Leg of deer, 180; of lamb roast, 221
Lemon cream dressing, 80
Length of buffet, 25
Lentil salad, 203
Lettering, truffle, 156
Lime cream dressing, 80
Liqueurs, 61
Liquid for salt water fish, 85
Little neck clams, 118
Liver pâté, 145; terrine, 145
Lobster, 98, 182; aspic of, 101, 130; with caviar,
    aspic of, 105; creole, 223; eggs, 34; Maine, 99;
    Maine and shrimp, aspic of, 102, 105; Maine,
    broiled, 222; Maine, en Bellevue, 107; Maine,
    Parisienne, 98; Maine, Victoria, 99; mousse,
    New England, 105; Newburg, 223; Parisienne,
    105; pounds, 91; salad, 218; seasons, 101;
    thermidor, 223; with truffles, aspic of, 104;
    Victoria, 101; in whiskey sauce, 223; cooking
    time, 101
Lobsters, dead, 101
Loin of pork, 175; with prunes, 184
Lorenzo canapé, 50; dressing, 78
Lorette salad, 203
Louie salad, 218
Louise salad, 212, 213
Low-price buffet, 19
Luncheon beef roast, 221

M

Mackerel, 182
Maine Lobster, 99; and shrimp, aspic of, 105;
    broiled, 222; en Bellevue, 107; Parisienne, 98;
    Victoria, 99
Manchette, 22
Mango, 60; chutney, 64
Margarine modeling, 41
Marinade, dry, 179; skimmed milk, 178; wine,
    179
Marinated fish, 62
Matjes herring, 44
Mayonnaise collee, 80; large quantity, 76; small
    quantity, 75
Meal from fruit, 61

Meat balls, 53; Swedish, 188
Meat hors d'oeuvres, 65; salads, 65; section, **cold,** 29
Meats, 21, 26, 47
Medallions, 159, 172; Langouste, 108; salmon, 93
Melon ball cocktail, 58
Melon balls, 58, 60
Melon basket, 59; centerpiece, 73; cocktail supreme, 59; ginger ale mold, 214
Menu for breakfast buffet, 189; for "brunch", 190
Milk marinade, skimmed, 178
Mimosa salad, 197
Miramichi salmon, New Brunswick style, 88
Mirror plate, 21
Mixed green salad, 197
Model tools, wooden, 31
Modeling butter, 41; margarine, 41
Mold for aspic, 126
Molded salad, avocado, 214
Molded and frozen salads, 212
Mollusks, 117; preparation of, 84
Monte Carlo salad, 204
Monterey crab delight, 114
Mother Hubbard salad, 204
Mothers' Day, decorated ham for, 158
Mousse, 132, 149; artichoke bottoms with, 152; avocado quarters with, 152; Celestine with, 152; cubes, decorated ham with, 150; cucumber barrels filled with, 152; cucumber boats filled with, 152; eclairs, salmon, 152; ham, 151; lobster, New England, 105; salad, avocado, 214; salmon, preparation of, 95, 96; tomatoes filled with, 152; tomato quarters filled with, 152
Mousseline, 151; sauce, 78
Museau de boeuf, 47
Mushrooms, 35
My Lady's choice salad, 208

N

Napkin folding, 22
Needles, dressing, 31; larding, 31
Newburg, lobster, 223
New Year buffet, salad for, 218
Noisettes, 172
Nuts, Pistachio, 37

O

Olive decorations, 36, 39
Olive rings, stuffed, for decoration, 40
Olives, 64; black, 35; ripe for decoration, 35
Onion tops for decoration, 32, 35
Onions, cocktail, 36; silver, 36
Orange cream dressing, 80
Orange sections, 58
Oranges, 60
Orlys, 53
Ox tongue, cured, 177; with Piquante salad, 177; salted, 65; smoked, 65; with tongue aspic, 176; Waldorf, 177
Oysters, cocktail, 54, 62, 117; Blue Point, 118; Cape Cod, 118; on the buffet, 118

P

Pain de foie, 148
Palm Beach salad, 212, 213

Panache salad, 197
Pantry Section, 29
Papaya slices, 60
Parfait de fois gras, 168
Pans, drip, 25
Parisienne spoons, 31
Parsley, for decoration, 40
Pasadena salad, 218
Paste, 136
Pastry, 18, 27
Pâté, 132, 136; baking the, 140; for buffet, 143; chimneys in, 143; of deer, 143; de foie gras dough, 144; de foie gras strasbourgeoise, 142; de lievre, 145; dough for, 140; family style, 144; filling for, 140, filling for salmon, 146; goose liver, 139, 144; liver, 145; pheasant, 145; preparation of, 139; preparation of aspic for, 141; salmon, 146
Peach and pecan salad, 208
Peaches, 36
Pears, 36, 58
Pecan salad, peach and, 208
Peppers for decoration, 40; green, 36
Pheasant, 22, 168; à la Bacchus, 168; galantine of, 136; pâté, 145; with cailles, 169; with pineapple, 170
Pickled beet salad, 204
Pickled fish, 62
Pies, 27
Pike, 46
Pimiento, red, 37; strips for decoration, 32
Pineapple, 37, 60, 61; and cottage cheese salad, 208; centerpiece, 73; chunks, 58; for decoration, 165; with pheasant, 170, sections, 60
Pistachio nuts, 37
Pizza alla Napoletana, 54
Placement, selection and, 15
Plantation salad, 204
Platter, cheese, 184; fish, 185; fruit, 184; wild fowl, 185
Platters, 21
Plaza dressing, 78
Poinsettia salad, 212, 213
Polynesian-style decoration, 139
Pompano, 222
Pork, 47; pork loin, 175; with prunes, 185
Portion-size salmon filets, 93
Potato salad, 209
Poularde à la Virginia, 161
Poultry, 47, 159; roast, 221
Prawns, 110
Preparation of aspic, 125; Caesar saald, 200, canapés, 65, 71; capon galantine, 132; whole cold salmon, 86, 87; crustaceans, 84; filling for pâté, 140; fish, 84; galantine, 133, 134; mollusks, 84; pâté, 139; prime ribs of beef, 174; roasts for display, 171; raw material, 43; salad bowl, 198; salmon filets, 93; salmon masterpiece, 89; salmon mousse, 95, 96; suckling pig, 137; terrine, 148
Presentation of food, 15, 18
Prime rib of beef, 174; cold, 175
Princess salad, 204
Printaniere, chaudfroid of capon, 160
Printemps salad, 204
Profiterolles of ham, 15
Progress salad, 212
Prunes, loin of pork with, 185
Purée, egg yolk, 119; Guacamole, 215
Pyramide d'Crevettes, 98

Q

Quail, 170
Quicke Lorraine, 54

R

Rabbit or hare pâté, 145; wild, 180
Rachel salad, 204
Radish decorations, 28, 39
Radish slices for decoration, 35
Radishes, 37
Rainbow Restaurant, 183
Rainbow trout, 98
Raspberries, 58
Ravigote sauce, 77
Raw material, selection of, 43
Reception, arrangements for wedding, 17
Refrigeration section, 28
Rejane salad, 204
Relationship of food, 15
Remoulade sauce, 77
Rib of beef, roast, 221; prime, 174
Riche, hors d'oeuvre, 57
Ring forms, 212
Ripe olives for decoration, 35
Rissoles, 55
Roast beef, 221
Roast beef tenderloin, larded, 221
Roast duckling, cold, 167
Roast leg of lamb, 221
Roast poultry, 221
Roast rib of beef, 221; round of beef, 221; sirloin of beef, 221
Roast turkey, 221
Roast spareribs, 188
Roasts, 18, 171; for display, 171
Robin Hood salad, 205
"Rollmops", 44
Rolls, sweet, 194
Roquefort dressing, 81
Round of beef, roast, 221
Rules for cooking fish, 85
Russian dressing, 79; salad, 215

S

Saddle of venison, Orientale, 179, 180
Salad, Alberta, 205; Alexandra, 205; Algerienne, 205; alligator pear, 198; Alma, 205; Alice, 205; American Beauty, 210; Anna, 210; Antoinette, 205; Argentine, 199; asparagus tip, 199; asparagus vinaigrette, 199; Assez, 210; Astoria, 210; Augustine, 210; avocado, 199; avocado, molded, 214; avocado mousse, 214; avocado stuffed with shrimp, 217; banana, 207; Beatrice, 199; Belge, 210, 211; Blackstone, 207; Bombay, 207; Bonton, 199; bowl, chicken, 211; bowl, preparation of, 198; bowl, shrimp, 216; Brazilian, 199; Bretonne, 199; Caprice, 210, 211; Carmelite, 200, 201; cauliflower, 200; Caesar, 200; Celery mayonnaise, 201; celery Victor, 201; Cendrillon, 201; Chatelaine, 201; Chefs', 201; chicken, 211; Chiffonade, 201; Cocette, 211; combinations, green, 197; containers, 196; Cosmopolitan, 202; Cosmopolitan, fish, 215; crab, 216; crab Louis, 219; crabmeat, 215; Cubane, 202; cucumber, 202;
dandelion, 202; Diana, 207; Diplomat, 207; Doctor's 212, 213; Dolly, 202, 203; Doucette, 203; dressings, 197; Dumas, 212, 213; endive and watercress, 197; Espagnole, 203; Excelsior, 208; Fantasie, 212; Florida, 208; Floridienne, 208; Frontenac, 208; frozen fruit, 214; garnishes, 196; Gaspacho, 215; Gauloise, 203; Geneva, 202; George, 202, 203; Grand Union, 203; greens, 196; Hawaiian, 208, 209; Hawley, 212, 213; health, 212; Herriot, 212; herring, 215; Hortense, 212, 213; Imperial, 203; iron, 212, 213; Italian, 215; Japonaise, 208, 209; Jeunesse, 212; Jockey Club, 203, 208; "Jonas", 183; Jordan, 203; Ladies' Delight, 208, 209; lentil, 203; lobster, 218; Lorette, 203; Louie, 218; Louise, 212, 213; Mimosa, 197; mixed green, 197; Monte Carlo, 204; Mother Hubbard, 204; My Lady's Choice, 208; for New Year buffet, 216; Palm beach, 212, 213; Panache, 197; Pasadena, 218; peach and pecan, 208; pickled beet, 204; pineapple and cottage cheese, 208; plantation, 204; poinsetta, 212, 213; pointers, 196; potato, 204; preparation of Caesar, 200; Princess, 204; printemps, 204; progress, 212; Rachel, 204; Rejane, 204; Robin Hood, 205; Russian, 215; Saratoga, 209; seafood, 216; specialties of other countries, 214; spring, 197; sunburst, 209; Swedish style, cucumber, 202; Tehachapi, 209; tomato and asparagus, 205; tomato and cucumber, 205; Tosca, 205; tossed, California, 199; tossed green, 198; tropical, 209; tunafish, 215; Veronique, 210; Waldorf, 210
Salads, 21, 26, 195; combined, 26, 195, 210; fish, 215; fruit, 205; general information on, 195; group of fruit, 206; meat, 65; molded and frozen, 212; simple, 195; vegetable, 198; vegetables and, 18
Salmon, 86; à la Norvegienne, 88; à la Parisienne, 88; aspic, 95; Chinook, Fantasia, 88; cold whole. 88; cold whole, preparation of, 87; filets, 94; filets, portion size, 93; filets, preparation of, 93; filets, Italienne, 92; fresh Gaspé, 88; garnishes for, 87, 91; Italian, filets of, 94; masterpiece, 91; masterpiece, preparation of, 89; medallions, sauce Verte, 92, 93; Miramichi, 88; mousse eclairs, 152; mousse, preparation of, 95, 96; Oregon, centerpiece of, 92; on plank, baked, 221; pâté, 146; pâté, dough for, 146; preparation of cold whole, 86; smoked, 38, 45, 182; steaks, broiled, 222
Salt water fish, liquid for, 85
San Francisco Bay shrimp, 110
Saratoga salad, 209
Sardines, 45, 64
Sauce, Andalouse, 80; brown chaudfroid, 82; Chantilly, 78; green chaudfroid, 82; Gribiche, 80; pink chaudfroid, 82; Cumberland, 83; Mousseline, 78; Ravigote, 77; Remoulade, 77; tartare, 77; Tyrolienne, 79; vinaigrette, 83; Vincent, 78; white chaudfroid, 81
Sausage, 65
Scaffolds, 24, for buffet, 25
Seafood salad, 216
Scallopini, 172, 221
Scallops, 117
Scampis, 110
Scandinavian smorgasbord, 56
Scotch woodcock, 55
Sculptures, 22

Seafood, 222; buffet, 100; cocktails, 58
Season, spawning, 84; lobster, 101
Selection and placement, 15; of raw material, 43; buffet, 26
Set-ups, table, 25
Shellfish, 117
Sherry, 183
Shrimps, 38, 64, 98, 99, 110, 182, 223; Alaska, 110; aspic, 129; and Maine lobster, aspic of, 105; avocados stuffed with, 217; cocktail, 72; cooking, 111; count, 110; curried, 223; eggs with, 119; frozen, 110; jumbo on the skewer, 223; salad bowl, 216; San Francisco Bay, 110
Silver, 18
Sirloin of beef roast, 221
Skimmed milk marinade, 178
"Skol", 182
Slicer, electric, 31
Slaw, 197
Smoked fish, hot, 193; salmon, 45
Smorgasbord, 25, 182, 186; Scandinavian, 56
Snapper, filets, fried in butter, 222
Socles, 22, 109; ice, 228
Soft shell crabs, 111
Soft boiled eggs, Bristol, 123; San Francisco, 123
Sole, 46, 95; filet of Calypso, 91; filet of Cecilia, 91
Soups, 17
Spareribs, roasted, 188
Spawning season, 84
Spoons, Parisienne, 31
Spring salad, 197
Steam hose, 227
Steaming fish, 86
Stewed fruit, 59
Strawberries, 58
Stroeming, 182
Stuffed boar's head, 181
Stuffed olive rings, 40
Stuffing for galantine, 133
Styrofoam, 104
Stew, kidney, 53
Suckling pig, 139; filling for, 138, galantine of, 136; preparation of, 137
Sunburst salad, 209
Supreme cocktails, 58, 59
Swedish hash, 188; meat balls, 188; cucumber salad, 202
Sweetbreads, creamed, 183
Sweet rolls, 194

T

Table set-ups, 25
Tallow sculpture, 24
Tarragon leaves, 38
Tartare sauce, 77
Tartlets, 55
Technique of ice carving, 228
Tehachapi salad, 209
Temperatures, 28

Tenderloin of beef, Wellington, 173
Terrine, 132, 147; from duck, 147; liver, 145; preparation for, 148
Thermidor, lobster, 223
Thousand Island dressing, 77
Tomato and asparagus salad, 205; aspic, 214; and cucumber salad, 205; quarters filled with mousse, 152; skins for decorations, 40; slices for decoration, 32
Tomatoes, 39, 172; for decoration, 40; filled with mousse, 152
Tongue, 37; aspic with ox tongue, 176; cured ox, 177; Waldorf, 177; with Piquante salad, 177
Tools for decoration work, 31; for ice carving, 226; wooden model, 31
Tosca salad, 205
Tossed green salad, 198
Tournados Richelieu, 176
Tropical salad, 209
Trout, 46, 95; Colorado or Idaho Amandine, 222; Rainbow, 98; in Sauterne aspic, 91; Royal, 98; truffle aspic, 157; lettering, 156; aspic of, with lobster, 104
Truffles, 39, 41
Tunafish salad, 215
Turkey, 22, 132, 163; galantine, 133; roast, 221
Tyrolienne sauce, 79

U

U-shape layout, 25

V

Veal, galantine of, 136; ham and, pie, 145
Vegetable salads, 198
Vegetables, 47; and salads, 18
Venison, saddle of, 179, Orientale, 180
Veronique salad, 210
Vinaigrette sauce, 83
Vincent sauce, 78
Virginia ham cornets, 150

W

Waiter, 21
Watercress for decoration, 40; salad, 197
Wedding, ice carving for, 225; reception, arrangement for, 17
White chaudfroid sauce, 81
Wild boar, stuffed head of, 180
Wine, dessert, 61; marinade, 179
Woodcock, Scotch, 55
Wooden modeling tools, 31

Z

Zabouska, Russian, 56